IMAGES
of America

AZTEC

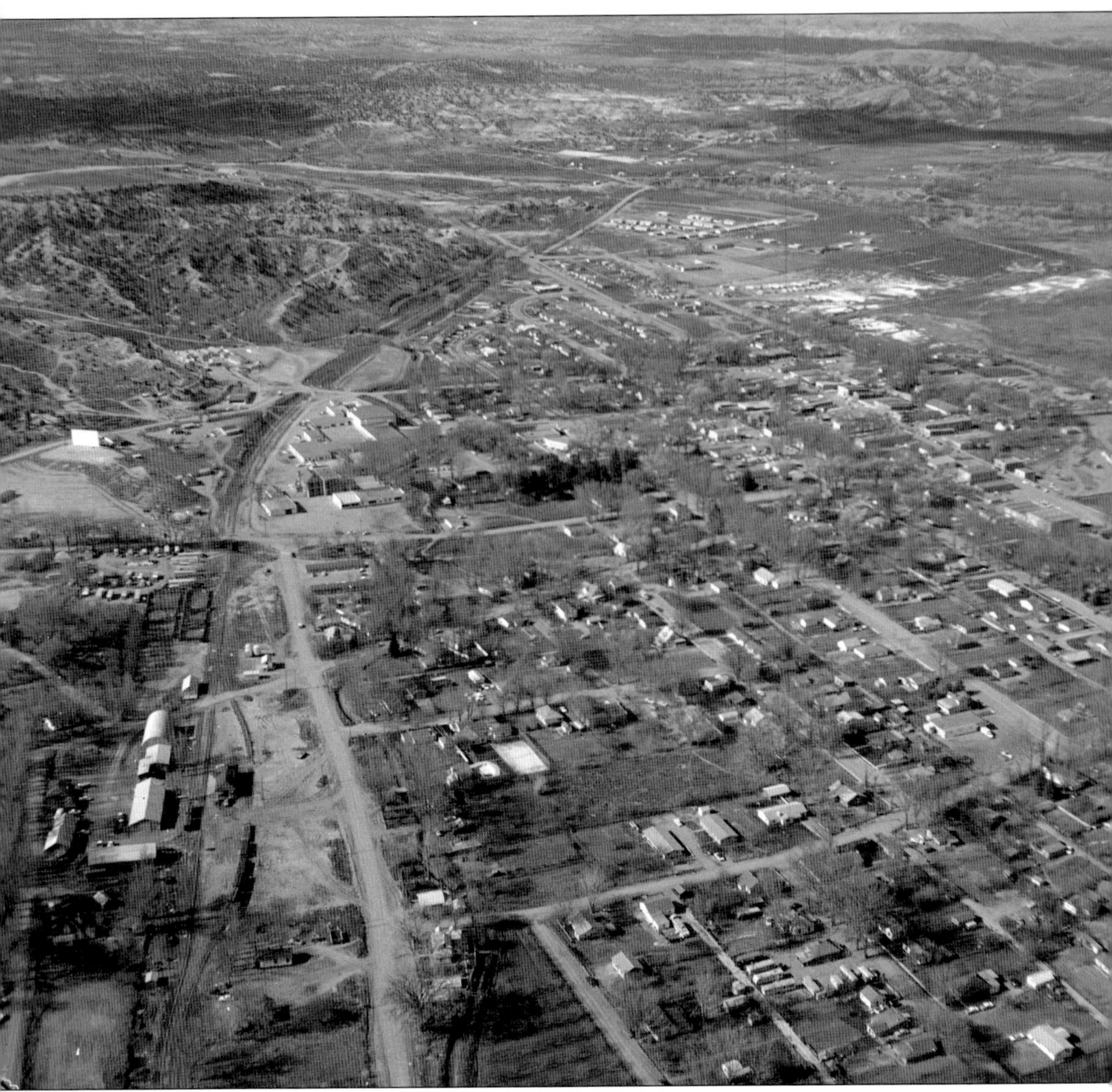

This aerial photograph of Aztec was taken by Henry Jackson and shows the community as it looked over 50 years ago. Note the Denver & Rio Grande Western railroad depot, yards, storage buildings, tracks, and railroad cars in the lower left corner. Today, the tracks are gone, the depot is a residence, and the area is full of houses. Most of the open spaces in the picture are now filled. (Courtesy Henry Jackson Collection, Aztec Museum.)

On the Cover: These girls are taking part in a 50-yard race during an Aztec schools event on Main Avenue on September 13, 1949. The day also included a tug-of-war, bicycle races, and a parade. (Courtesy Henry Jackson Collection, Aztec Museum.)

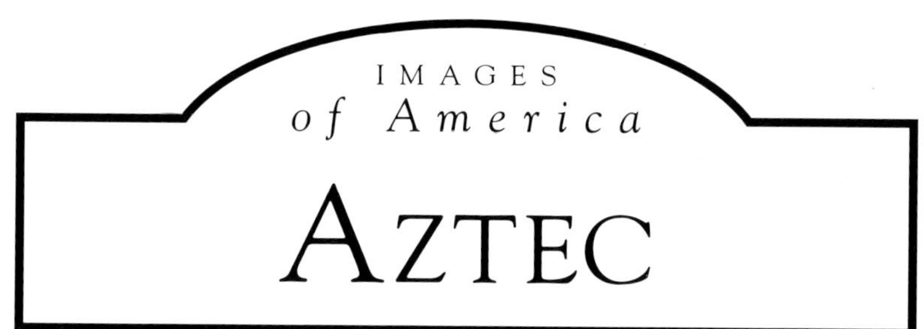

Marilu Waybourn
City of Aztec

To Beth –
read and enjoy
Marilu Waybourn

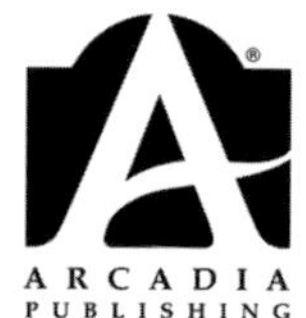

ISBN 978-0-7385-8495-9

Published by Arcadia Publishing
Charleston, South Carolina

Printed in the United States of America

Library of Congress Control Number: 2011929766

For all general information, please contact Arcadia Publishing:
Telephone 843-853-2070
Fax 843-853-0044
E-mail sales@arcadiapublishing.com
For customer service and orders:
Toll-Free 1-888-313-2665

Visit us on the Internet at www.arcadiapublishing.com

To the pioneer families who cared for their photographs through floods, moves, and other ups and downs. Thanks to them, we have a view of the past.

Contents

ACKNOWLEDGMENTS

The biggest thank you goes to Catherine Davis, who spent hours looking up and verifying information through the San Juan County Historical Society archives and the San Juan College microfilm library. She also read the proof and checked for historical accuracy.

Thanks is not a big enough word to cover the cooperation and involvement of the pioneer families who opened up their homes and their photo albums. They are Bob and Pat Pawley, Deanna Morrison Blythe, Art and LaVada Jones, Audrey Glazebrook, Judy Hollar, Bernice and Jim Bowra, and Raymond Johnston. They not only loaned pictures but also were willing to answer questions and give more details as needed. Others who loaned pictures include Phyllis Gilkey, Cleofas Montoya, Esther Jacquez Smith, Nellie Howard, and Linda Williams.

Aztec Museum Association members Vicky Ramakka, Dale Anderson, and Linda Williams kept an eye out for items that might fit in the book. They allowed unlimited access to the museum archives and were willing to loan photographs for the book. Linda stumbled onto a scrapbook filled with information applicable to this project. She is a fifth-generation Aztecan and read the proof with the eye of a pioneer.

Farmington Museum staff members—director Bart Wilsey and Debbie Doggett—were most helpful with photographs from their Aztec collection.

Henry Jackson was a local photographer who donated his extensive collection to the Aztec Museum and the San Juan County Historical Society. Unless otherwise credited, the photographs in this book are from the Aztec Museum's Henry Jackson Collection.

Photographers Connie Pruitt and Kelly West shot pictures all around Aztec to capture the current scenes.

Ron Nott, a self-professed railroad nut, loaned a classic photograph and furnished details on the Denver & Rio Grande railroad.

Gary Brown, acting supervisor of the Aztec Ruins National Monument, was most helpful in answering questions about the ruins.

Roshana Moojen, Aztec's community development director, was instrumental in getting the book going. She worked with Arcadia Publishing to get things started. After I became involved, she continued to be helpful with information and encouragement during the process.

And finally, thank you to my husband, Jim Waybourn, who puts up with the mess and stress of an author. Without his encouragement, getting books out would be much harder.

INTRODUCTION

The Aztec area was first inhabited by early Pueblo people. They left behind a virtual history book of villages filled with artifacts that help educate us about what was going on before the pioneers arrived. That ancient history is the reason Aztec was misnamed. Information from the Aztec City Library helps us resolve how Aztec got its name. One early reference to this area is on Baron Alexander von Humbolt's 1804 map of New Spain. This location is cited as "First abode of the Azteques from Aztlan." On an 1810 map of Mexico by Aaron Arrowsmith, it is also marked as "First settlement of the Azteques from Aztlan." Henry S. Tanner's 1823 and 1846 maps both cite the area as the "former residence of the Aztecs." Finally, on an 1849 US map by J.H. Colton, this area is noted as "Supposed residence of the Aztecs in the 12th Century."

Current knowledge explains that they were not Aztecs but ancestral or early Pueblo people who left the area around 1300. A few hundred years later, new settlers began the establishment of Indian reservations and the moving around of tribes. On May 20, 1862, Pres. Abraham Lincoln signed the Homestead Act, and when the law took effect on January 1, 1863, the move westward was in full swing.

The Aztec area, which later became San Juan County, New Mexico, went through several steps before it was opened to homesteaders. An executive order dated March 25, 1874, and signed by Pres. Ulysses S. Grant set aside this region as part of the Jicarilla Apache Reservation, and thus, the land was withdrawn for sale and settlement. The boundary ran along the edge of the Navajo Reservation. A couple of years went by, and the area remained mostly empty; according to historical record, the Jicarilla Apache did not want to live so close to the Navajo.

Rumors began to circulate about the area being opened for settlement. Those rumors turned to fact when Ulysses S. Grant signed another executive order on July 18, 1876, that negated the previous one and returned the lands to public domain. The focus of this book begins when the lands were opened for homesteading.

John A. and Emaline Koontz left their home in Pennsylvania to head west. They were among the first pioneers to settle in what is now Aztec. In 1878, Koontz erected a building of adobe bricks that became the family home and the first general store of the area. The Park Avenue site of the Koontz home now houses the Aztec Community/Senior Center.

More settlers arrived, and the Koontz family continued to look forward. On July 16, 1884, they filed homestead papers on the spot they had selected, and it was surveyed by J.E. Harper in 1887.

The first squabble for the newcomers began when Rio Arriba County was split in two in 1887. The western portion became San Juan County, but no county seat was named. After much debate, petitions, elections, and general turmoil, Aztec was officially named the county seat in 1892.

When the dust settled, John and Emaline Koontz continued to look to the future. They received a US patent for the land on March 21, 1889, and paid $200, or $1.25 per acre, for the 160 acres. It was time to form a structured community, and on September 13, 1890, they filed a plat to establish the town of Aztec on 50 acres of their homestead. The original town site was sold to the Aztec Town Company, with W.H. Williams as trustee. Thus, the town of Aztec was born.

This date was heralded in 1984 when the City of Aztec, at the request of the Aztec Museum Association, issued a proclamation to commemorate each September 13 as Founder's Day. The annual celebration continues to expand and now includes a parade and several special activities.

The incorporation of the town and the arrival of the railroad were highlights of 1905. Civic-minded citizens of Aztec petitioned the San Juan County Commission for incorporation on January 4, 1905. The official resolution granting incorporation was issued on May 4 and then filed with the state on May 8, 1905. On this date, the residents of Aztec held their first municipal election. The incorporation—on September 3, 1905—was treated as just another step in the growth of the community, but the arrival of the railroad was a monumental event.

Getting from here to there was a major problem for area residents in the early 20th century. Roads were sparse and in poor condition, and the nearest railroad was 35 miles away in Durango, Colorado. Livestock had to be driven and freight hauled by wagons. Finally, track was laid from Durango to Farmington, and the first train rolled into Aztec on August 24, 1905. A new phase in the story of Aztec began as the railroad brought in more people and businesses and ensured easier contact with the outside world.

Aztec endured a flood in 1911, statehood in 1912, the Great Depression, and two world wars. Each milestone brought changes to the community. The biggest change came with a natural gas boom in the 1950s, when population and commerce grew at a staggering pace.

Long before that boom, Aztec opened the first commercial natural gas well in the state of New Mexico in 1921. It was a hurdle to modernization that had good and bad points. The gas from the well was not regulated, and as townspeople turned the gas on or off, the pressure went up and down. Several fires resulted before steps were taken to fix the problem.

Aztec Ruins National Monument was established in 1923 to preserve the largest ruin in the neighborhood. The ruins have since become part of a United Nations Educational, Scientific and Cultural Organization (UNESCO) World Heritage Site. Farmers and construction crews continue to turn up artifacts when plowing or excavating, proving that there may be more sites to find as time goes on.

One of the best examples of the community working together is illustrated in the building of the Navajo Dam Road and the subsequent selection of Aztec as an "All-America City" in a 1963 issue of *Look* magazine. After the Navajo Dam was erected and Navajo Lake State Park became an attraction, Aztecans had to drive extra miles through Bloomfield and Blanco to get to the recreation site. Since the physical distance was a mere 18 miles, residents worked together to plan a more direct route from Aztec to the dam and then brought this dream to fruition in 1963.

Today, Aztec is a gateway to New Mexico's myriad tourist attractions, including the Aztec Ruins National Monument. Aztec hosts a UFO Symposium each March, with tours to the nearby site of an alleged 1948 UFO crash. The Symposium and the associated Alien Run Mountain Bike competition bring numerous travelers to the area. The city boasts dozens of registered historic buildings and a historical walking tour that helps visitors and locals check them out. With its authentic pioneer village and extensive collection of oil and gas memorabilia and equipment, history buffs and travelers are attracted to the Aztec Museum.

Aztec's population has grown from 126 in 1890 to 6,763, according to the 2010 census. From a few scratches on the surface of the fertile lands to a thriving community, Aztec has come a long way and continues to move forward.

One

Aztec Is Born

The San Juan Basin area in Northwest New Mexico was originally part of Taos County. The western part of Taos County was annexed to Rio Arriba County on February 10, 1880. The location of the county seat—Tierra Amarilla—created problems for residents, as any county business required a long trek across part of Rio Arriba County, the Carson National Forest, and the Jicarilla Apache Reservation.

Citizens of the area clamored for a separate county with a closer seat of government. Finally, on February 24, 1887, San Juan County was created out of Rio Arriba County's western end. Due to an oversight, the Territorial Act did not specify a location for the county seat. Although this resulted in problems, elections, and a general uproar that has been published in countless documents with several different versions of events, this book will only touch on the results.

Territorial governor E.G. Ross appointed the first set of county officials, and on February 25, 1887, the appointees were sworn in by justice of the peace E.G. Berry. The temporary county seat was in Aztec. The first county officers chosen by the people were elected on November 6, 1888.

The 1890 election set the permanent location of the county seat in Junction City (on the peninsula across the Animas River from Farmington), and the battle began. Originally, Junction City got 255 votes, Aztec got 246, and Farmington got 1. The next two years were spent wrangling over whether or not the election was legal and who was eligible to vote. The district court process resulted in many votes being disqualified because a person was too young, did not live in the district, was bribed, and so forth.

The Territorial Supreme Court finally settled the disputes on August 24, 1892, when the seat of San Juan County was permanently situated in Aztec.

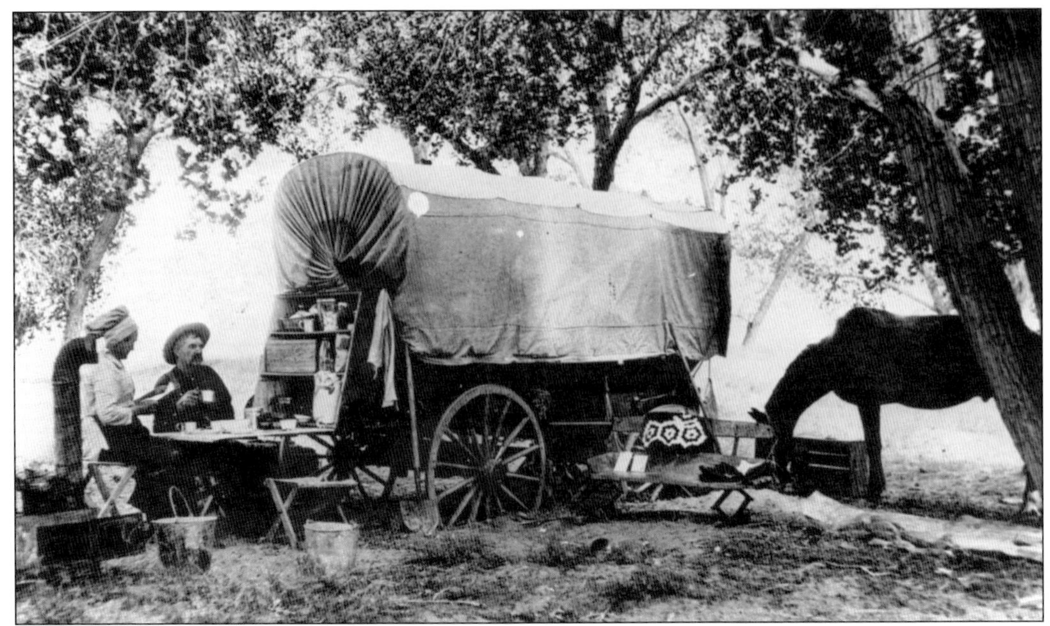

The area now known as Aztec opened for homesteading in 1876. Mr. and Mrs. Estes, shown here with their covered wagon, were typical of the settlers who came to Aztec. The table is part of the wagon that lowers for access to the provisions. The wagon seat has been removed and serves as a bench or cot. Perhaps the Estes Arroyo that goes under Ruins Road into the Animas River is named after them. (Courtesy Farmington Museum.)

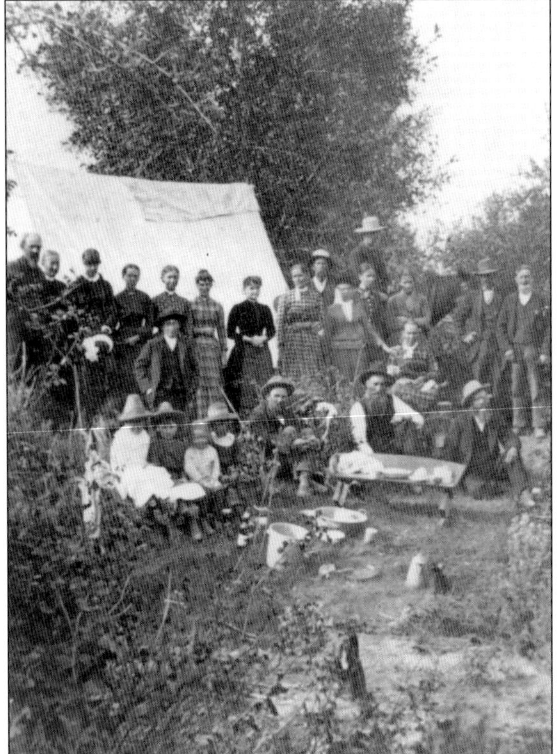

The pioneers built shelters, dug irrigation ditches, planted crops, and then made sure their children and families had churches and schools. This 1887 camp meeting is an example of an early religious gathering. The Reverend Hugh Griffin, of the Methodist Episcopal church, came to the area in 1878 and rode the circuit to spread the gospel to at least 11 settlements, including Aztec. (Courtesy Aztec Museum.)

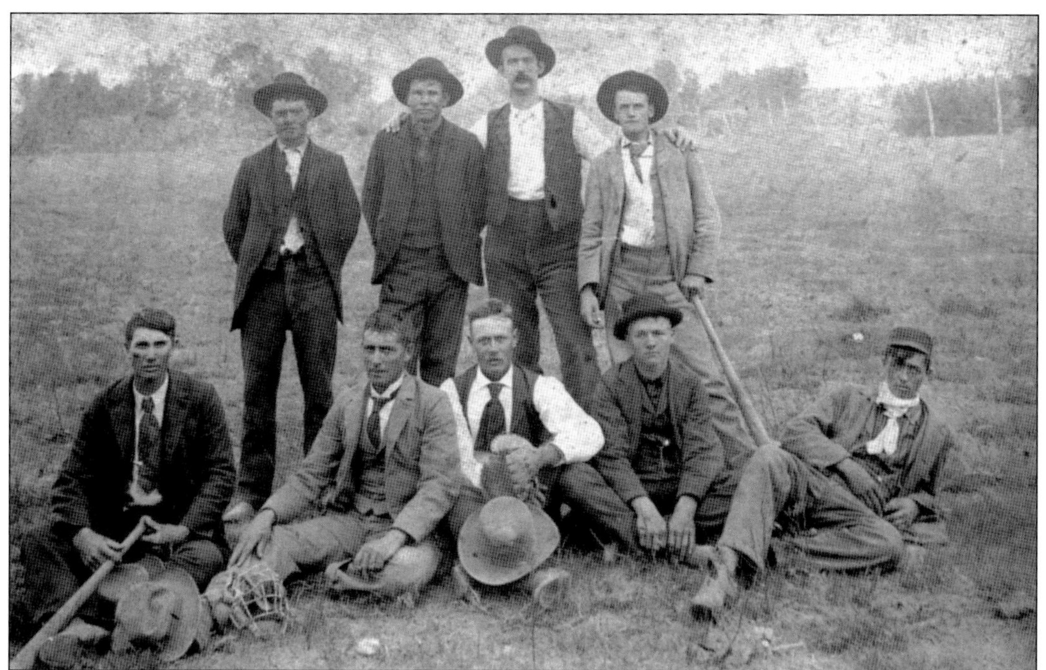

Baseball became a great outlet for the early settlers, and teams soon formed in each community. Competition was intense, and each town came out in force to support their players. This 1898 photograph shows one of Aztec's first baseball teams. Pictured here from left to right are (first row) J.M. Palmer, Charles Safford, Leonard Boat, and two unidentified players; (second row) A.C. Scott, Frank Baker, John Rogers, and Bill Lenfesty. (Courtesy Aztec Museum.)

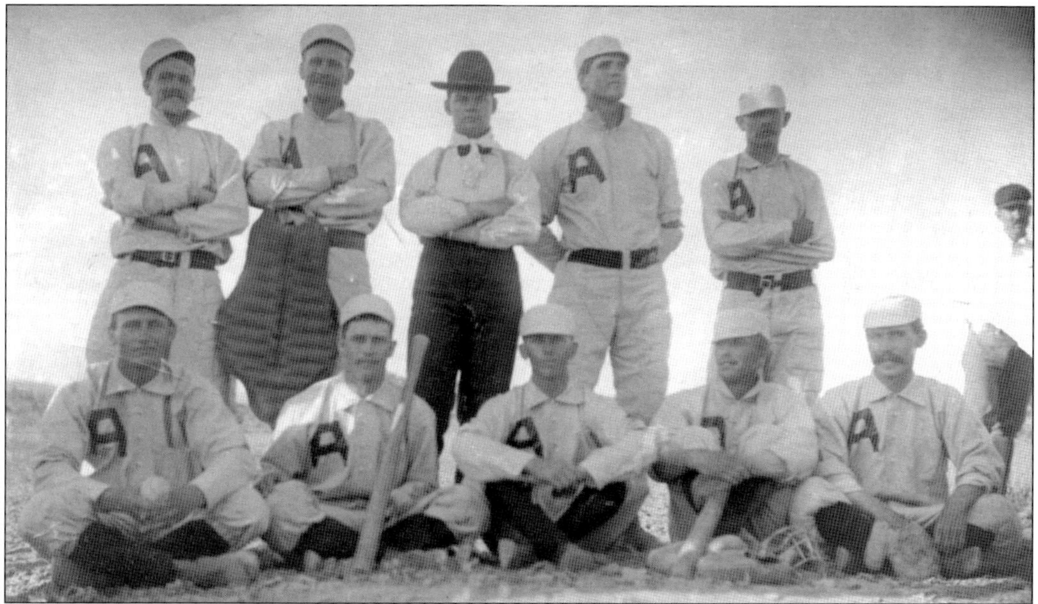

By 1900, the Aztec baseball team sported uniforms. From left to right, the team members are (first row) Byron Baker, John Austin, Albie Hiblie, Charlie Safford, and George Grable; (second row) Bill Lenfesty, Frank Baker, manager Joe Pendleton, Tony Hustkin, and Leonard Boat. (Courtesy Aztec Museum.)

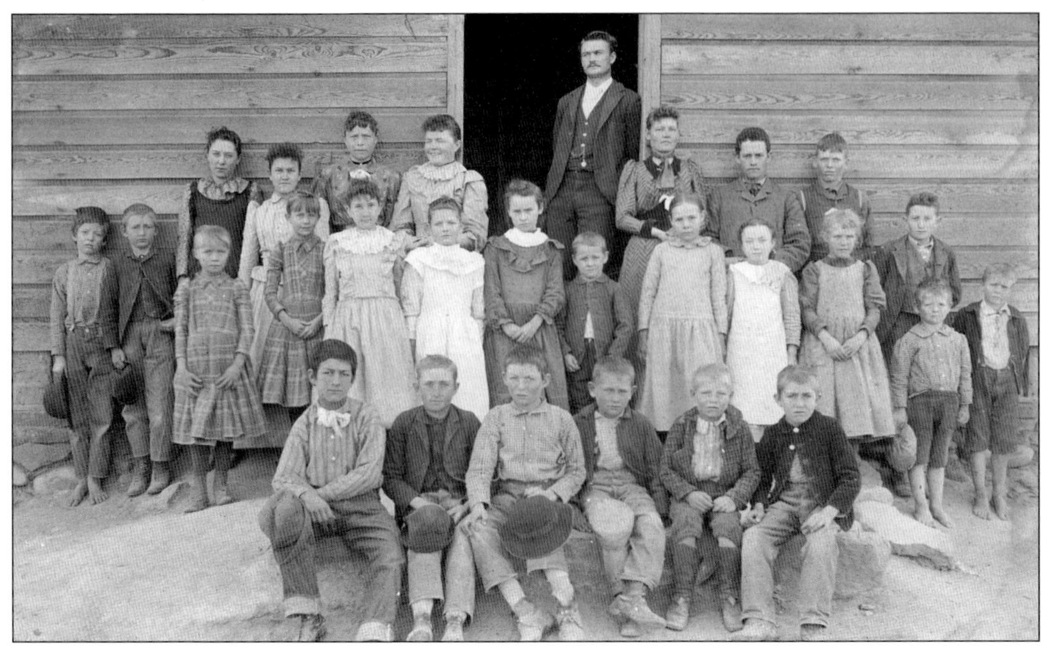

Aztec students and their teacher pose in a photograph from about 1890. They are, from left to right, (first row) George Watkins, Jay McCoy, Bur Knickerbocker, Lyle Koontz, Jess Carmine, and Len McCoy; (second row) two unidentified girls in matching dresses, Stella Stowell, Wanda Atterbury, Bessie Austin, Timothy Allen ("Allie") Austin, Rena Watkins, Eva Gillam, Ethel Smith, Harvey Knickerbocker, and Bart Smith; (third row) Frank Knickerbocker, Arch McCoy, Zoe Rash, Flora Stowell, Lee Atterbury, Lena Austin, Mr. Yeager, Jenny Danner, John B. Austin, Barnet Knickerbocker, and Everet Fields. Note the many pioneer family names. (Courtesy Aztec Museum.)

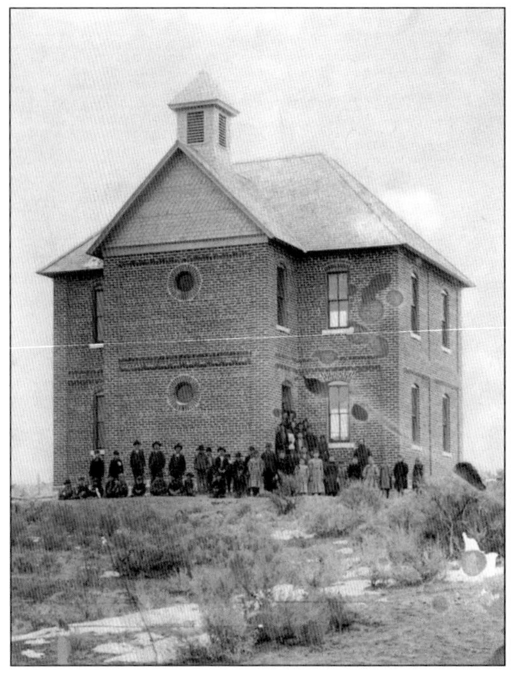

Aztec school students moved from a temporary frame building into this impressive two-story brick structure in 1899. The bricks were made from nearby soil and fired at a local kiln. According to a Bureau of Immigration brochure, the building cost $2,500. (Courtesy Aztec Museum.)

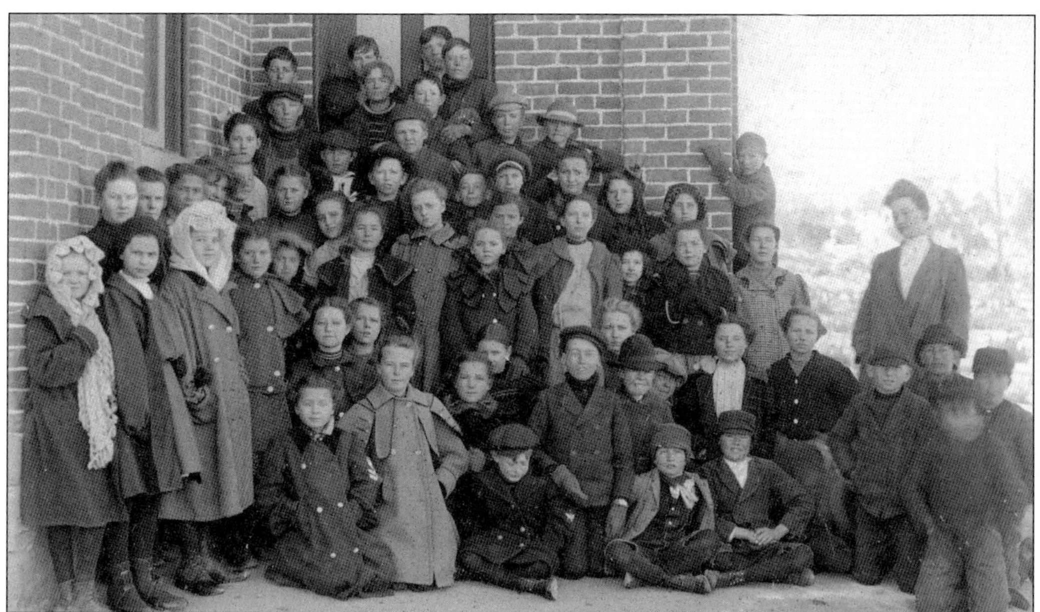

These two photographs show how students dressed in the Aztec school system in the 1900s. The image above shows the third-grade class in 1905. Below, students of varied ages pose in 1908, when school was held in the courthouse. Pictured below are, from left to right, (first row) Ray Morrison, Henry Thomas, unidentified, Everett Pollard, Tom Marcotte, Don Jones, and Joe Pollard; (second row) Ora Whitfor, Lily Colton, Marguerite Kirk, Ertel Current, Golden Bell, Flossie Benton, Cora Williams, Ruth Hartman, unidentified, Mark Current, and Lois Fifield; (third row) Gilbert Hatfield, Essie Kirk, Dick Williams, Ona Eblen, Bess Martin, Thetis Lair, Esther Keel, Maude Van Vorst, Art Walters, Hazel Brown, Anna Whitehead, Earl Revell, Bruce Walters, unidentified, and teacher Sherman Coon; (fourth row) Kip Bell, unidentified, Clayton Pollard, Robert Van Vorst, Earl Dalton, Lyle Cutting, and Jim Green. (Both courtesy Aztec Museum.)

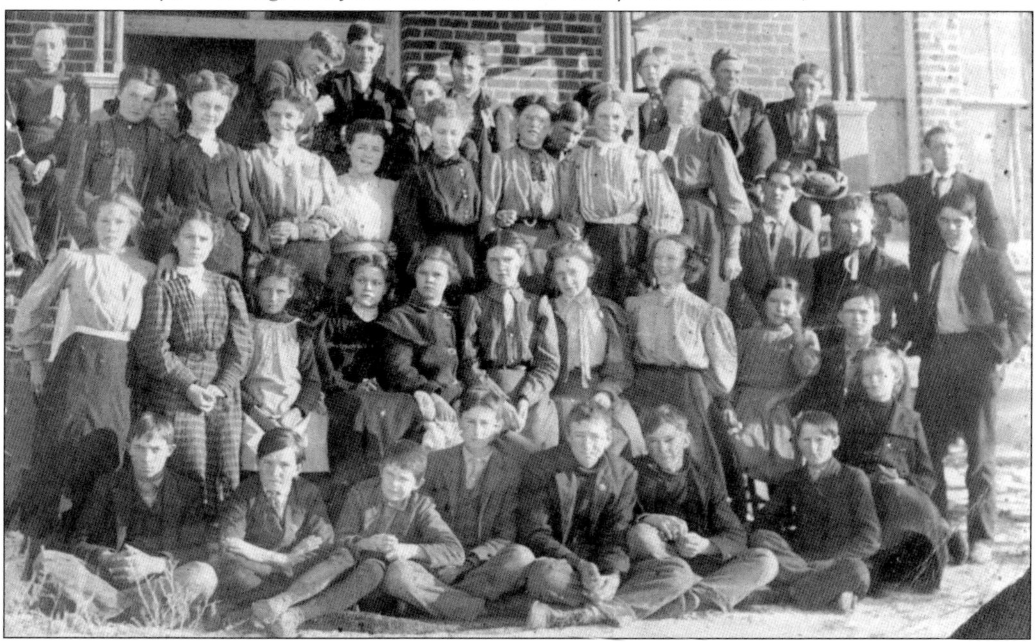

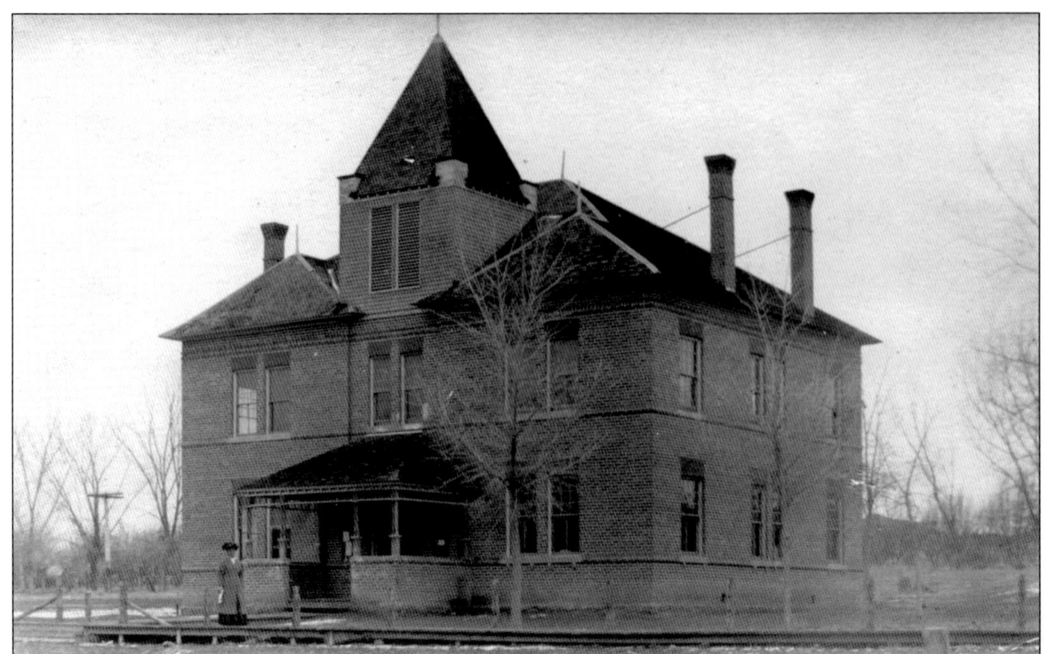

After the dust settled over the debate of where the county seat should be, the people of Aztec built this courthouse in 1898. According to Brewer family records, C.G. Brewer and his oldest son, Truman, burned the brick on the grounds with material from the sides and bottom of the nearby irrigation ditch. This courthouse served the community until it was demolished and replaced in 1950. (Courtesy Aztec Museum.)

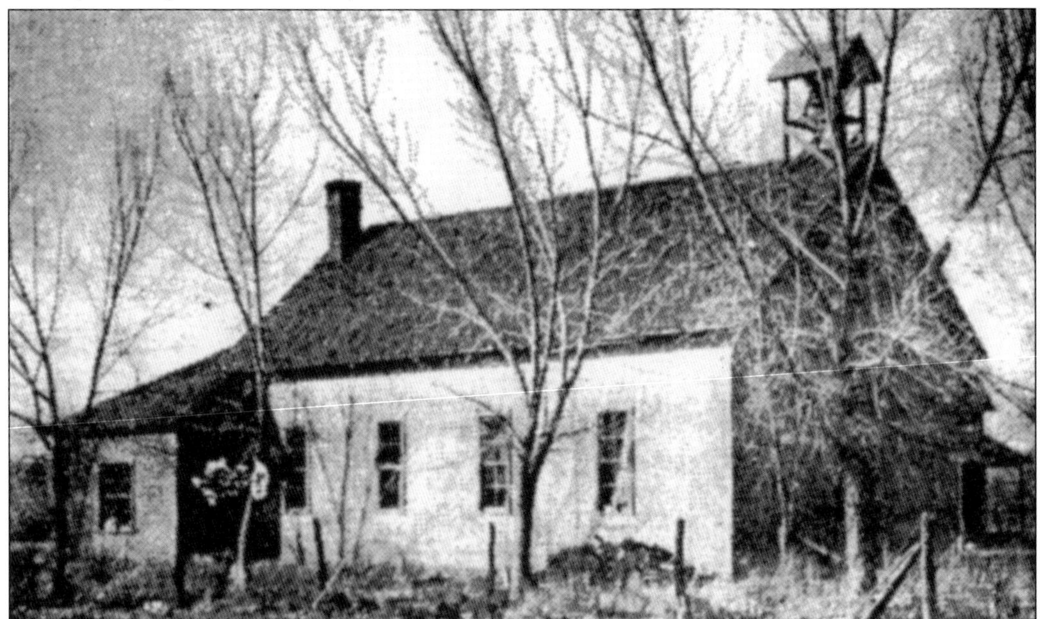

The Aztec Presbyterian Church was built in 1889 with adobe bricks made from ground just north of the church site. This postcard photograph was taken about 1910, and the building looks much the same today. It is on both the National and New Mexico State Historic Registers. (Courtesy Aztec Museum.)

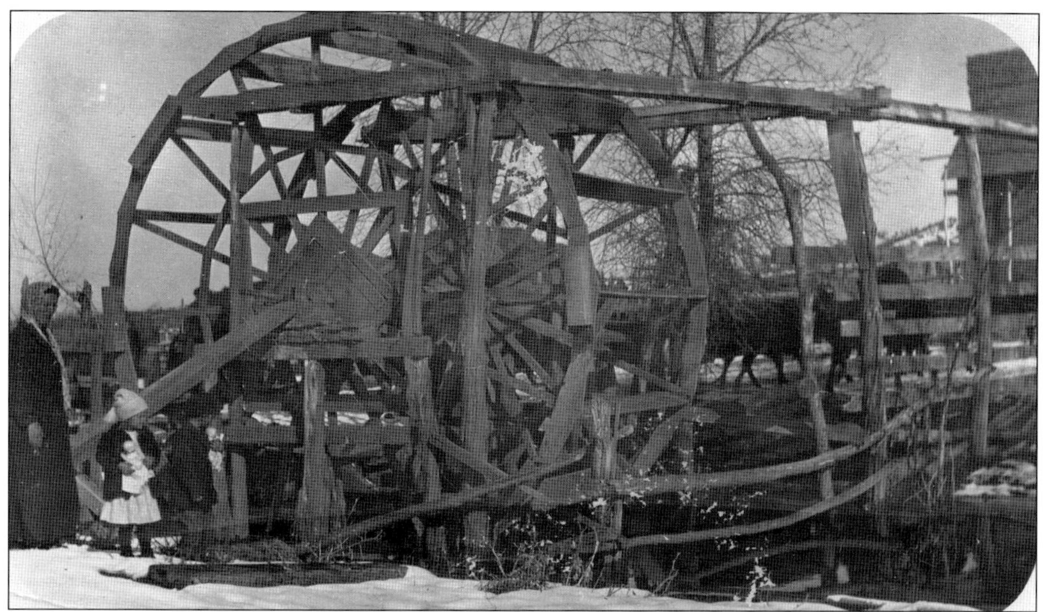

This homemade wooden waterwheel is an example of the ingenuity the pioneers used to get water to their fields. Mrs. J.M. McGee and children are shown on this 1906 postcard. (Courtesy Aztec Museum.)

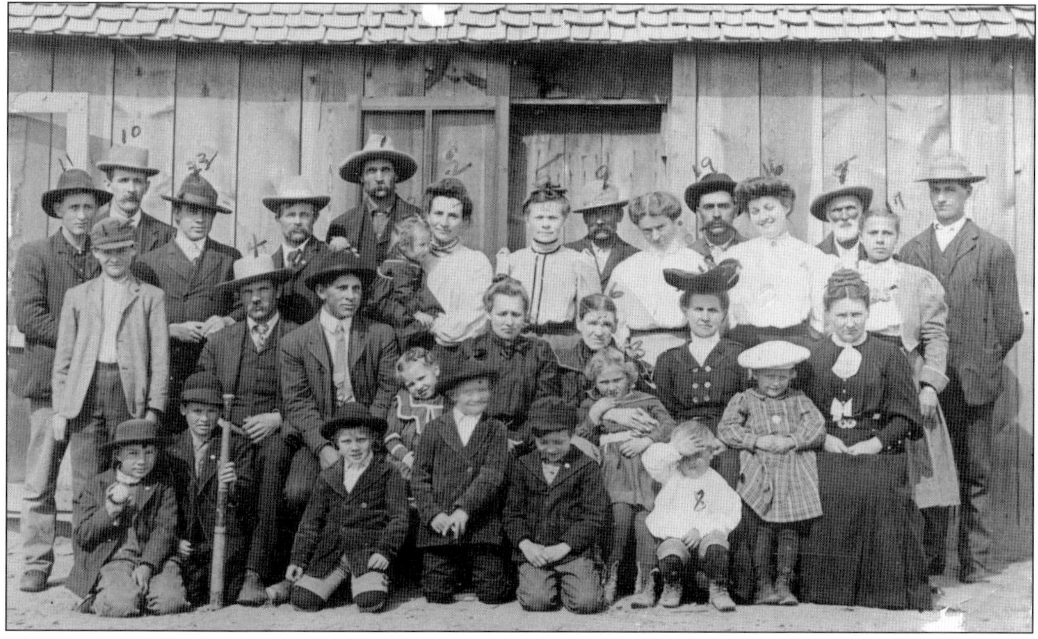

The McGee family and friends are shown here in 1905. They are, from left to right, (first row, children) Daley Hildebrand, Walter McGee, Elmer McGee, Mary McGee, Harold Titt, unidentified, Beulah McGee, Frank McGee, and unidentified; (second row) Fred Lawson (standing), Tom McGee, Rhoder Hildebrand, unidentified, Lucretia McGee, Mary Hildebrand, and Mary Titt; (third row) Arthur Lawson, Will McGee, Floyd Hildebrand, unidentified, James R. McGee, Catherine McGee holding her daughter Ona, Dorah McGee, Frank Titt, unidentified, J.R. Hildebrand, Sadie McGee, William Micager McGee, Etta Hildebrand, and Davis McGee. (Courtesy Aztec Museum.)

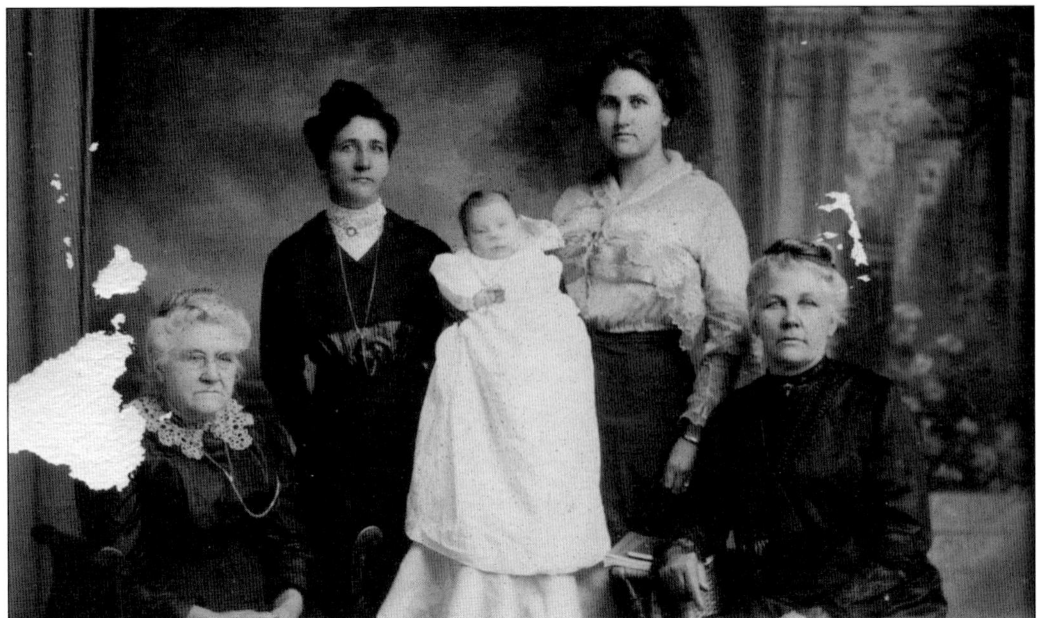

This damaged photograph represents women from some of the early pioneer families. From left to right are Mrs. Moses Blancett, Lula McCoy Rathjen, Rathjen's daughter Lena Southard (holding her son Billy), and Blancett's daughter Ella McCoy. Moses Blancett served as commissioner with the first set of San Juan County officials and also on the first board of directors for the Aztec Presbyterian Church. (Courtesy Aztec Museum.)

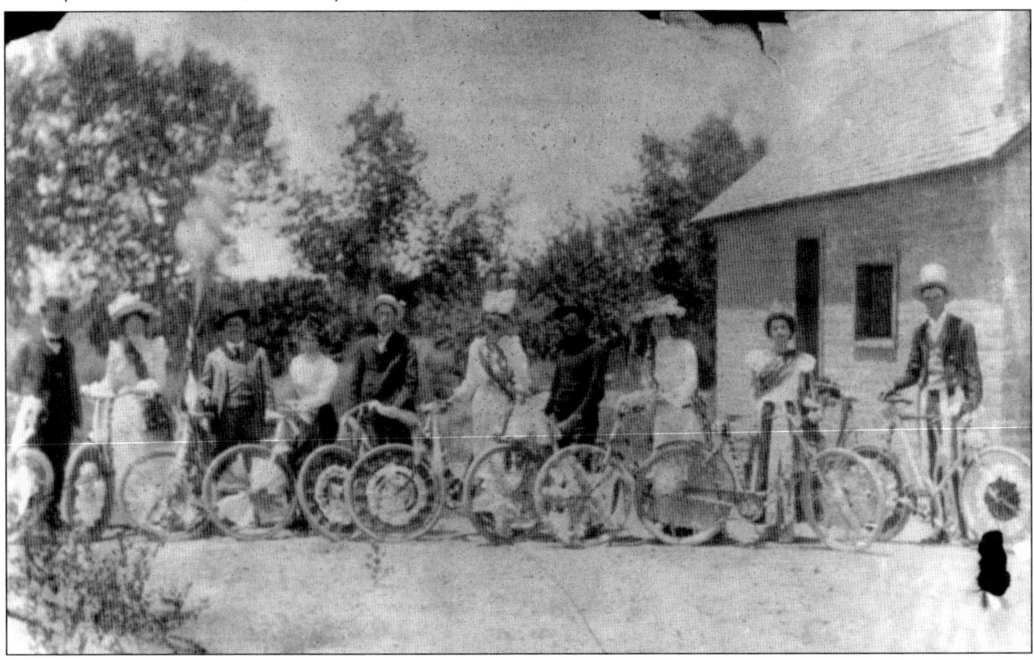

The Fourth of July meant celebrations, parades, music, and other entertainment. These bicyclists decked out themselves and their bicycles for the parade in 1902. Pictured here are, from left to right, L.C. Grove, Esther Brown, John Austin, Maud Austin, James McCoy, unidentified, Oren Randall, Bessie Austin Randall, Lizzie Randall, and John Koontz. (Courtesy Farmington Museum.)

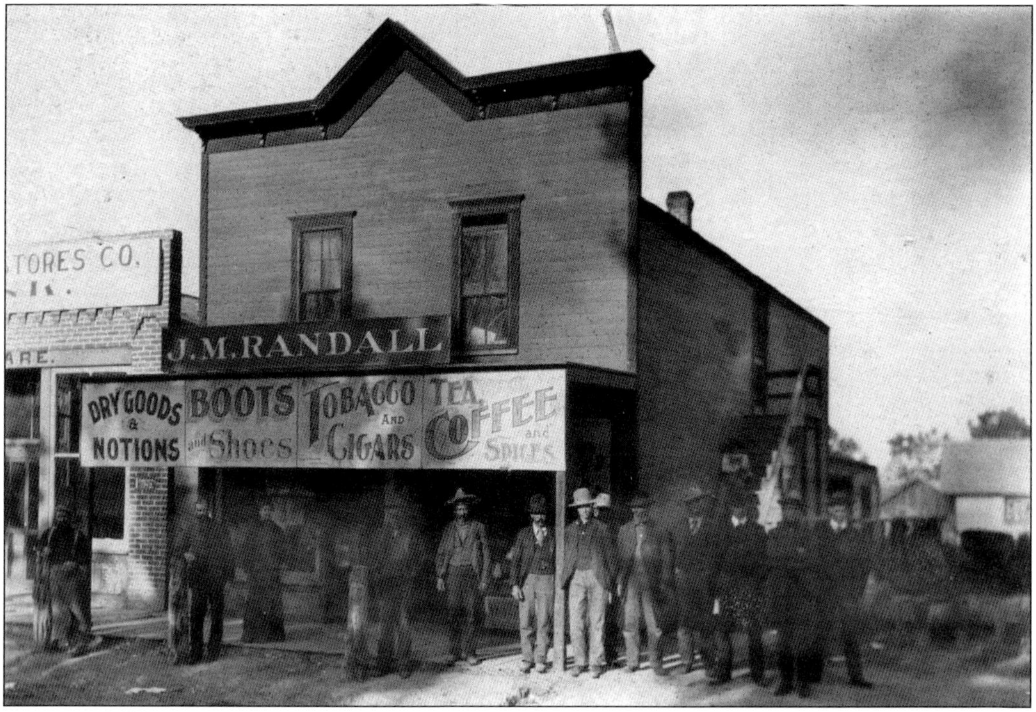

J.M. Randall built this wooden general merchandise store in 1901. The Randall family was among the early pioneers. Their 160-acre homestead was east of Aztec. (Courtesy Aztec Museum.)

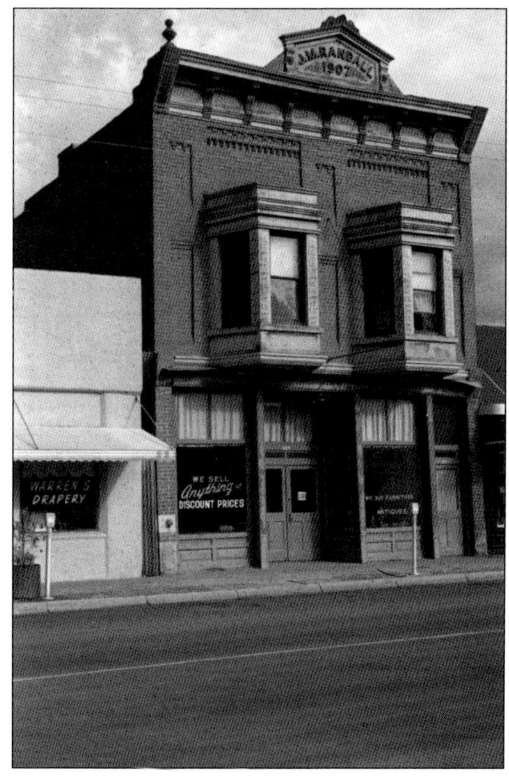

Business was good in Aztec, and J.M. Randall built this two-story brick building in 1907. Living quarters were upstairs. The building, at 117 South Main Avenue, is on both the State and National Historic Registers. This 1966 photograph looks much the same as it did when new, and even today. (Courtesy San Juan County Historical Society.)

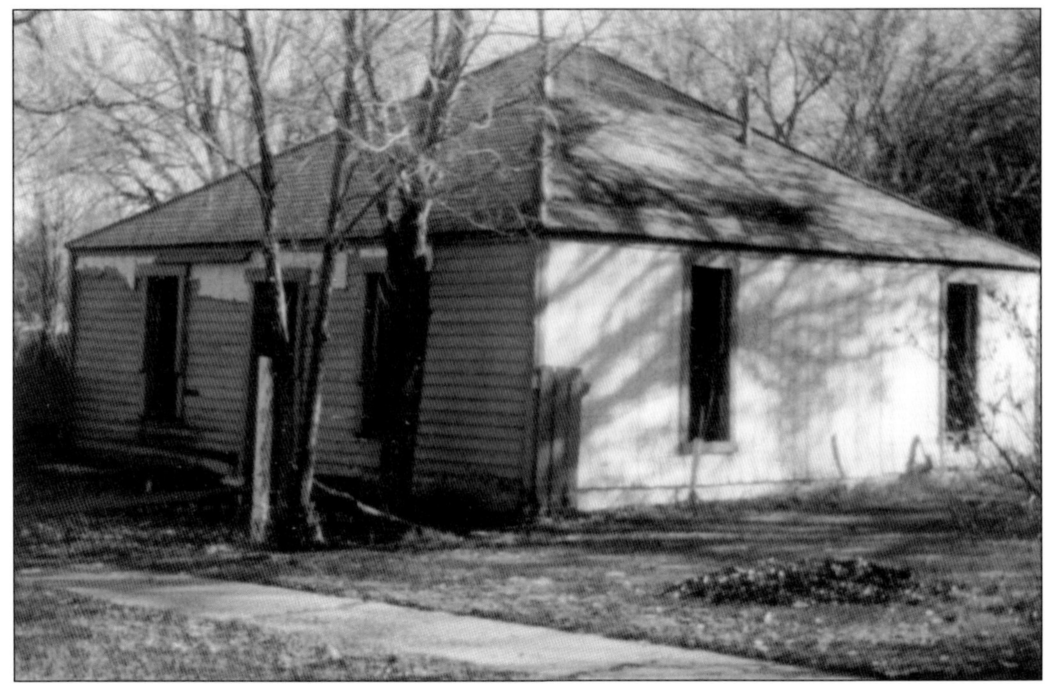

The railroad arrived in 1905, generating changes all over the area. It is said that 13 of these square houses were built for railroad workers and scattered around town. Each house had four rooms and a path to the outhouse. A few remain, but many have been torn down. This one, located on North Church Avenue, has been extensively remodeled. (Courtesy Phyllis Gilkey.)

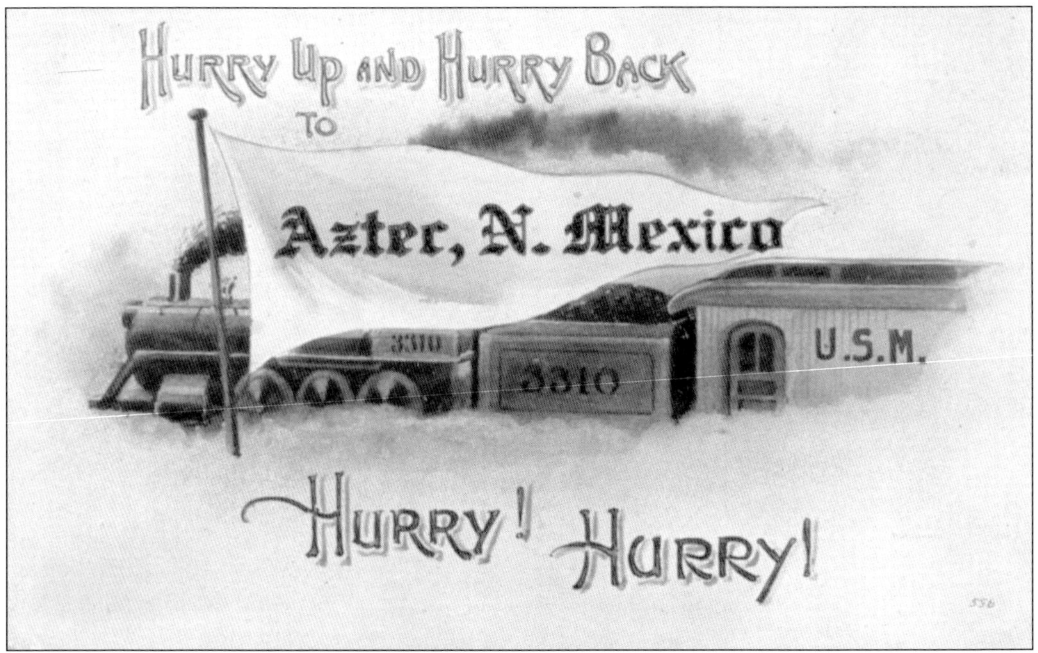

This 1905 postcard was issued to celebrate the arrival of the Denver & Rio Grande railroad. With more people coming to the area, the future of Aztec changed, as the community was suddenly in need of commerce and buildings. (Courtesy Aztec Museum.)

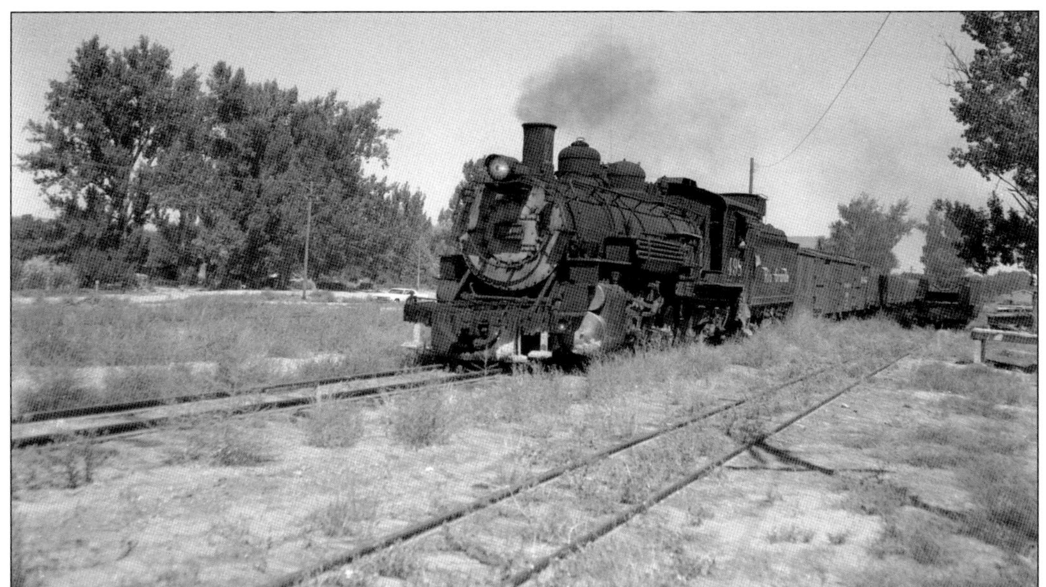

The first Denver & Rio Grande engine chugged into Aztec on August 24, 1905, on a standard-gauge rail. It was thought that the rail would go through Farmington and on to Gallup; several surveys were made with that in mind. It never happened, though, and the struggles of changing from standard-gauge cars to narrow gauge in Durango ended in August 1923 when a large crew moved one track over to narrow gauge. Only one day of scheduled runs was affected.

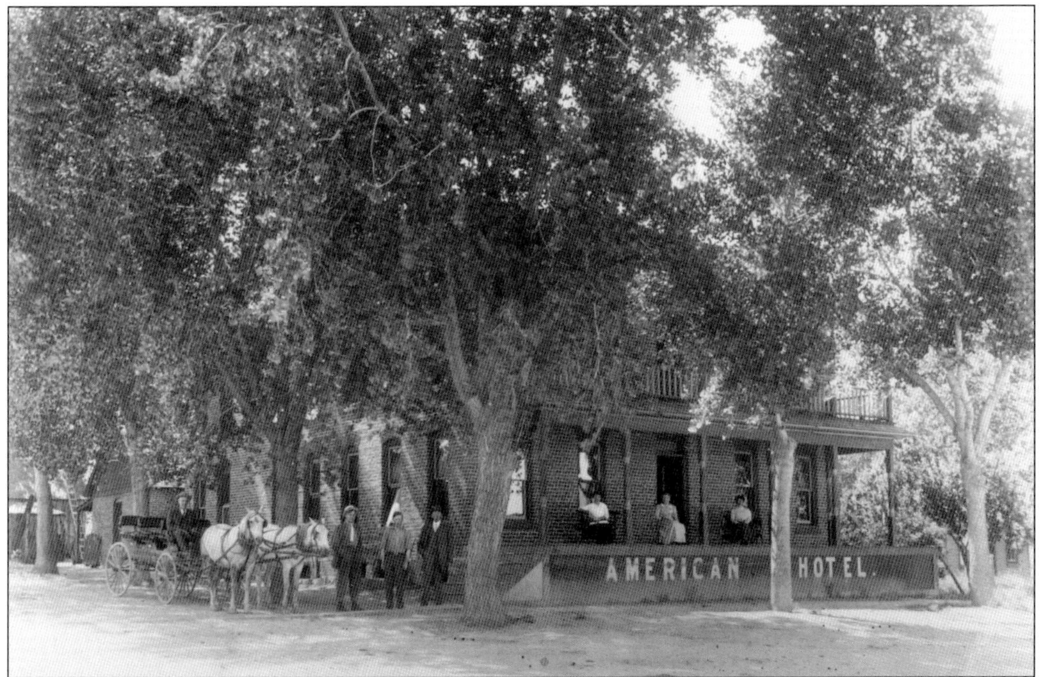

George W. Stone saw the need for a larger hotel in Aztec to service the increased traffic brought in by the railroad. In 1906, brick masons C.G. Brewer and sons built the American Hotel on the corner of Zia Street and Main Avenue. The Stone family had eight daughters, so there was plenty of help on hand. By March 1907, H.L. Lair was proprietor of the hotel. (Courtesy Aztec Museum.)

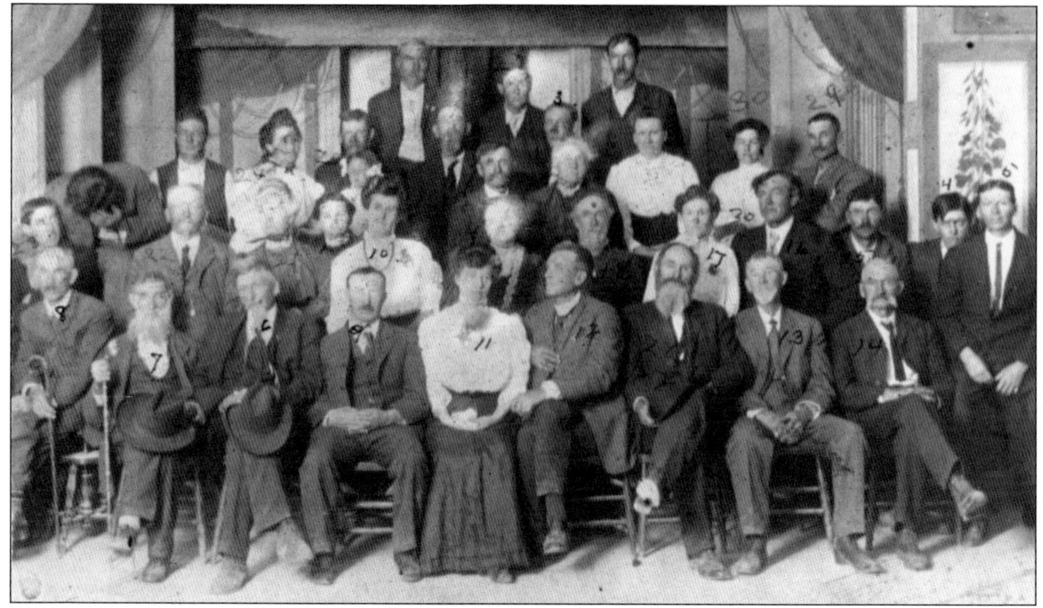

Green's Opera House was a popular place to meet in 1905. Pictured here are, from left to right, (first row) Mike Real, Allen McCoy, Peter Knickerbocker, Al Hubbard, Lizzie Vaughan, Boone Vaughan, D.J. Craig, unidentified, A.F. Stump, and Ernest Knickerbocker; (second row) Will Rash, Fred Bunker, Kate Bunker, Martha Morrison, Ella Hubbard, Mary Howe, Joe Howe, Arrie Stowell McCoy, Lee Brown, John Swire, and Linn Blancett; (third row) unidentified, John Morrison, Kate Townsend, Fred Townsend, Eva Townsend (on Fred's lap), G. Will McCoy, Harvey McCoy, George Blancett, Lucienda Blancett, Mrs. Earl, Lillie Blancett McWilliams, and George Allen; (fourth row) Charles McKinney, Dean Howe, and Jim Brown. (Courtesy Farmington Museum.)

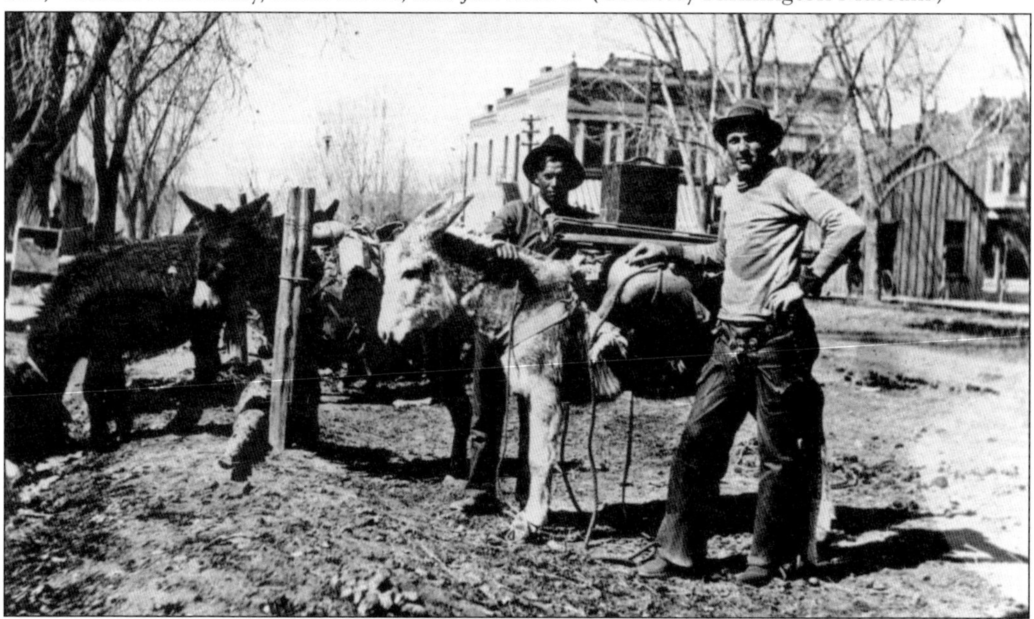

This 1909 image shows two young men with their mules in downtown Aztec. The Pinkstaff building, erected in 1906, is in the background. George F. Bruington's law office was upstairs in the Pinkstaff building. (Courtesy Farmington Museum.)

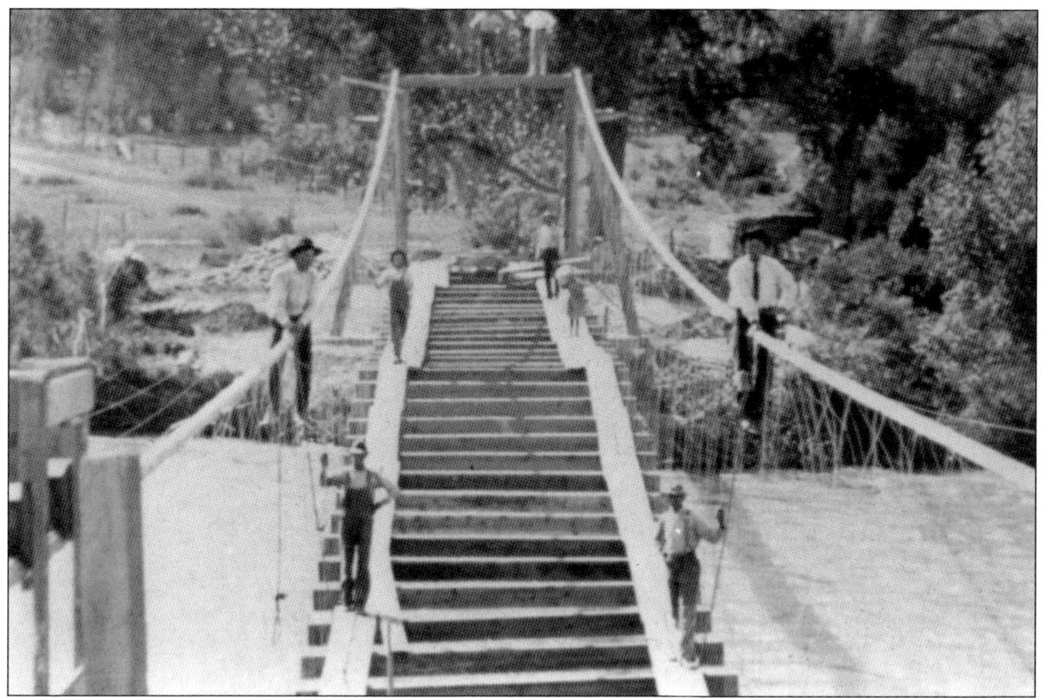

J.S. Thurston, possibly the man in the tie at right, and his sons Bill and Tom built this suspension bridge over the Animas River in 1908. The bridge was located at the mouth of the Estes Arroyo, just north of the present cement bridges. (Courtesy Judy Hollar.)

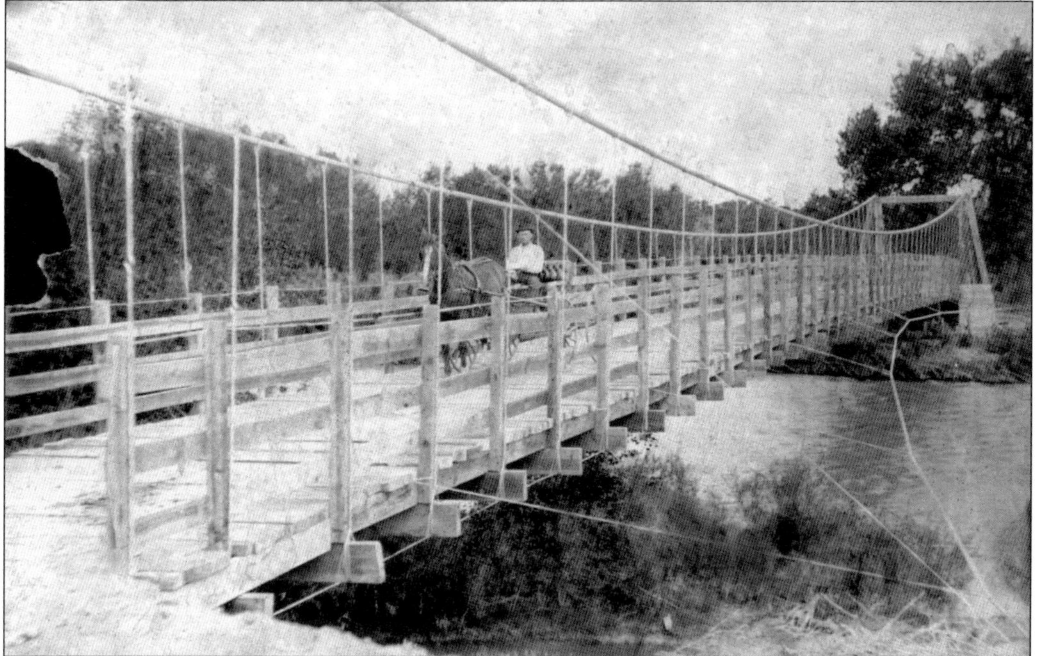

Aztec's first bridge, built farther down the river in the 1890s, washed out in a flood in 1905. This suspension bridge opened in 1908. Cy Cameron, pictured here, was said to be the first to cross. This was the only bridge in the county that survived the 1911 flood. (Courtesy Aztec Museum.)

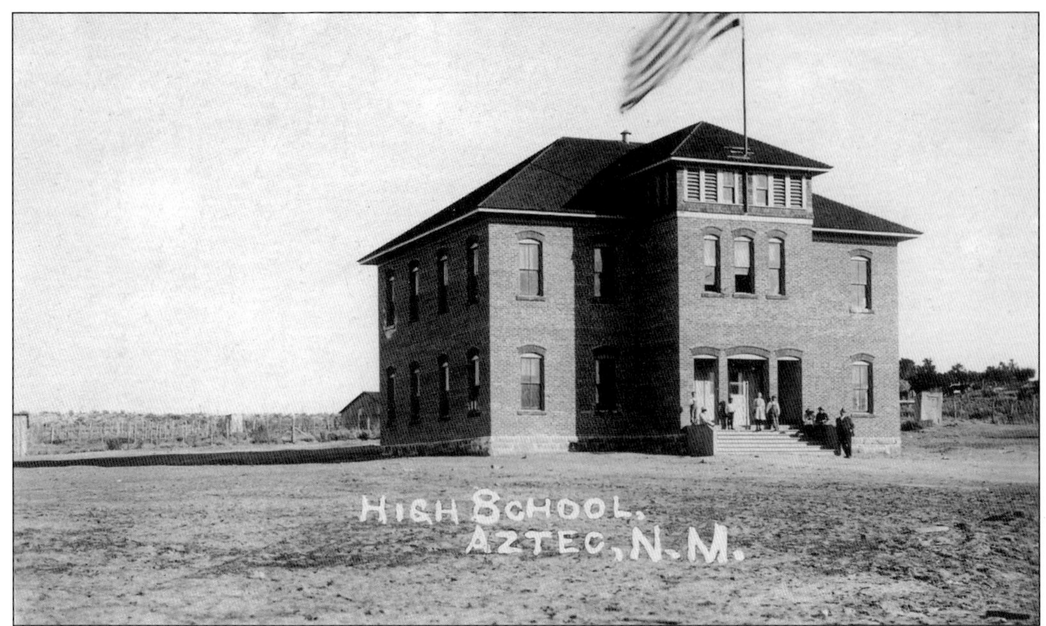

Schools remained a primary priority for the Aztec citizens. This is Aztec's first high school, built in 1909. The population of Aztec in 1910 was 509 (975 when including the surrounding rural area). (Courtesy Aztec Museum.)

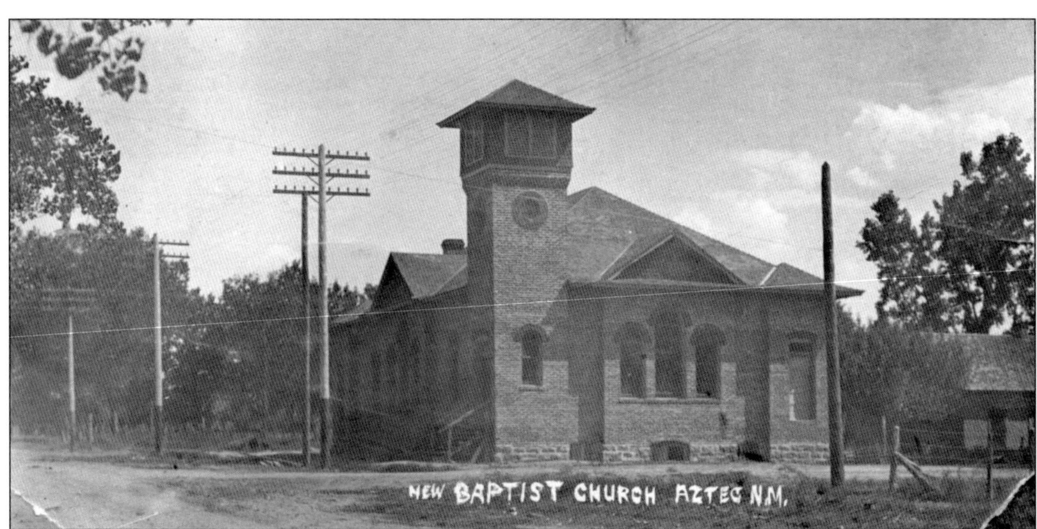

The new Aztec Baptist Church, built in 1909 at Chaco and Church Streets, is shown on this c. 1915 postcard. Before this building was constructed, the church met in the school and the courthouse. In 1909, the church had 95 members. It was destroyed by fire in 1922 and rebuilt with a stucco exterior on the same site. (Courtesy Deanna Morrison Blythe.)

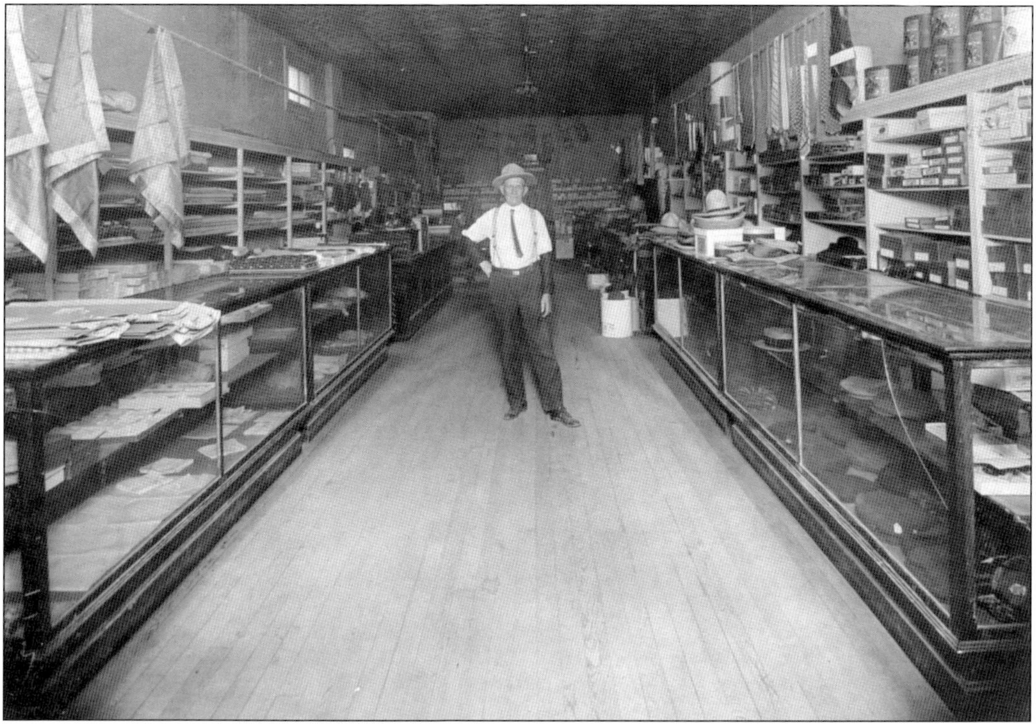

Richard S. Ridenour, shown here, purchased the Bailey portion of the Bailey and Howe General Store in 1908. The store was located in the Pinkstaff building—today's 123 South Main Avenue. (Courtesy Bernice Gardner Bowra.)

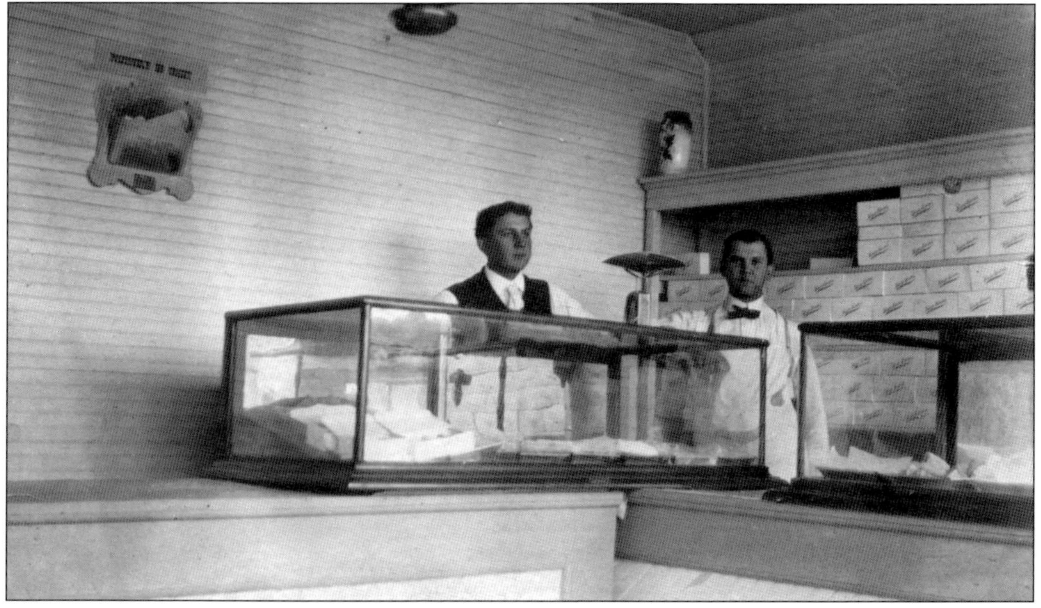

In this 1908 image, Clare (left) and Tom Uptegrove pose in Aztec's first candy store, which was located inside the Bunker building. That building was destroyed by fire in 1910. In 1913, the Uptegroves built a new store on North Main Avenue; there are plenty of photographs of that site. (Courtesy Aztec Museum.)

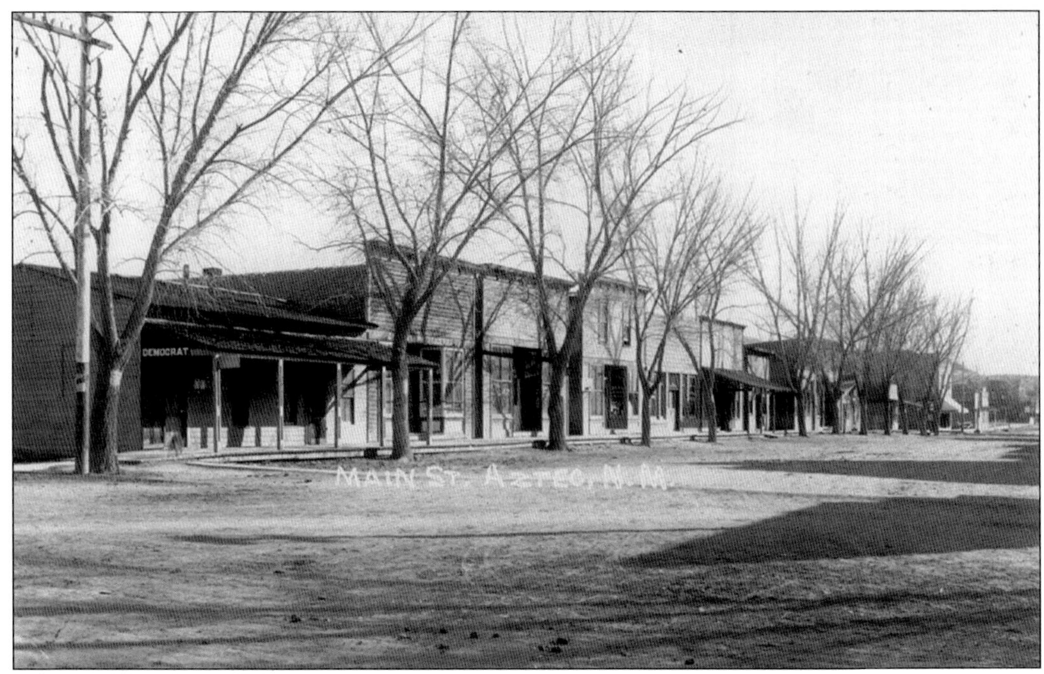

These two photographs show parts of Main Avenue in 1910. The above picture is the east side of Aztec's Main Avenue, looking south. The first building on the left houses a local newspaper, the *San Juan Democrat*. The *Democrat* ran weekly from July 19, 1906, to September 25, 1914. On October 4, 1914, the *Democrat* merged with the *San Juan County Index* to form the *Aztec Independent*. The last building, at far right, is the two-story brick American Hotel. The picture below is the west side of Main Avenue, looking north. The large building, L.F. Bates & Co. Aztec Livery, is about where Citizens Bank is today. The buildings with signs, going north, are the McGee & Rathjen Blacksmith Shop, Louis Grauel's tailor shop, a meat market and, at the corner, the Brewer building. The second block is recognizable as part of Aztec's present-day historic district. (Both courtesy Aztec Museum.)

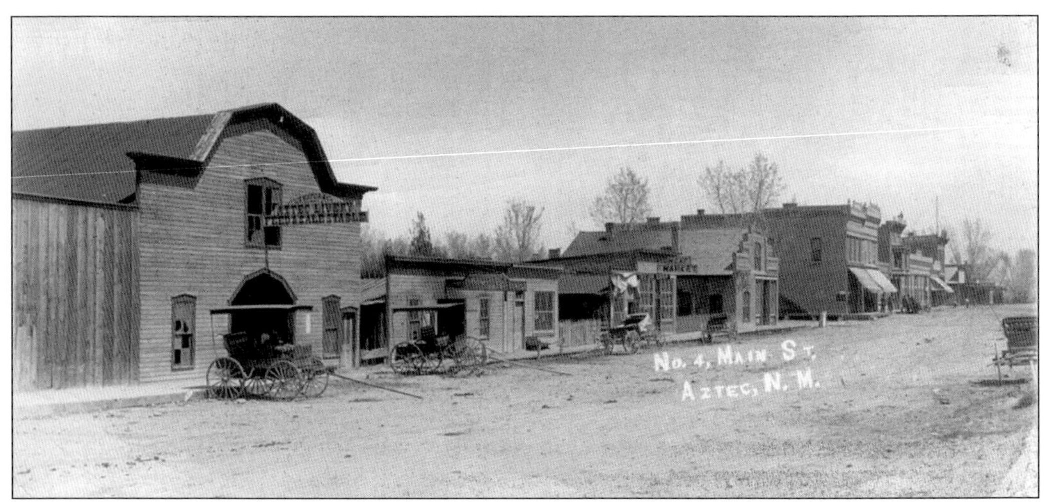

Two

Aztec Is Growing

Aztec residents were plagued nearly every spring with high water runoff and, often, a flood. The most publicized and damaging flood was on October 6, 1911. The summer had brought lots of rain, and the soil was soaked. Heavy rains began above Durango, Colorado, and residents there sent word to Aztec, Farmington, and Shiprock that a flood was on the way.

The *Farmington Times-Hustler* reported the event on October 12, 1911. The paper's short sentences tell the bare facts: "Twenty-five miles of railroad washed away, 150 miles of river bottoms devastated with the San Juan and Animas Rivers higher than ever in the memory of the oldest residents. About 50 families in the county lost their homes." One life was lost.

Statehood was another hurdle for the Aztecans, as it did not come easy. In 1889, a special election sent two delegates to a constitutional convention in Santa Fe. Ten years later, on December 18, 1899, a statehood rally was organized, and petitions were sent to the US Congress in support of statehood.

Nothing happened during the next several years, and due to frustration, some decided to take another tack and try to become part of Colorado. Several memorials were sent to the president and Congress, requesting that San Juan County be annexed to Colorado as Orchard County.

This project didn't go anywhere, so the citizens intensified their efforts to acquire statehood for New Mexico. In 1910, San Juan County again sent delegates to the constitutional convention. On Monday, August 21, 1911, word came that President Taft had signed the Smith-Flood resolution, assuring New Mexico statehood. This initiated celebrations throughout the county.

The festivities proved premature when word came that, in reality, President Taft had vetoed the resolution. A second resolution, entered by Sen. Henry Flood of Virginia, was worded in such a way as to avoid a veto; this resolution passed. New Mexico finally officially entered the union on January 6, 1912.

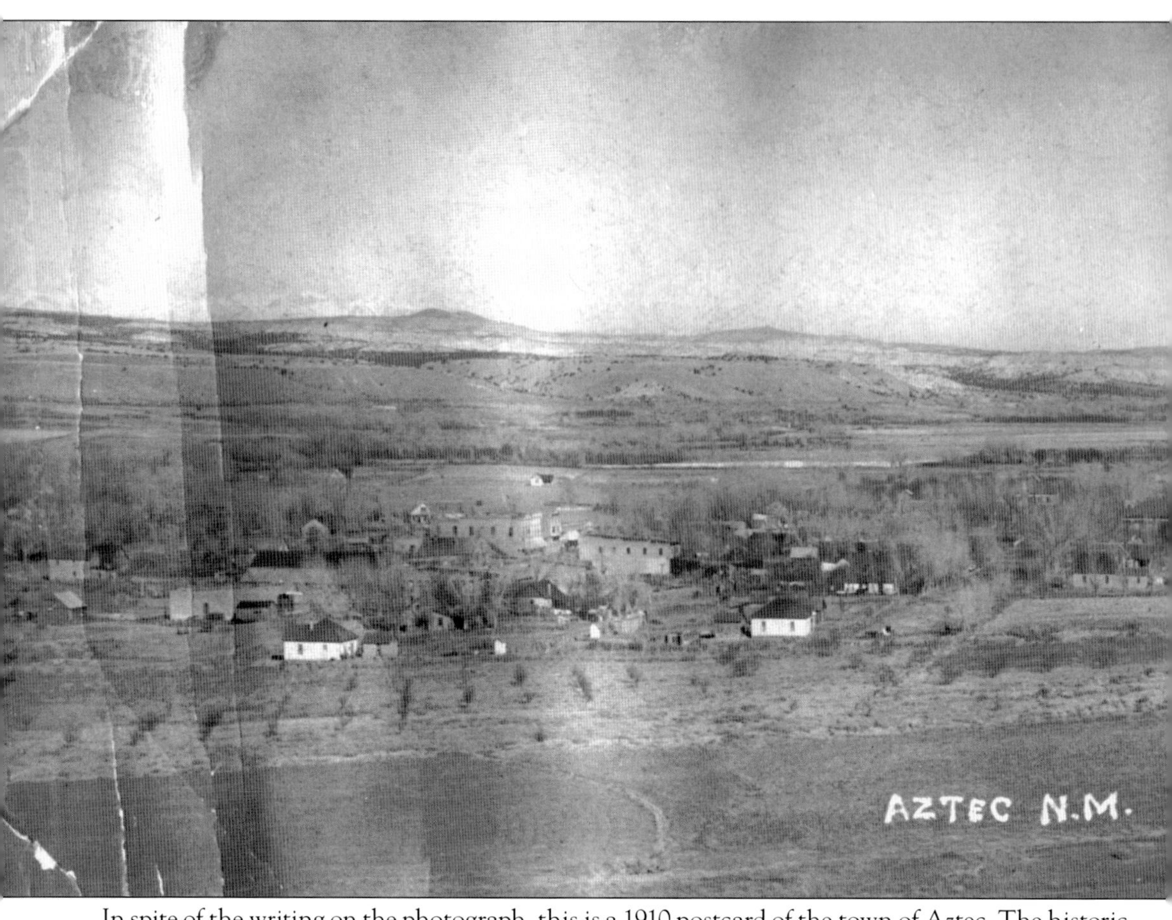

In spite of the writing on the photograph, this is a 1910 postcard of the town of Aztec. The historic district of today was already taking shape. At the time of this picture, the population of Aztec was

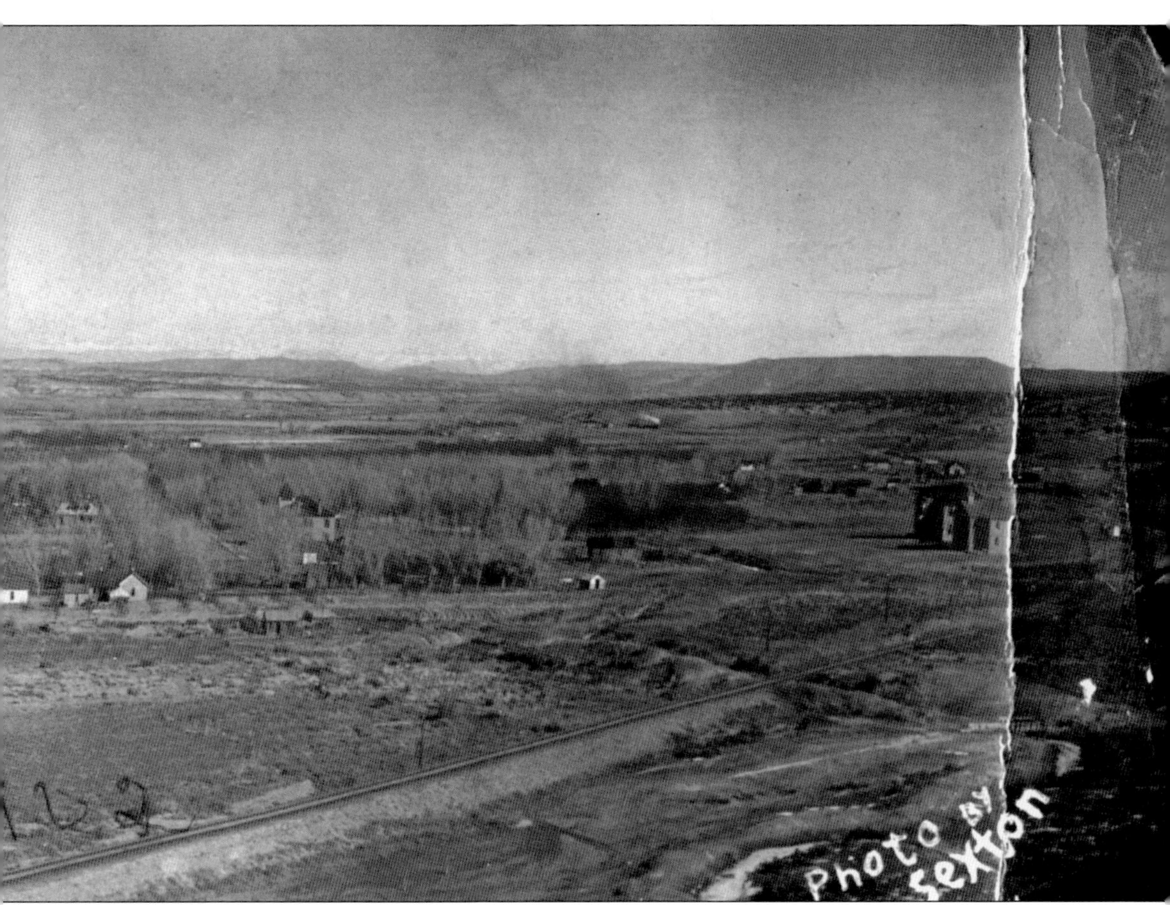

about 500. The courthouse, a two-story brick school, a hotel, and multiple businesses were already settled in. Note the railroad track in the foreground. (Courtesy Deanna Morrison Blythe.)

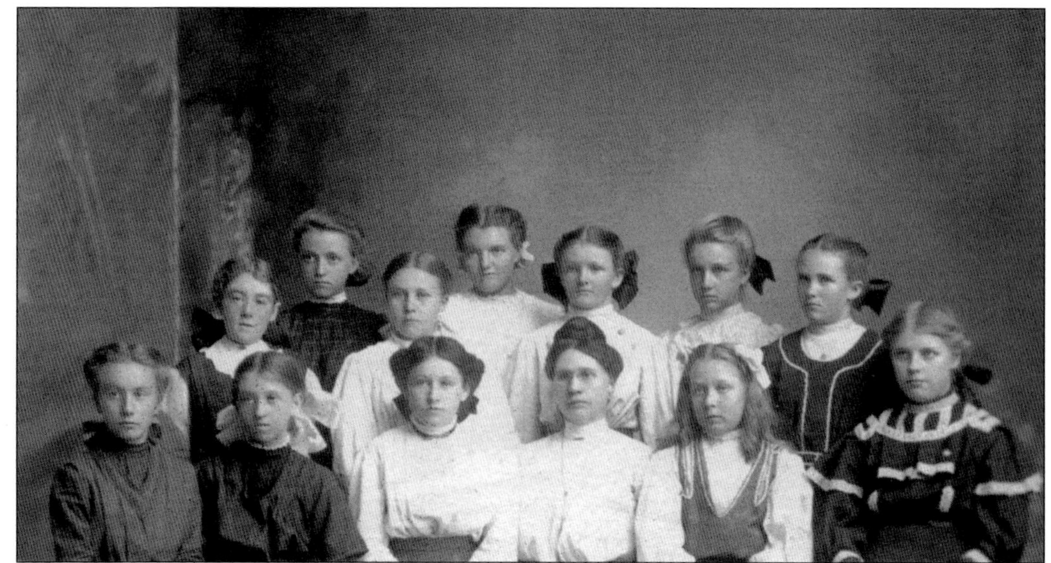

The Aztec Methodist Church Sunday School class of 1910 poses for a photograph. Pictured here are, from left to right, (first row) unidentified, Anna Williams, Eva Sharp, teacher Mrs. Oley Owens, Eva Gerheart, and Olive Ransom; (second row) Mable McCoy, Lucy Thurston, ? Fuller, and Linnie Donals; (third row) Gertrude Morrison, unidentified, and Winona Walters. (Courtesy Aztec Museum.)

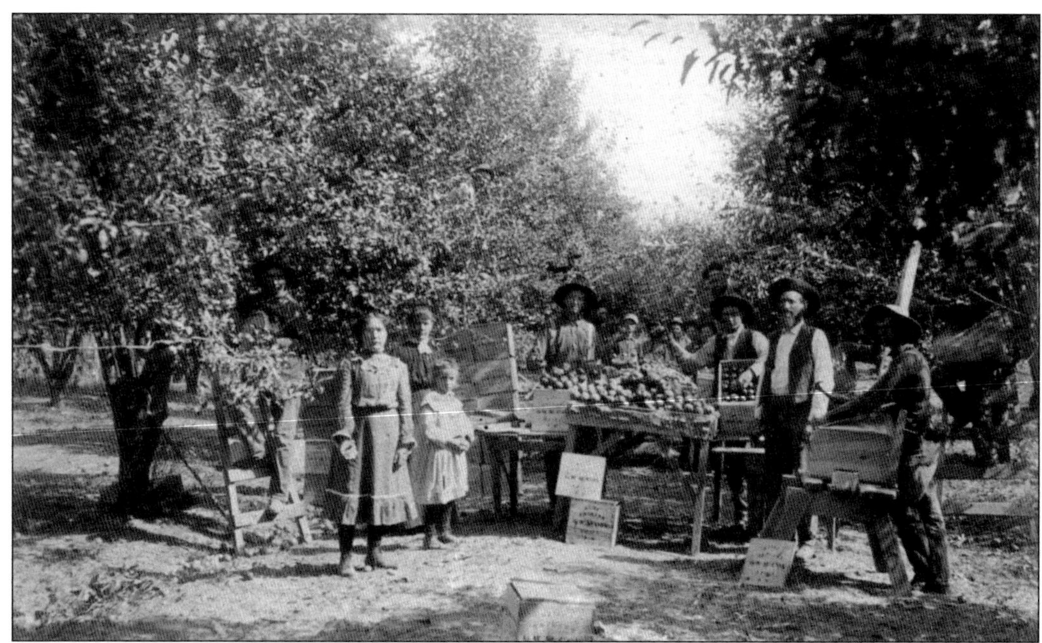

Apples were a major industry in the early years. According to a newspaper account from 1890, San Juan County fruit was known for its "size, flavor and lack of worms." This group pauses while picking apples in the well-established McCoy orchard about 1910. The orchard's location is north of the school on today's McCoy Avenue. (Courtesy Deanna Morrison Blythe.)

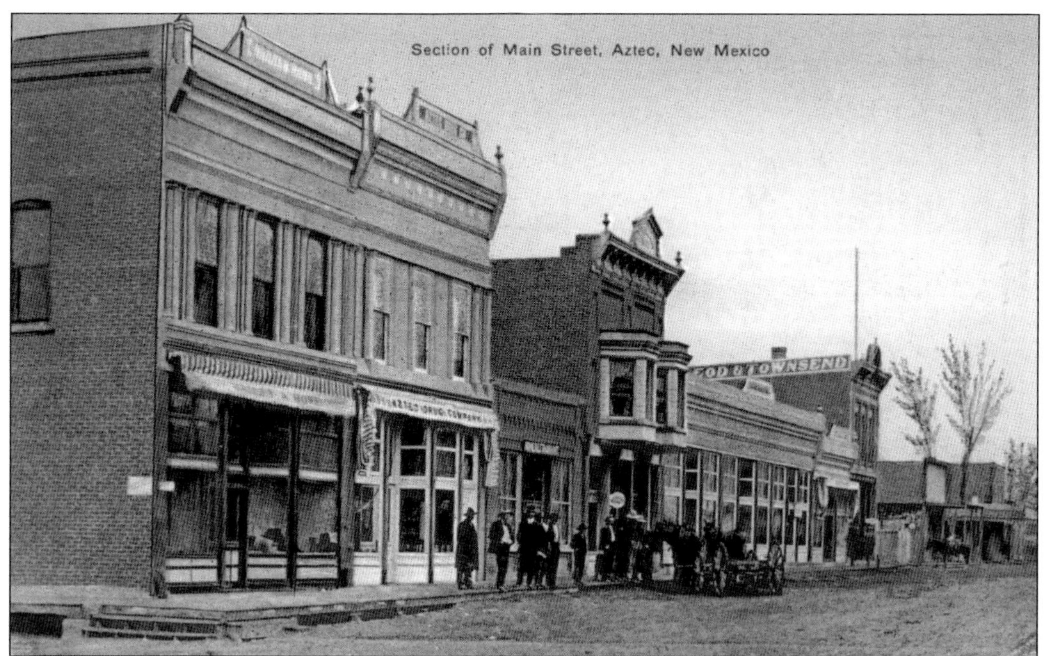

There was a big fire on Main Avenue in 1910. The image above is a postcard showing a full block of buildings. The large, one-story structure fifth from the left is the Bunker building; the small store next to it with the awning is Fred W. Townsend's meat market. Both were destroyed in the fire. Tenants in the Bunker building included Dr. McRee, Waring & Mangham Jewelry, Uptegrove Brothers Confectionery, McClure & Jackson Real Estate, and the post office, where Lucy P. Waring was postmaster. The photograph below, taken from the opposite direction, shows the new two-story Fred W. Townsend building, a still empty space with remnants of the fire, and the new Citizens Bank building. Electricity arrived in 1909. The above picture shows no wires, but the one below displays wires, poles, and a streetlight. (Above, courtesy Kelly West; below, courtesy Aztec Museum.)

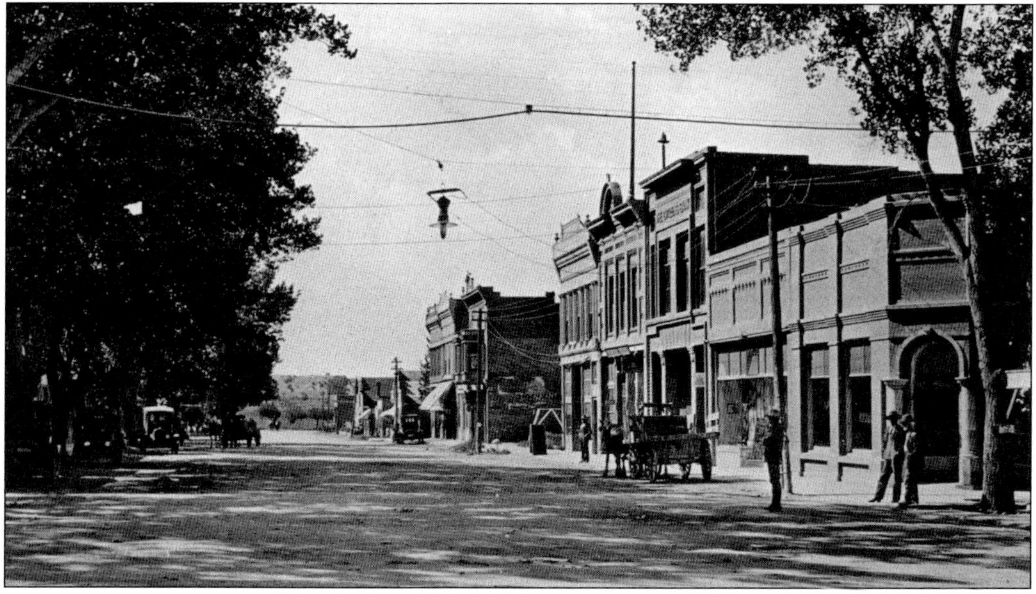

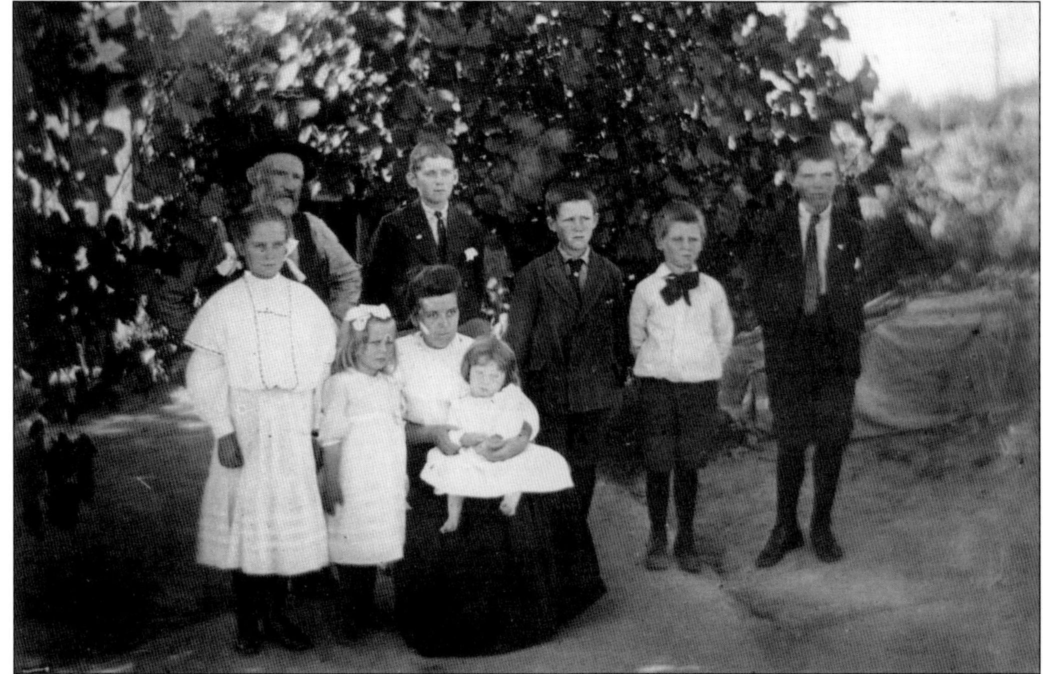

The Bowras came from England through Canada to settle in Aztec. Pictured here around 1911 are, from left to right, (first row) Ethel Bowra (Kohl), Dorothy Bowra (Burrows), Florence Annie Bowra, and baby Walter Bowra; (second row) Henry Bowra, Harry Redman Bowra, Edgar Bowra, Frank Bowra, and George Bowra. George Bowra grew up to be one of San Juan County's most noted newspapermen, who always "called a spade a spade." (Courtesy James Bowra.)

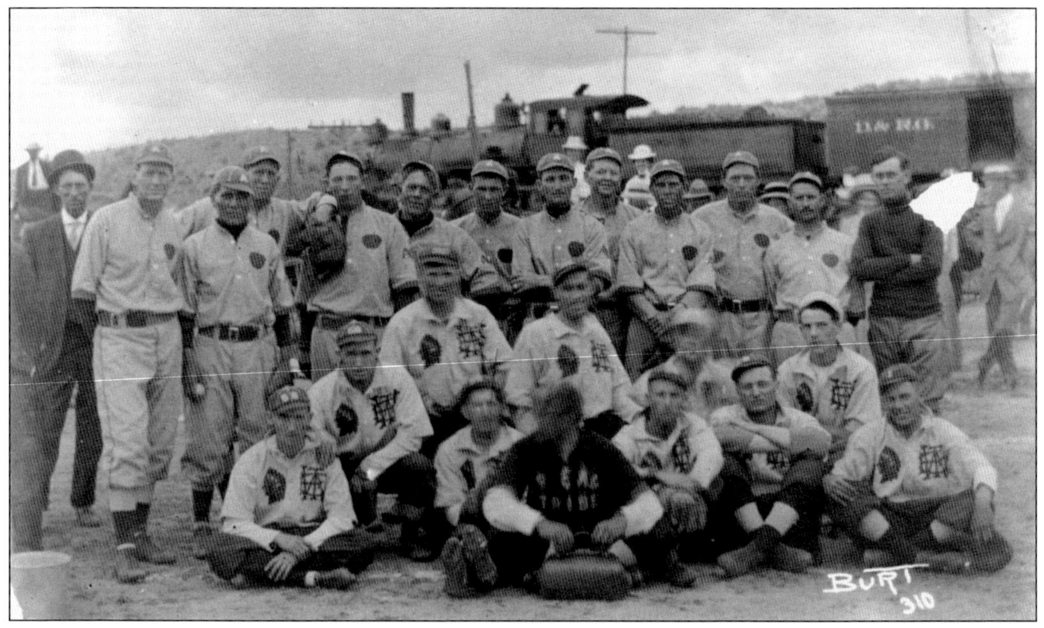

People turned out in large numbers to support their community baseball teams. This postcard, dated July 7, 1911, shows the Denver War Eagles in front of the Aztec Red Apples with red apples on their shirts. Note the D&RG Red Apple Flyer in the background. (Courtesy Aztec Museum.)

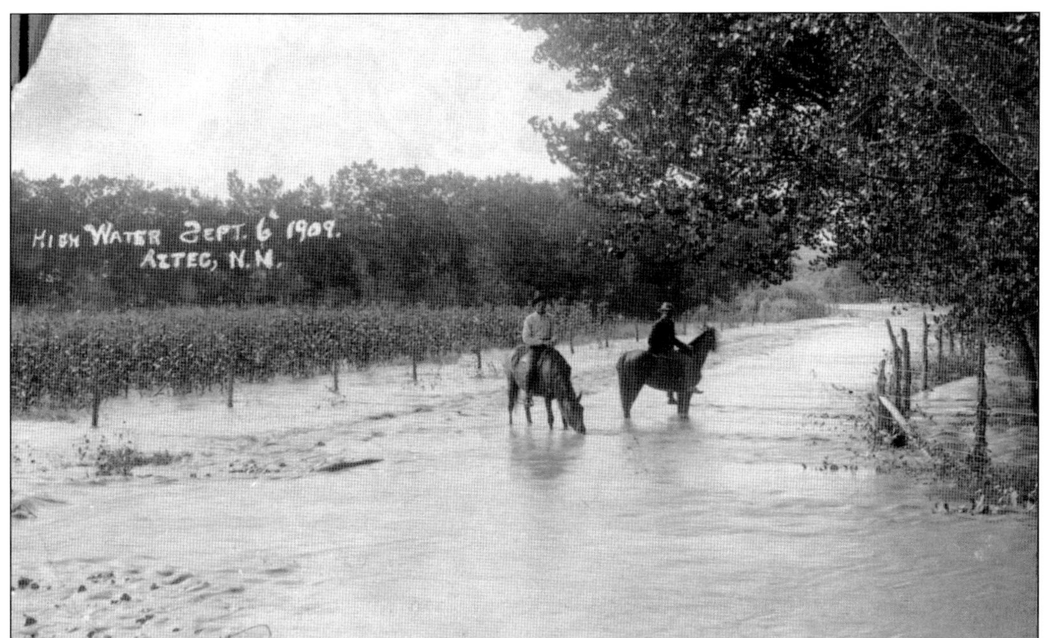

The rivers often ran rampant, and floods came fairly frequently. This postcard from September 6, 1909, shows high water on present-day Ash Street. (Courtesy Aztec Museum.)

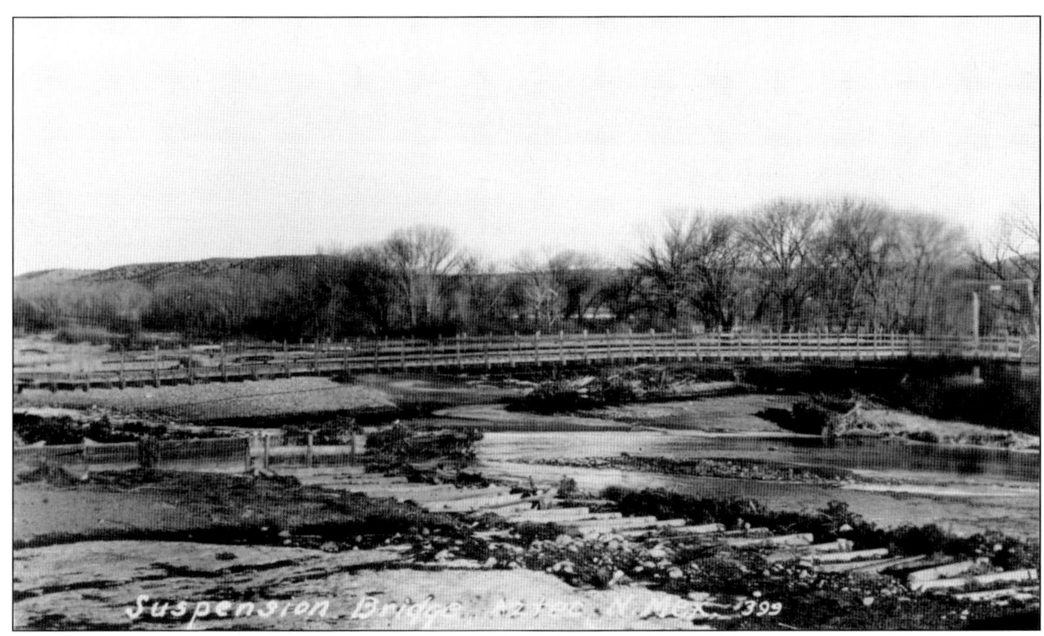

Aztec's worst flooding was on October 6, 1911, and thankfully has not been equaled since. This postcard shows the suspension bridge in Aztec shortly after the flood. It is a tribute to the builders that this was the only bridge in San Juan County that survived the flood. One man drowned, and property damage was extensive from Durango to Shiprock. (Courtesy Deanna Morrison Blythe.)

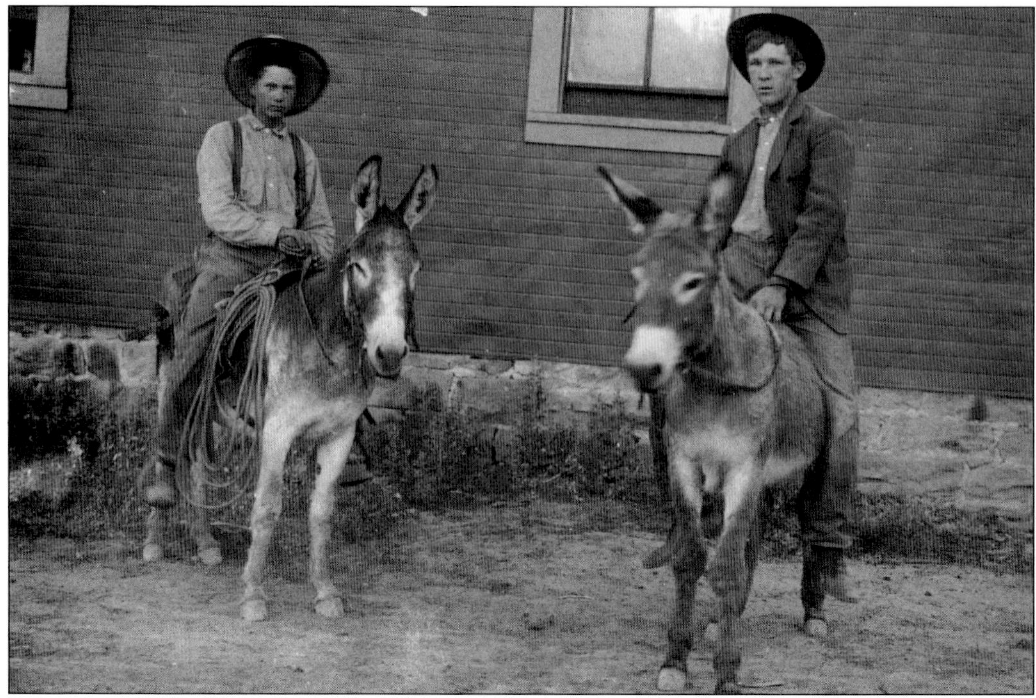

Bruce and Artemus Walters pose on their donkeys. Their parents, pioneers Price and Mary Bates Walters, came to Aztec from La Jara, Colorado, about 1900. Price and Mary also had a daughter, Winona. Price was one of Aztec's first educators and taught in the little schoolhouse on the southeast corner of Main Avenue and Zia Street. (Courtesy Aztec Museum.)

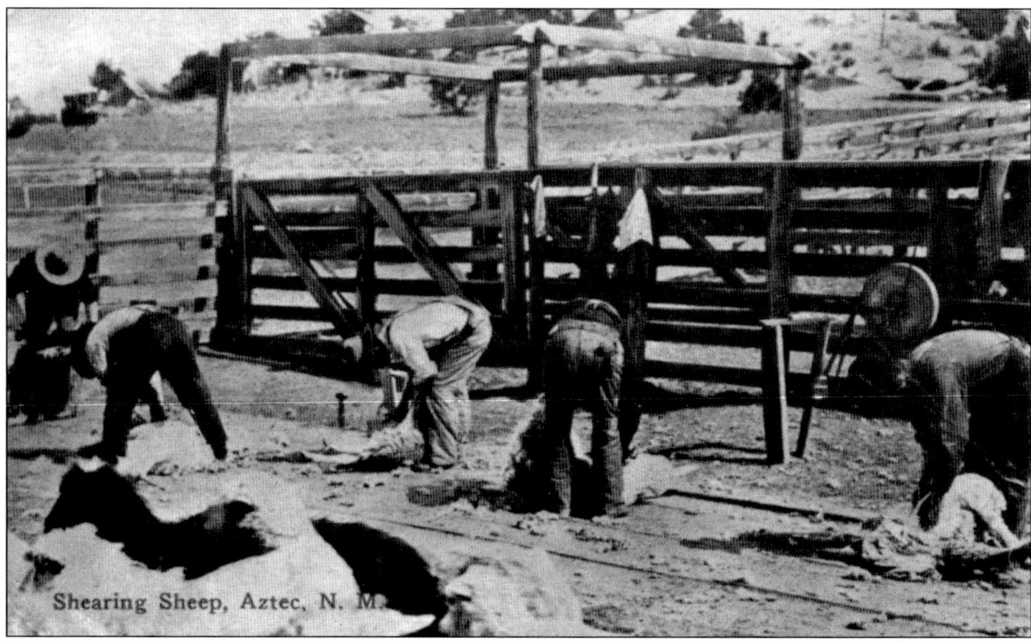

These men are shearing sheep at the Aztec stockyards. Livestock was a major industry, which expanded quickly when the train came to town in 1905 and made shipping easier. (Courtesy Aztec Museum.)

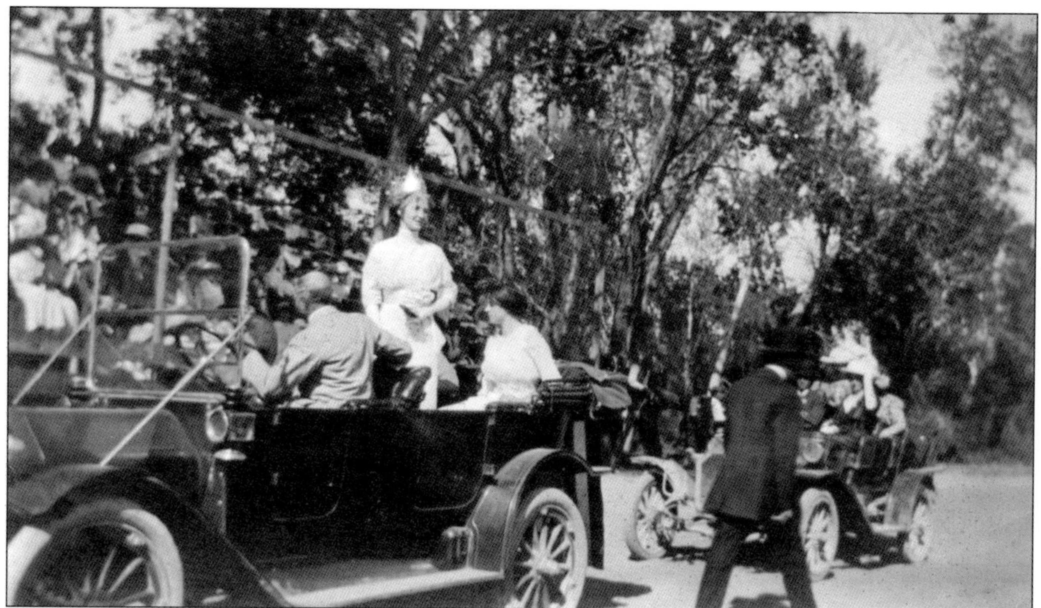

Miss Clyde Calloway, standing in a new two-seated convertible, reigned as San Juan County Fair Queen in 1912. The theme of the fair was celebrating statehood, and it was held at the Aztec fairgrounds near the river. New Mexico became the 47th state in the union on January 6, 1912. (Courtesy Aztec Museum.)

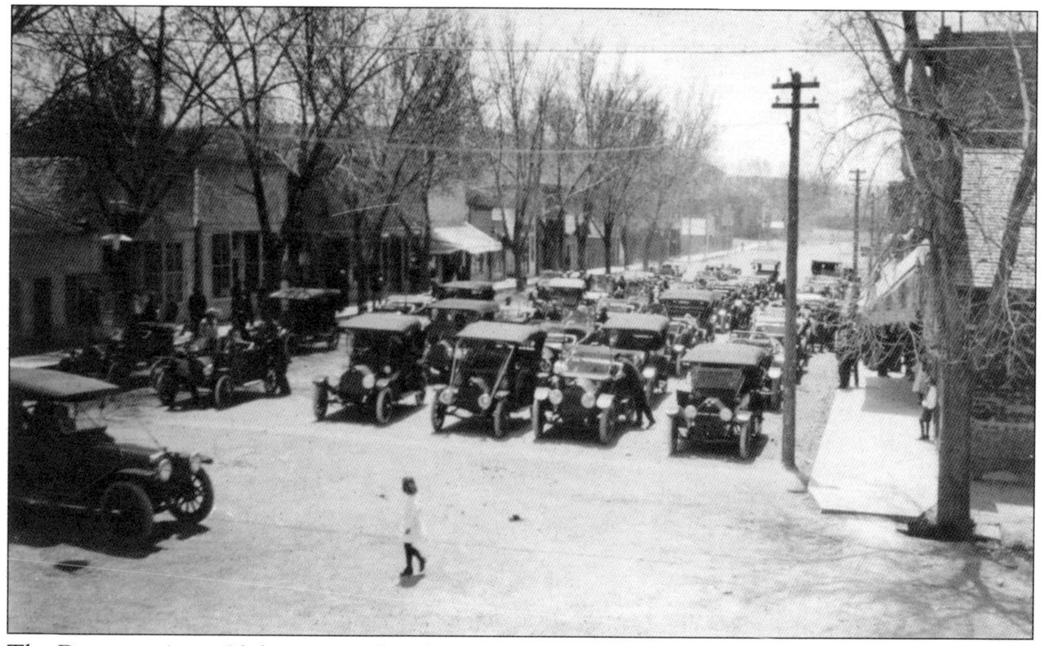

The Durango Auto Club convened in Aztec in 1912. It is interesting to note that the east side of Main Avenue is still mostly small, one-story shops. At the same time, the west side of the street was much more developed, with brick and concrete structures. (Courtesy Aztec Museum.)

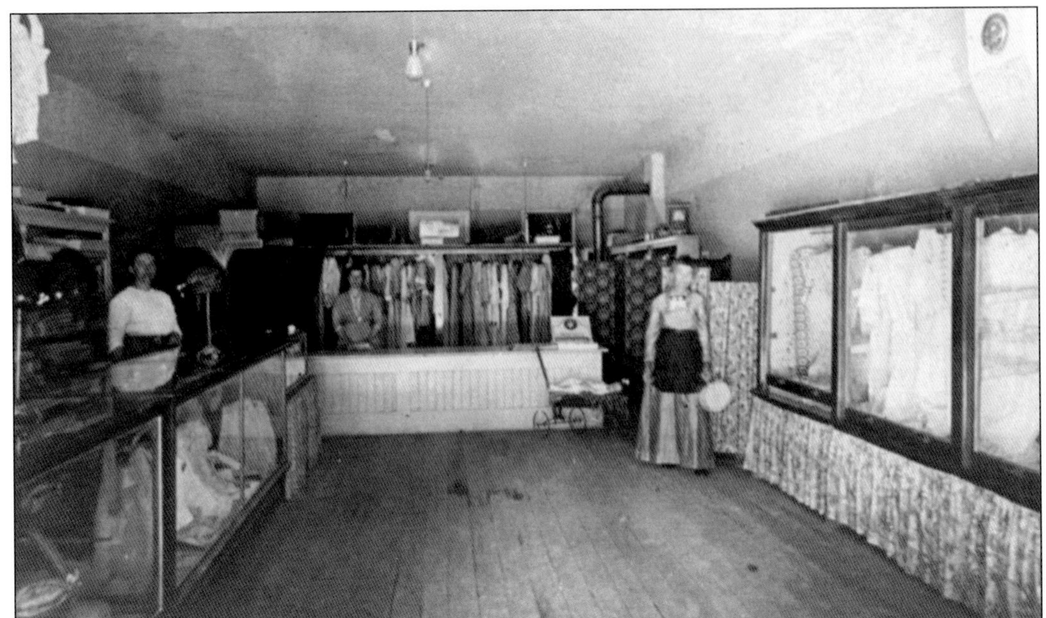

The interior of the Owens & Tatum Millinery is shown here in 1915. The women in the store are Louise Graves Tatum (left), Elizabeth Owens (center), and Grammy Graves. The shop handled all types of women's clothing. When women came to buy high-top shoes, they left the old worn ones at the shop. The shoes were made of silk from the ankle up, so Tatum cut the tops off and used the silk in patchwork quilts. (Courtesy Farmington Museum.)

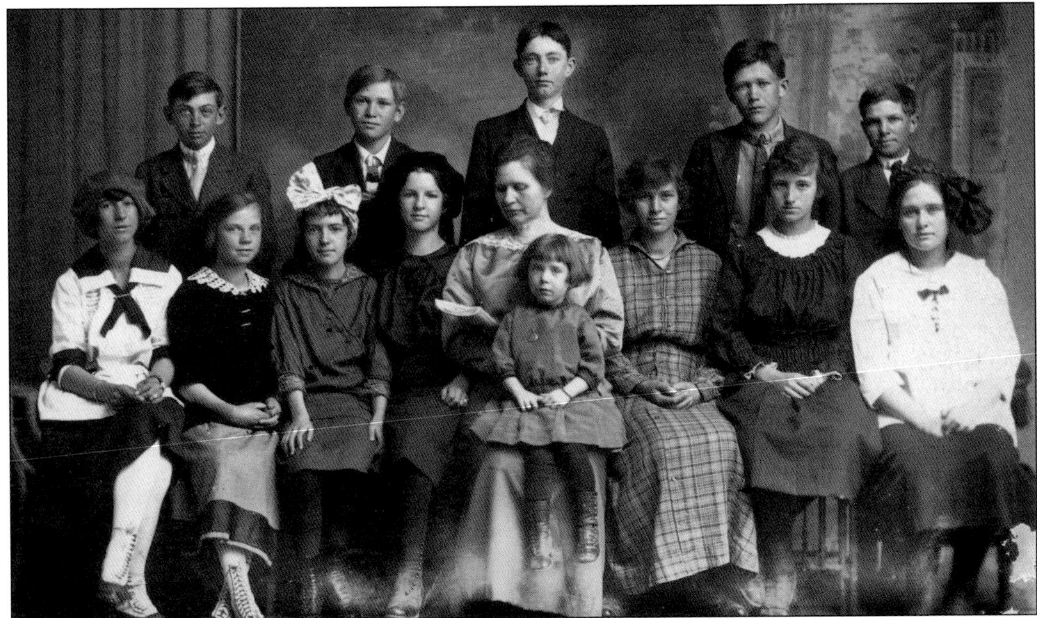

The Aztec Methodist Church Sunday School class of 1915 sat for this photograph. Pictured here are, from left to right, (first row) Helen Jackson, Ruth Heflin, Eleanor Lenfesty, Dortha Wagner, teacher Elizabeth Owens holding daughter Leona Mae, Beulah McGee, Edna Koontz, and Ethel Bowra; (second row) Roswell Chrisman, Joe Hartman, Grider Johnson, Edgar Bowra, and Frank McGee. (Courtesy Aztec Museum.)

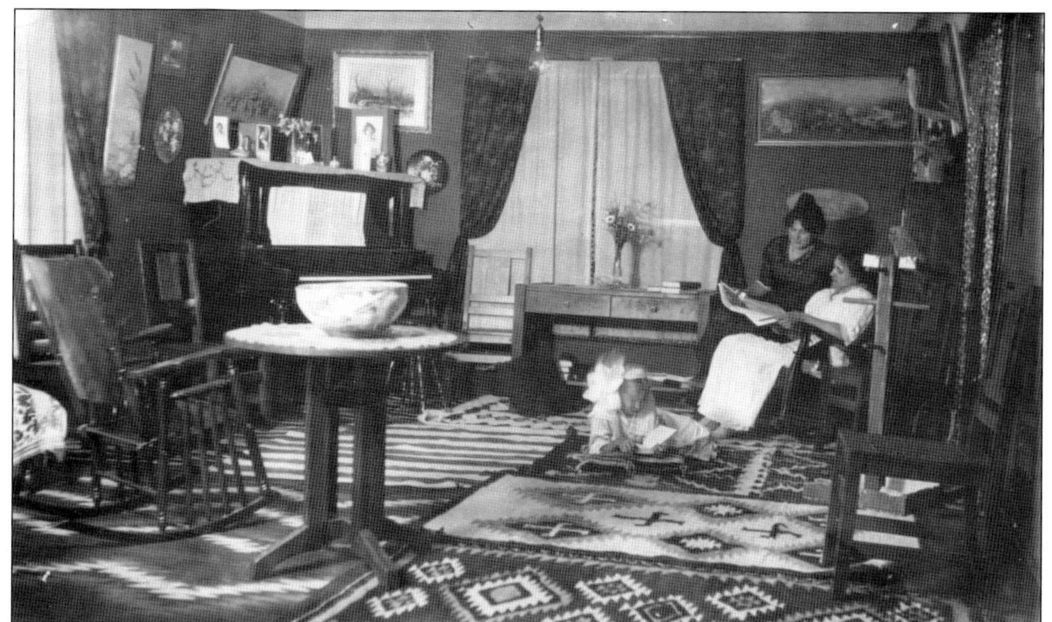

Homesteaders came a long way from the covered wagon and a few household items. This 1914 postcard shows Adele A. Pinkstaff seated in her living room with her two daughters, Zelda (on the floor) and Rhoda. Note the floor covering of Navajo rugs, the upright piano, and the varied styles of furniture. It is a cozy scene. (Courtesy Aztec Museum.)

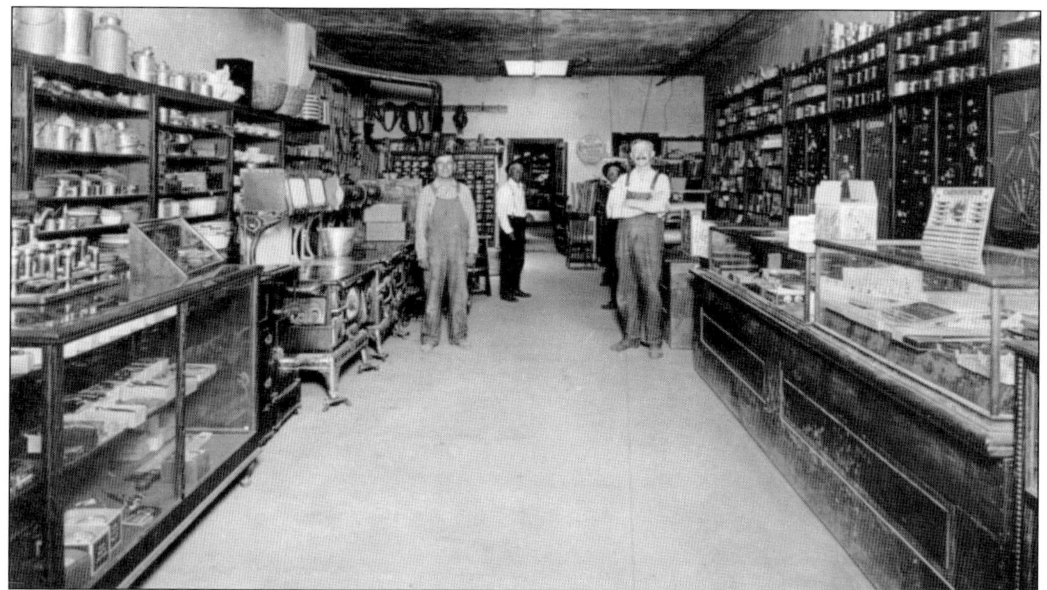

Pictured here in 1919 at the Hillstrom & Fisher Hardware store are Manuel M. Fisher (far left) and Frank T. Hillstrom (far right). Notice the merchandise array ranging from kitchen cookstoves to horse collars, with all sorts of hardware and baskets in between. (Courtesy Aztec Museum.)

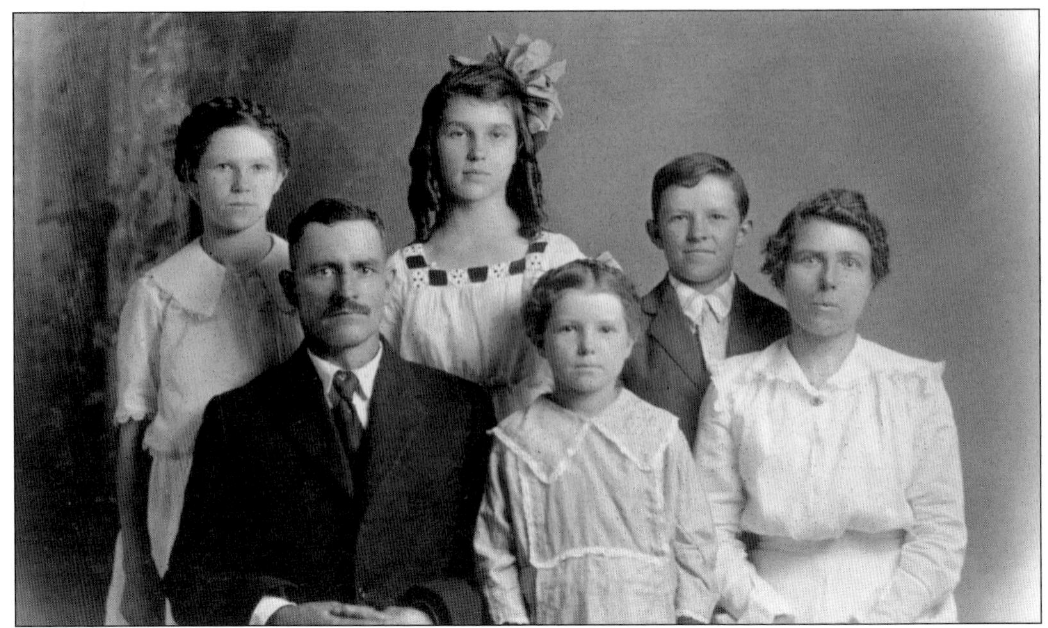

The John H. Austin family came to the area in 1887 and immediately jumped into community and Presbyterian church affairs. John H. Austin's son John B. followed in his father's footsteps. John B. Austin's family is pictured here in 1917. From left to right, they are Ethel May, John B., Nellie Ruth, Hazel Catherine, Montie Allen, and Maud. (Courtesy Deanna Morrison Blythe.)

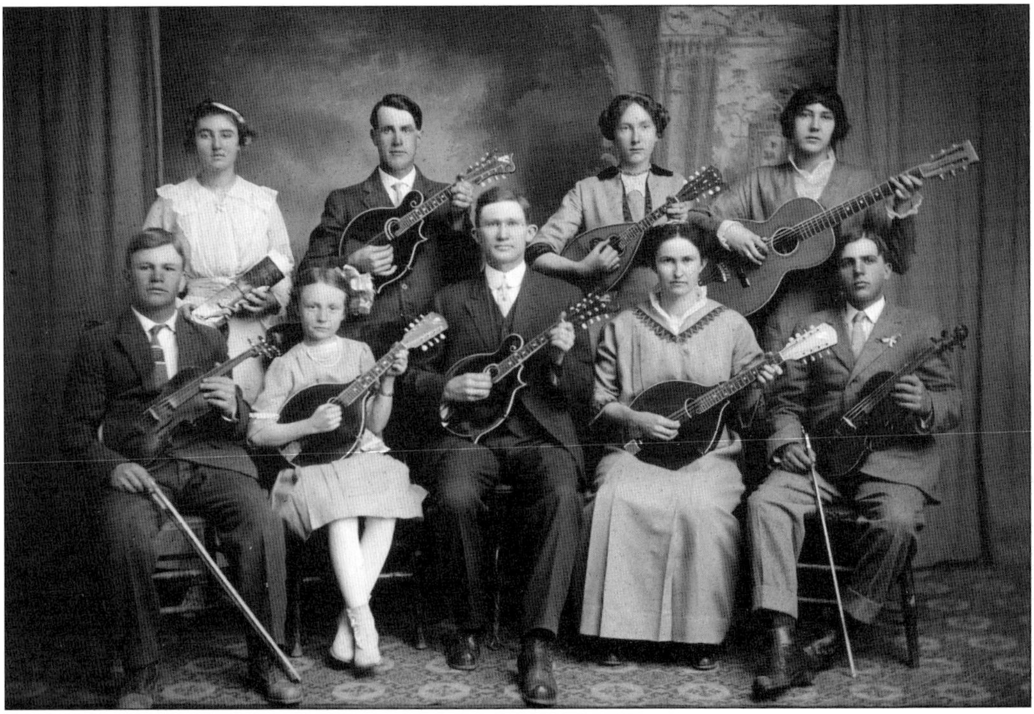

The Aztec string orchestra members shown here around 1917 are, from left to right, (first row) Tommy Brett, Florence Wilson, Frank Ridenour, Lulu Ridenour, and Paul Winchell; (second row) Edith Whitford, Fred Utton, Edith Fields, and Clara Sweeny. (Courtesy Bernice Gardner Bowra.)

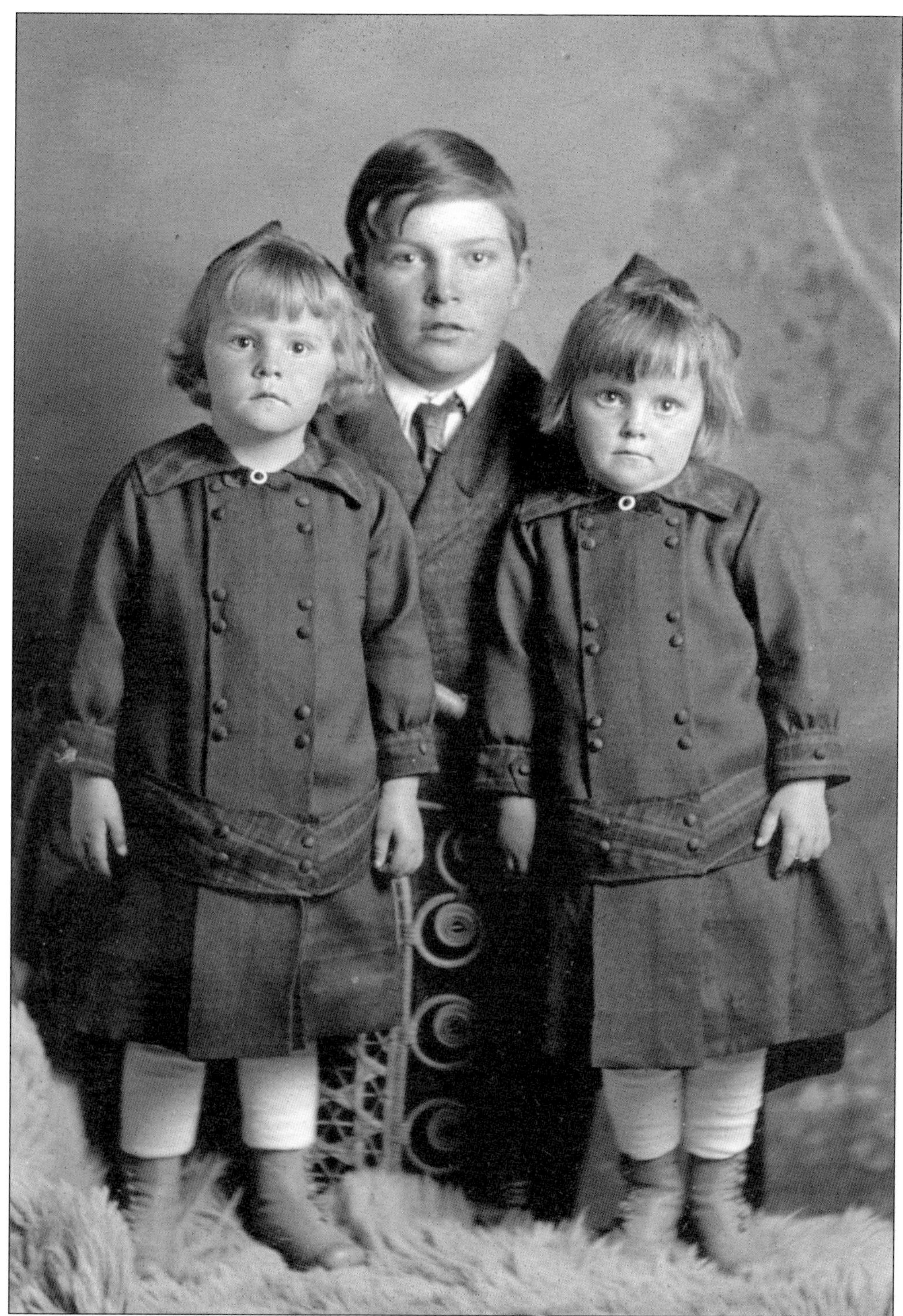

The Pawley family came to the area around 1908 and homesteaded about three miles north of Aztec on Ruins Road. Shown here are siblings Lorene (left), Frank, and Norene Pawley. Note the interesting clothing worn by the twin girls. (Courtesy Audrey Glazebrook.)

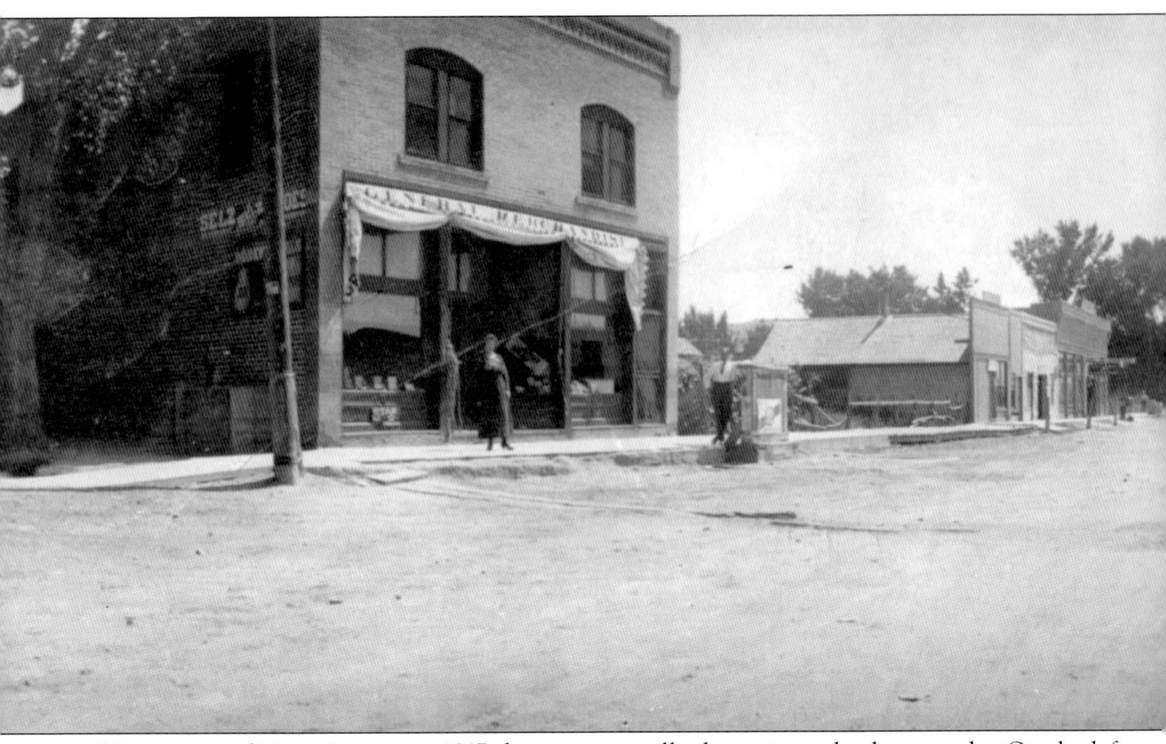

Here is part of Main Avenue in 1917 that is not usually shown in early photographs. On the left is the J.M. Thomas building, which was constructed in 1906 as a general merchandise store, later serving as the post office. At right is the Brewer building. C.G. Brewer and his son Truman were

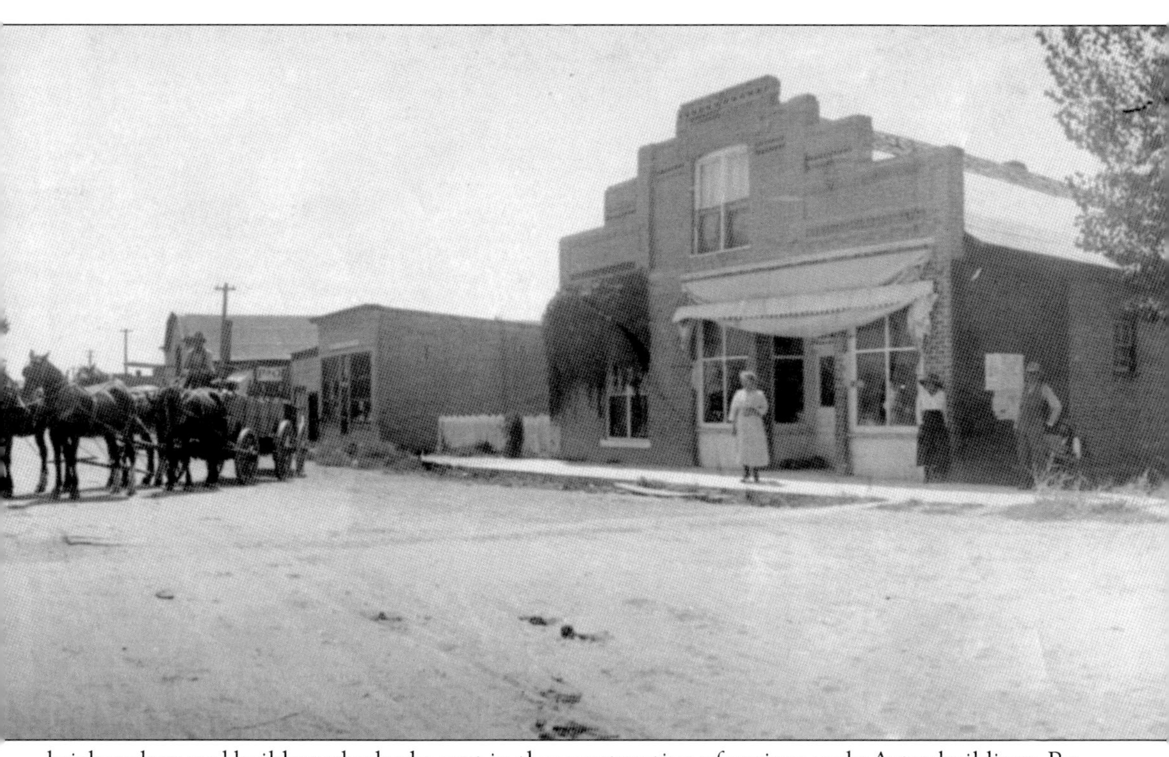

brick makers and builders who had a part in the construction of various early Aztec buildings. By 1926, the Brewer building was the home of the Dial Hardware. (Courtesy Aztec Museum.)

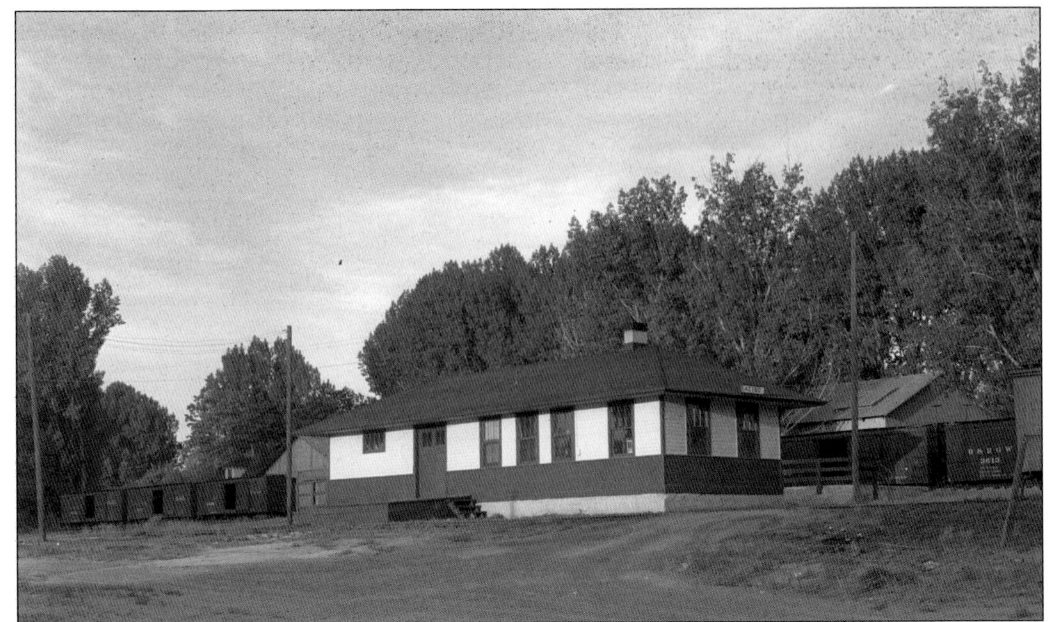

When the Denver & Rio Grande railroad came to town in 1905, a depot was erected. That building burned in 1915 and was replaced with this structure. This 1950s photograph shows the back side of the depot as it looked until the trains stopped coming in 1968 and the building subsequently became a residence.

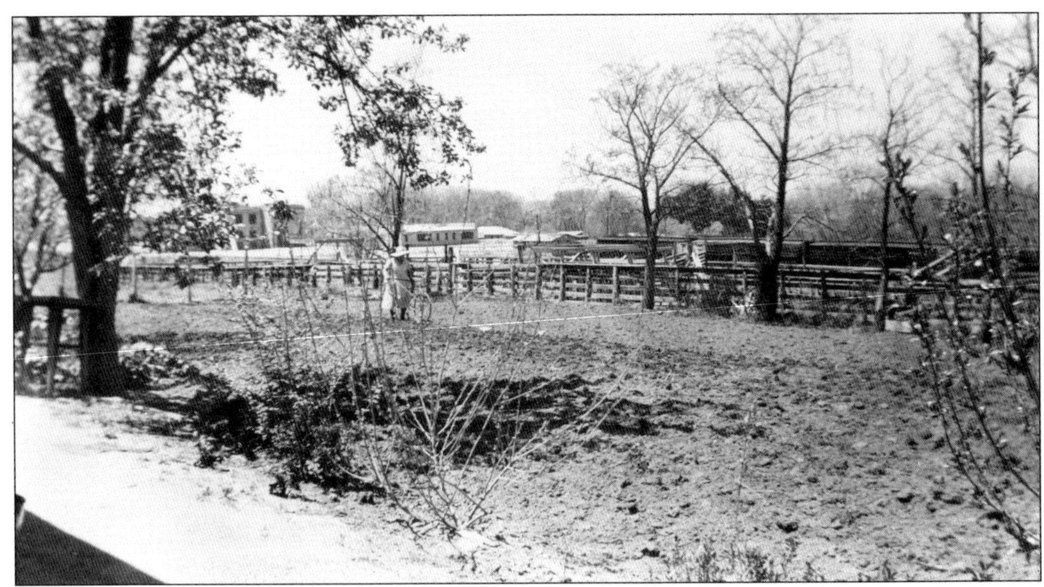

The Aztec stockyards were located south of the depot. The large building in the background is the school. Note the woman plowing up ground that possibly became a garden plot in the 1930s. (Courtesy Aztec Museum.)

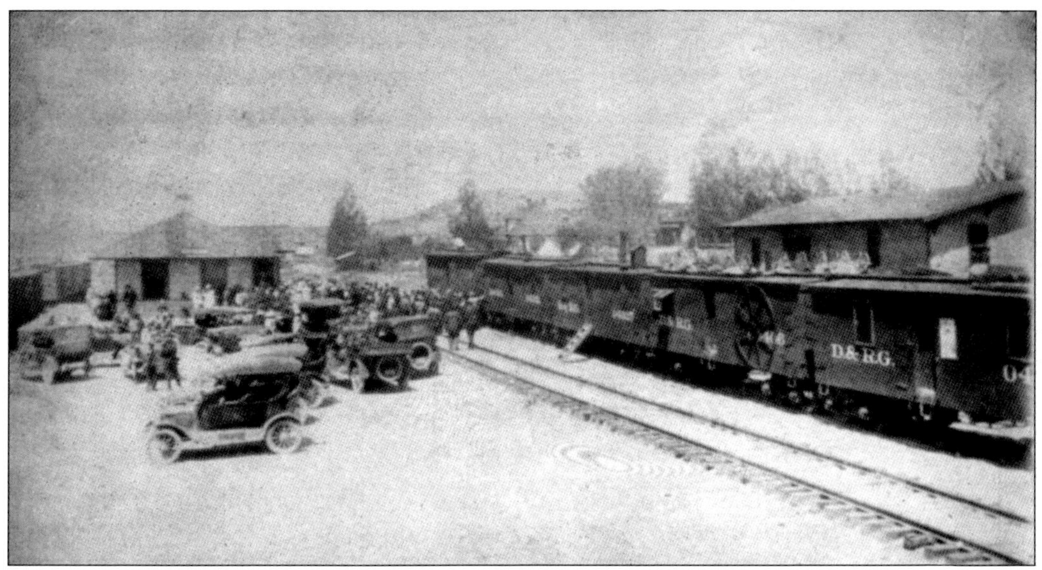

This faded photograph shows World War I soldiers preparing to board the train in 1917. (Courtesy Aztec Museum.)

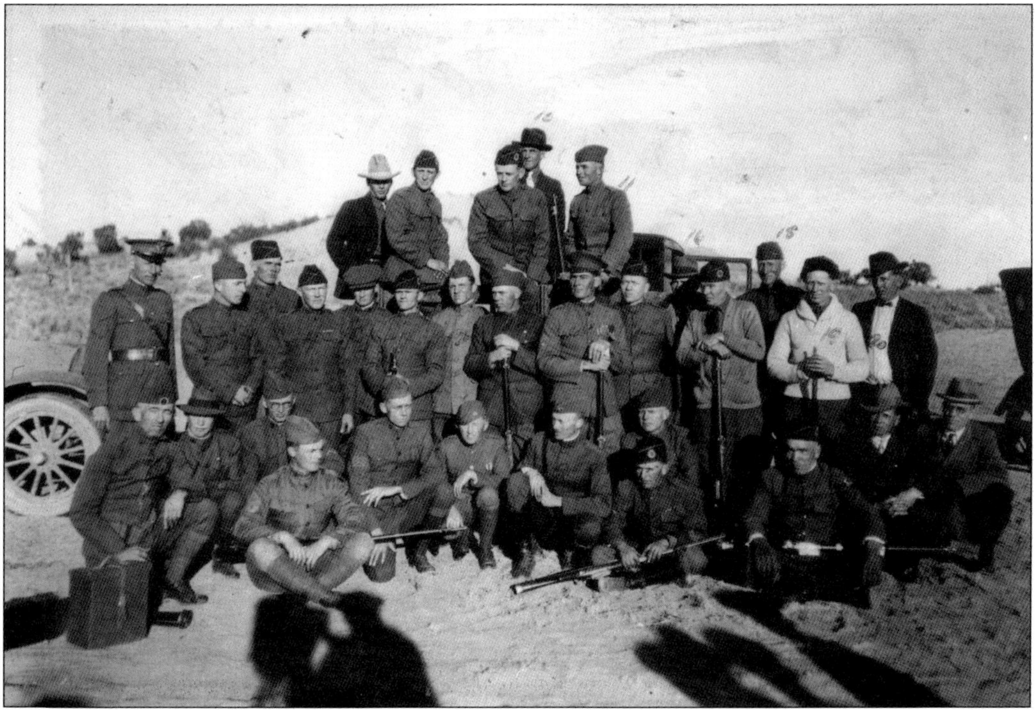

In this 1921 photograph, the war is over and the soldiers are home. Someone numbered the veterans in this image, but that list could not be found, so the names are unknown. (Courtesy Aztec Museum.)

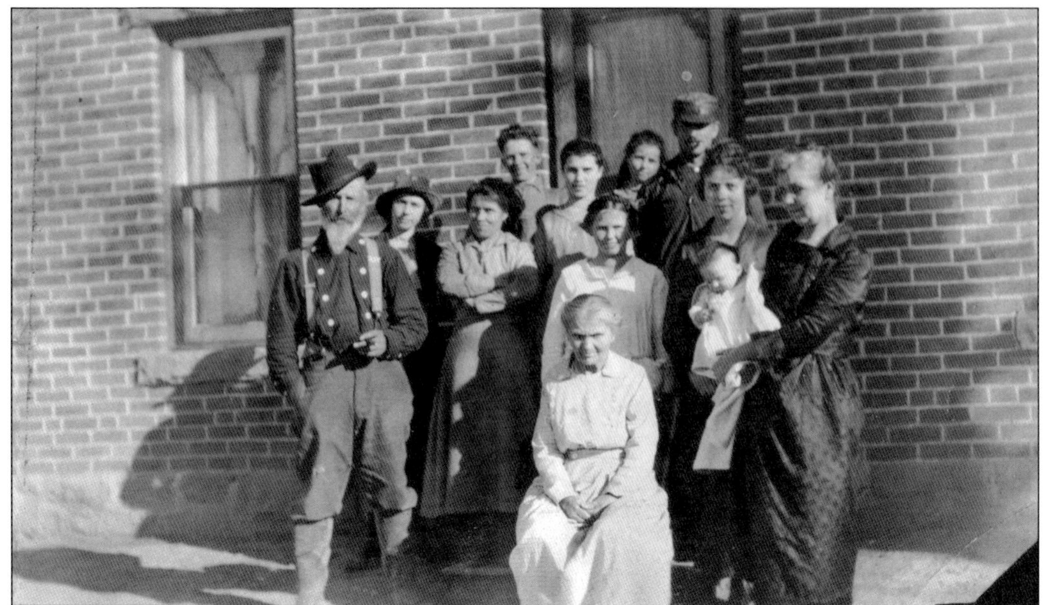

The Brown family assembles in 1917 by a brick home (possibly theirs) on North McCoy Street. Clarence Thomas Brown is at left and his wife, Eliza Catherine Brown, is seated. Others are unidentified. (Courtesy Deanna Morrison Blythe.)

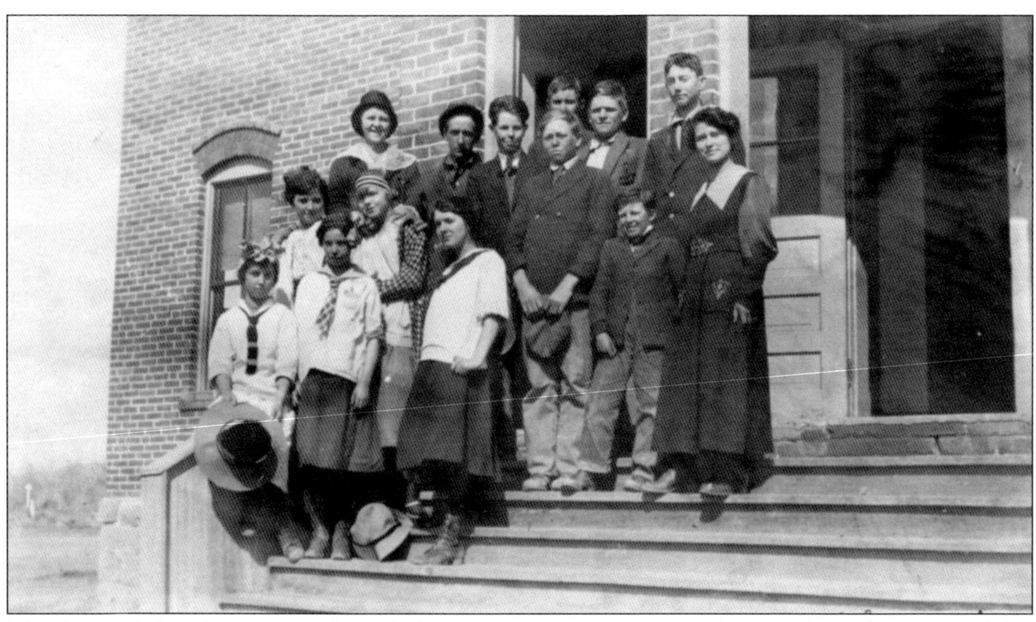

Members of the Aztec school's eighth-grade class in 1917 are identified on the back of the photograph as: "front five girls, Nellie Austin, Celia Jaquez, Vivian Skrifvars, Kathleen Ricketts (blonde), and Eleanor Lenfesty. At back are Edna Black, Charles Utton, Raymond Smith, (upper) Welton Armstrong, Carry Lively, Harrold (Pug) Titt, Montie Austin, Grider Johnson, and teacher Olive Frazier." (Courtesy Deanna Morrison Blythe.)

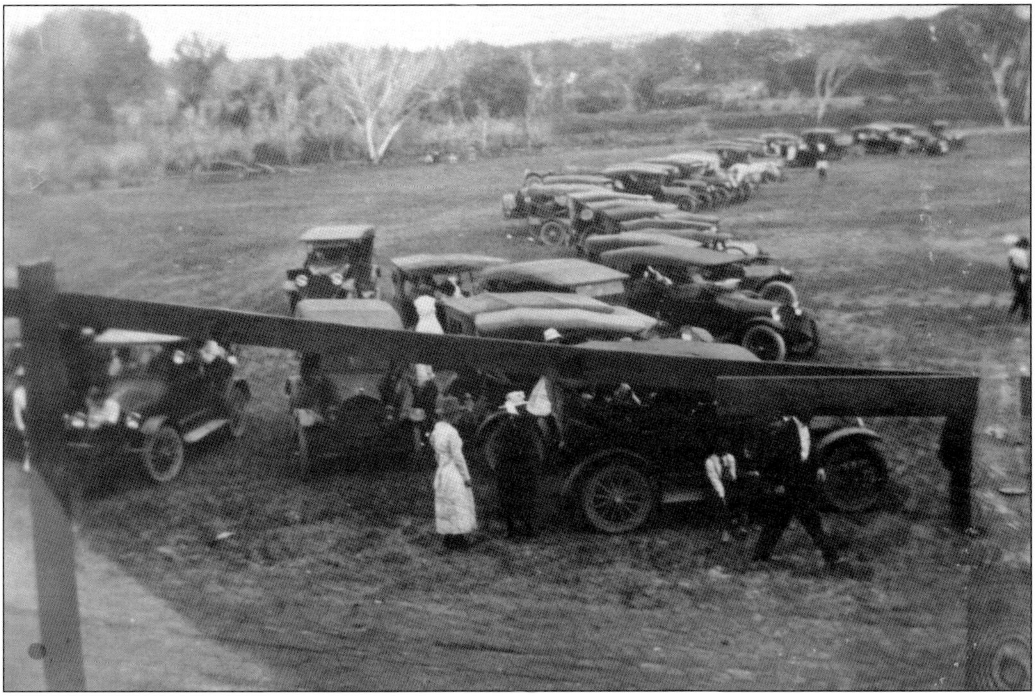

A crowd gathers for an event at the Aztec Fairgrounds in 1919. In the above picture, cars are lined up as though the action could be seen from the vehicle. Perhaps they are ready for a baseball game or the county fair? The photograph below is across the field from the cars. The announcer or judge's booth is decorated with flags, and the bleachers are filling with fans. This area across from the A&W has recently been cleared of underbrush. (Both courtesy Aztec Museum.)

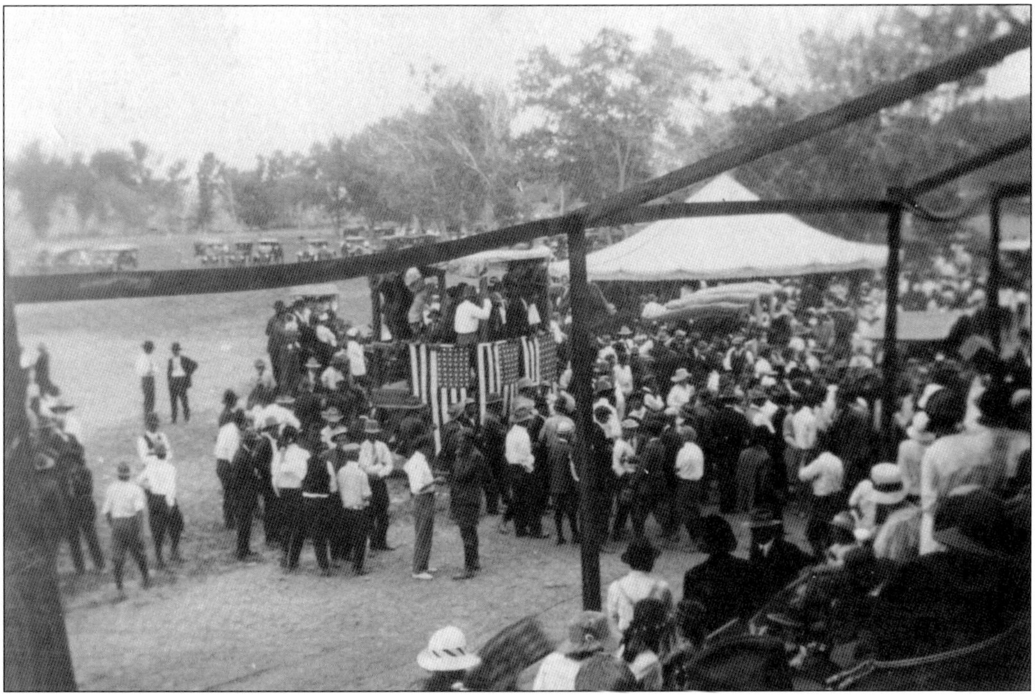

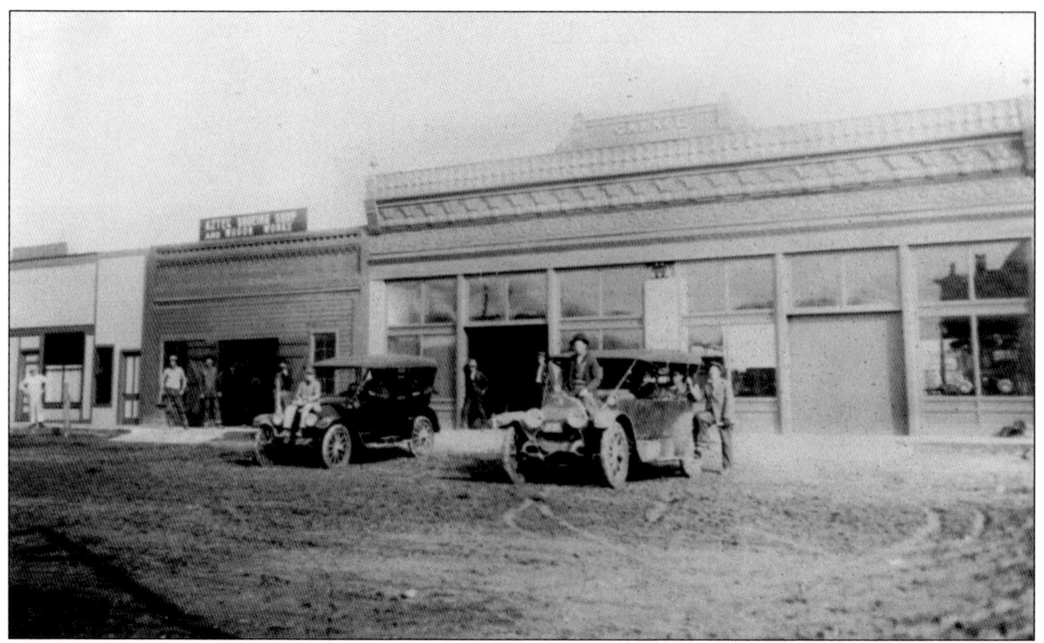

This Buick agency garage, built in 1913, was established by J.S. Hartman, John B. Austin, and Oren Randall. Austin and Randall were both mechanics. It was later owned by Carl Neitzel and was partially destroyed by fire in 1926. This is the present-day location of Aztec Feed & Supply, and smoke-stained bricks can still be seen in the warehouse. (Courtesy Aztec Museum.)

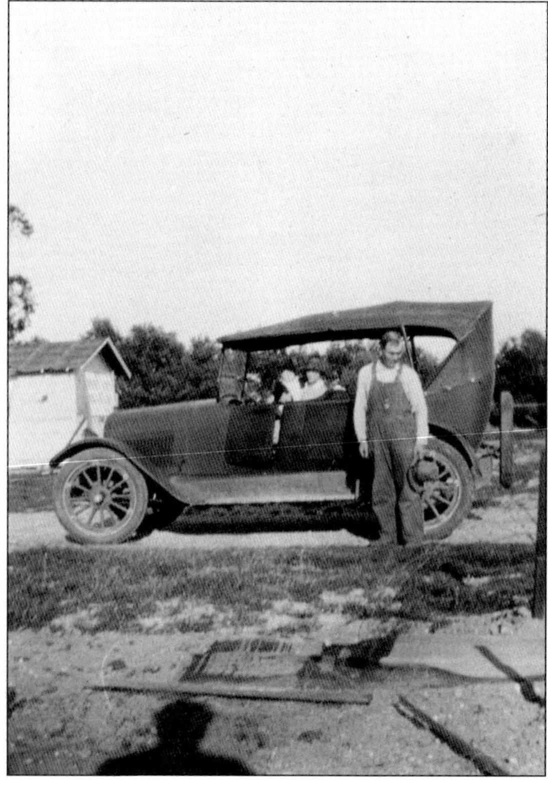

This vehicle is an example of the automobiles of the time, estimated to be between 1925 and 1928. Robert Ellis Pawley stands beside the car. (Courtesy Pawley family.)

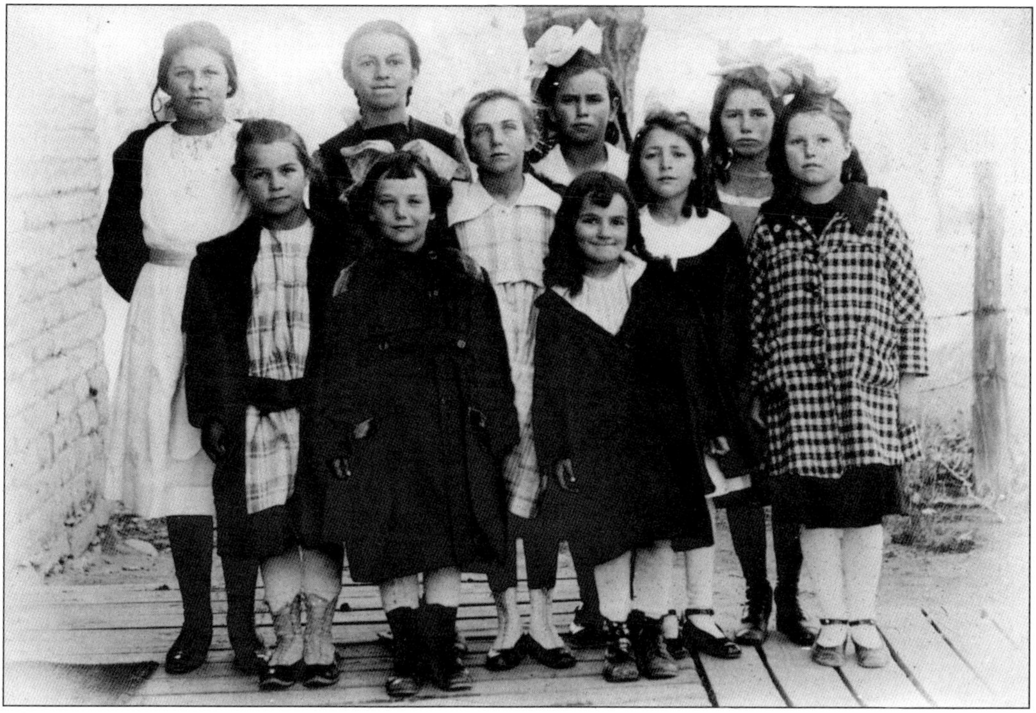

The Aztec Presbyterian Church Sunday School class of 1920 poses for a photograph. The students pictured here are, from left to right, (first row) Marie Neitzel and Maida Brewer; (second row) Clara Brewer, Mildred Sutiff, Louise McGee, and Hazel Austin; (third row) Ethel McClure, Bertha Brewer, Ramona Frazier, and Louise Dunning. (Courtesy Aztec Museum.)

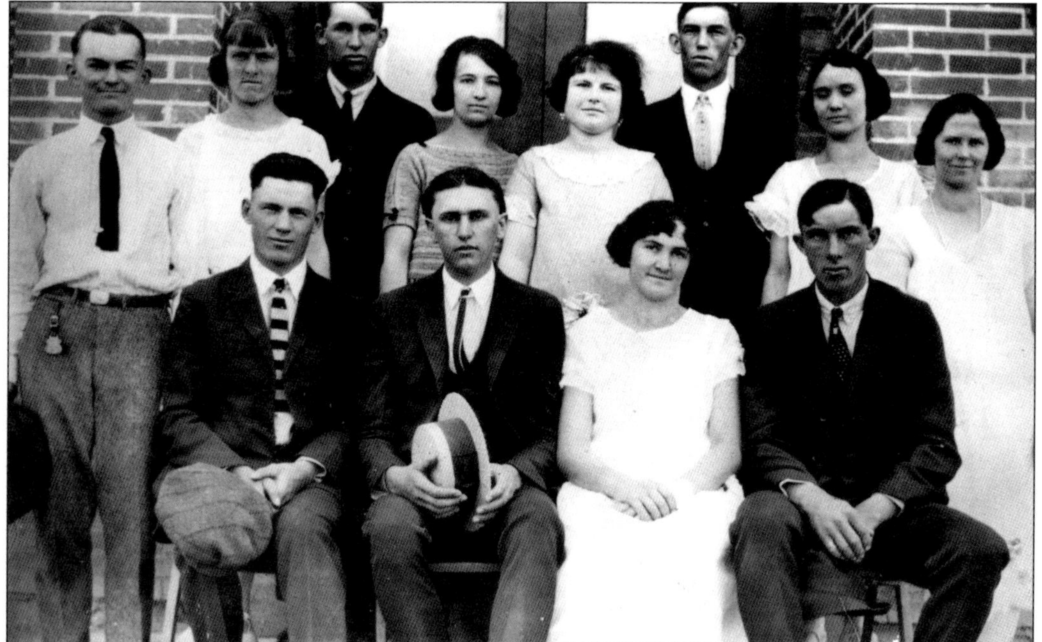

The Aztec High School class of 1924 poses on the steps of the school. There were 18 graduates that year, so some of them are missing from the photograph. (Courtesy Aztec Museum.)

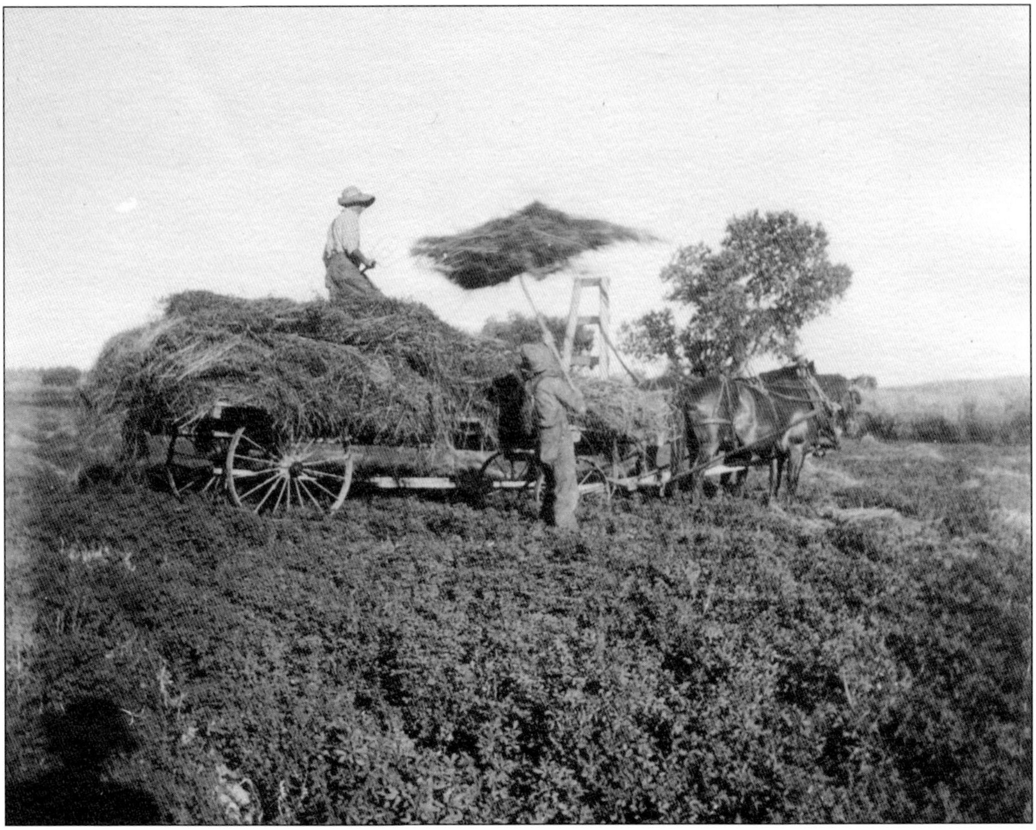

These photographs from around 1920 demonstrate how gathering hay sometimes became a project that called for neighbors to get together and help each other out. Above, men load hay onto a wagon. Below, men work a hay stacker at the Calloway farm. (Above, courtesy Deanna Morrison Blythe; below, courtesy Aztec Museum.)

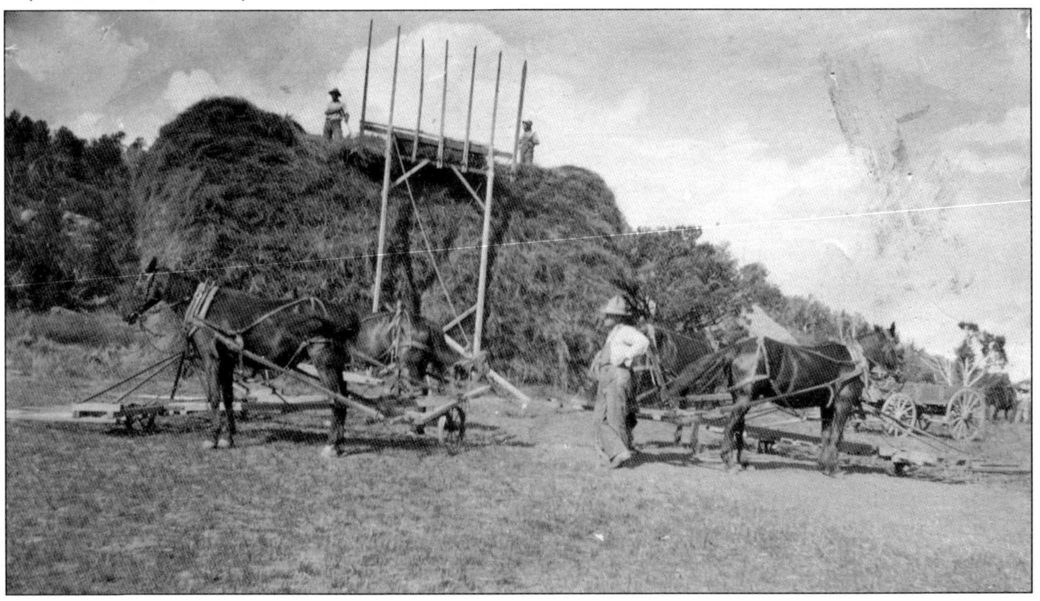

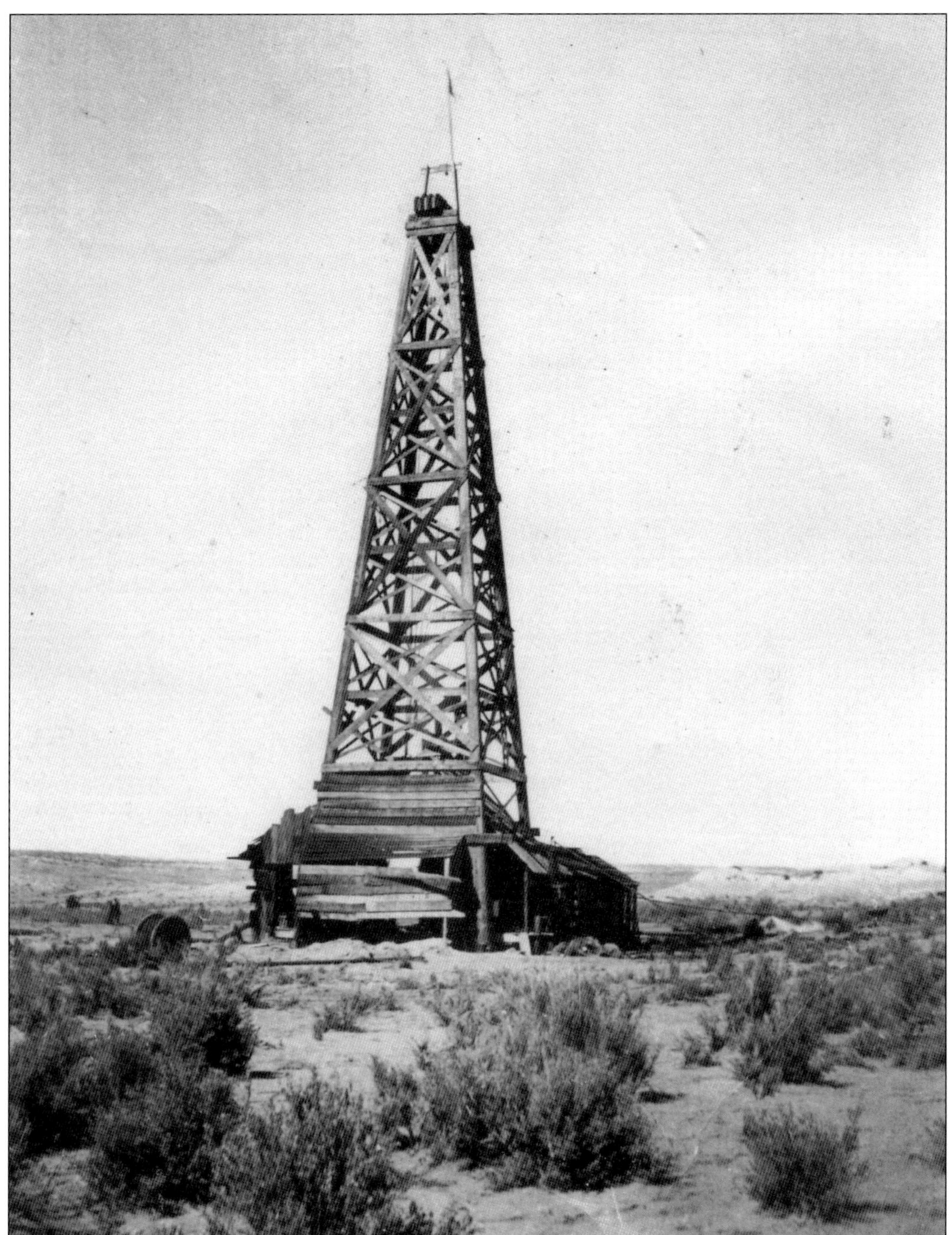

Aztec can boast having the first commercial natural gas well in the state of New Mexico. The Aztec Oil Syndicate drilled the well a couple miles south of town. On October 21, 1921, the well came in with a large amount of natural gas. The town had been watching, taking lunch to the workers, and hoping for success. Now, there could be natural gas heat in their homes, and many were quick to begin using the product. There were several missteps—a few houses and a church burned—but the end result was that, by December 1921, retail natural gas was being sold in New Mexico for the first time. (Courtesy Tom Dugan.)

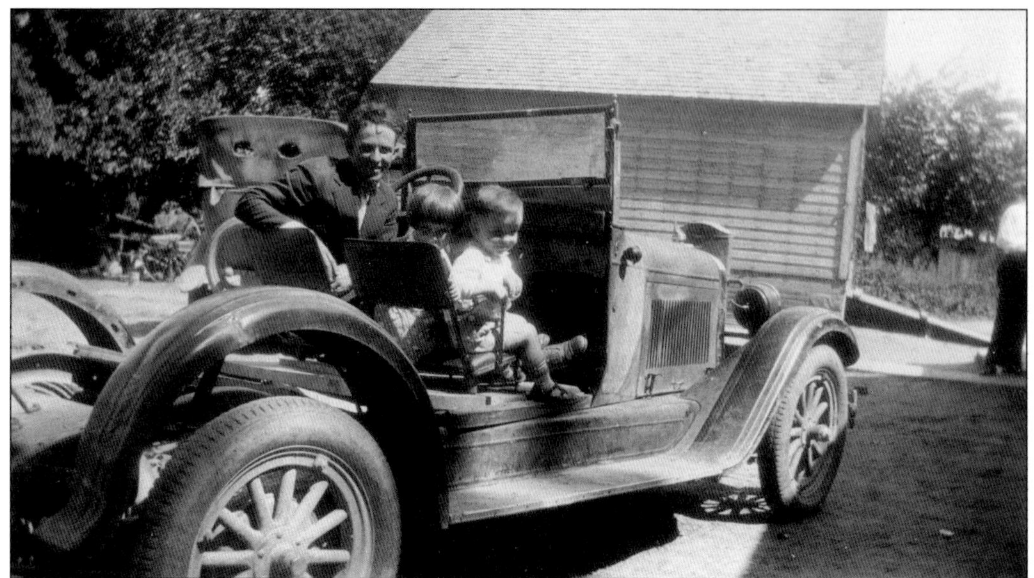

Montie (left), Evelyn (center), and Johnny Austin prepare to take a spin in this modified car. With the seat belts and protective devices in modern cars, things have changed since 1928. (Courtesy Deanna Morrison Blythe.)

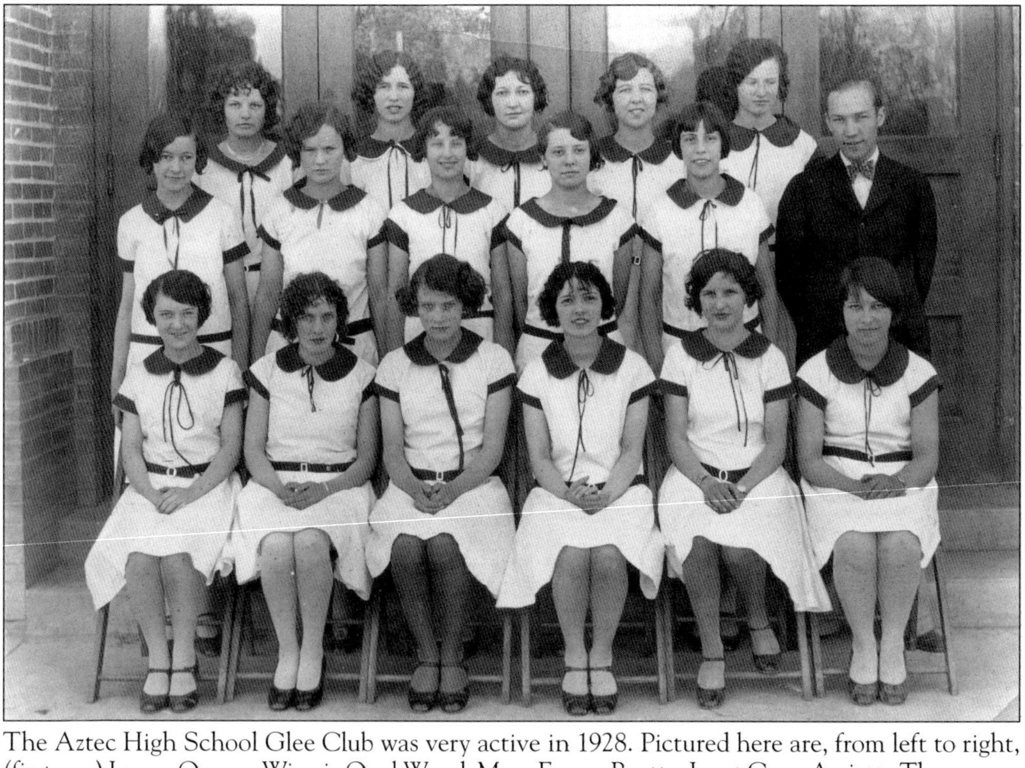

The Aztec High School Glee Club was very active in 1928. Pictured here are, from left to right, (first row) Leona Owens, Winnie Opal Wood, Mary Emma Beatty, Janet Case, Arrietta Thompson, and Annabell Hendricks; (second row) Mary Taylor, Ethel Scott, Martha Smith, Jo Bruington, Catherine Case, and instructor Stanley Stout; (third row) Leona McWilliams, Louise Dunning, Louise McGee, Genevieve Coon, and Betty Smith. (Courtesy Aztec Museum.)

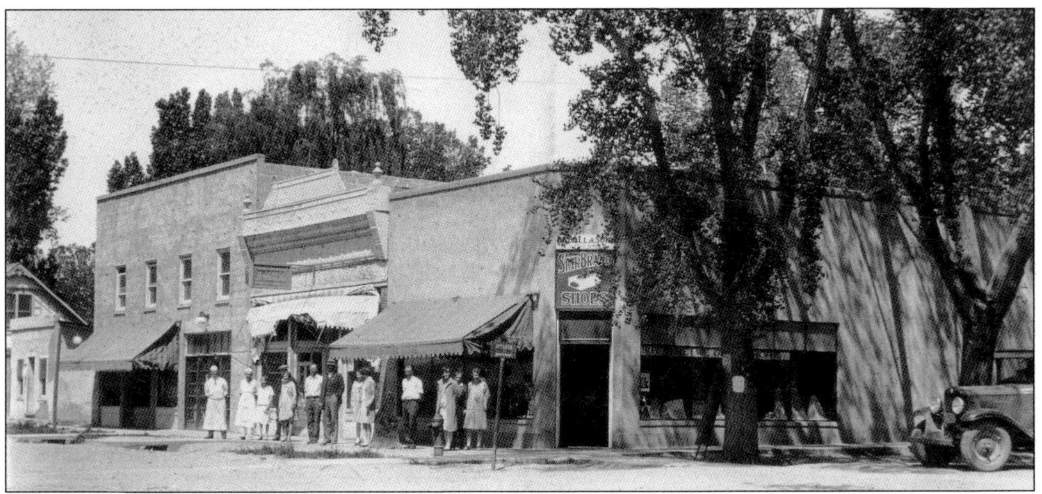

This is how the corner of Chaco Street and Main Avenue appeared in 1927. On the corner is the D.C. Ball & Son Dry Goods store built in 1910. Next to it is the Uptegrove Confectionery and Bakery built in 1913, with the family posing out front. Clare and Tom Uptegrove moved their renamed business here after the Bunker building burned in 1910. Next to the Uptegrove Confectionery is the Mayan Theater, which was built in 1927 by J. Oscar Manning. (Courtesy Aztec Museum.)

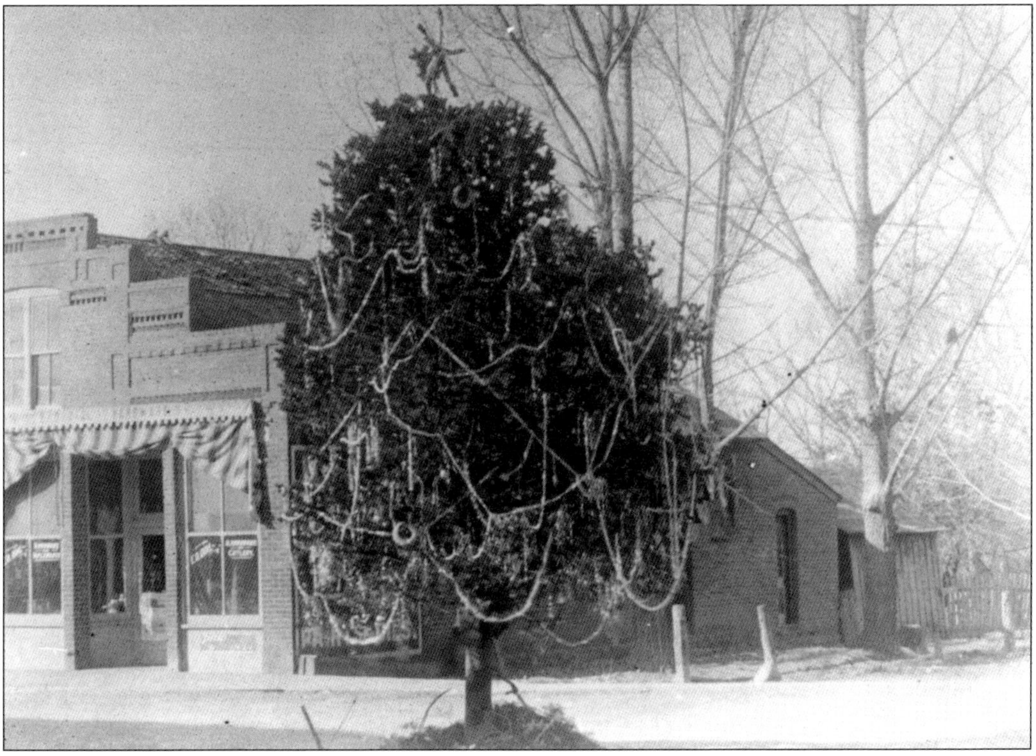

Everett O. Dial bought the Brewer building at the southwest corner of Main Avenue and Chuska Street in 1926 and opened a hardware store. Later, the living quarters were removed from the top, and it was remodeled into a one-story building. This is one of only a few photographs that features Christmas decorations. (Courtesy Aztec Museum.)

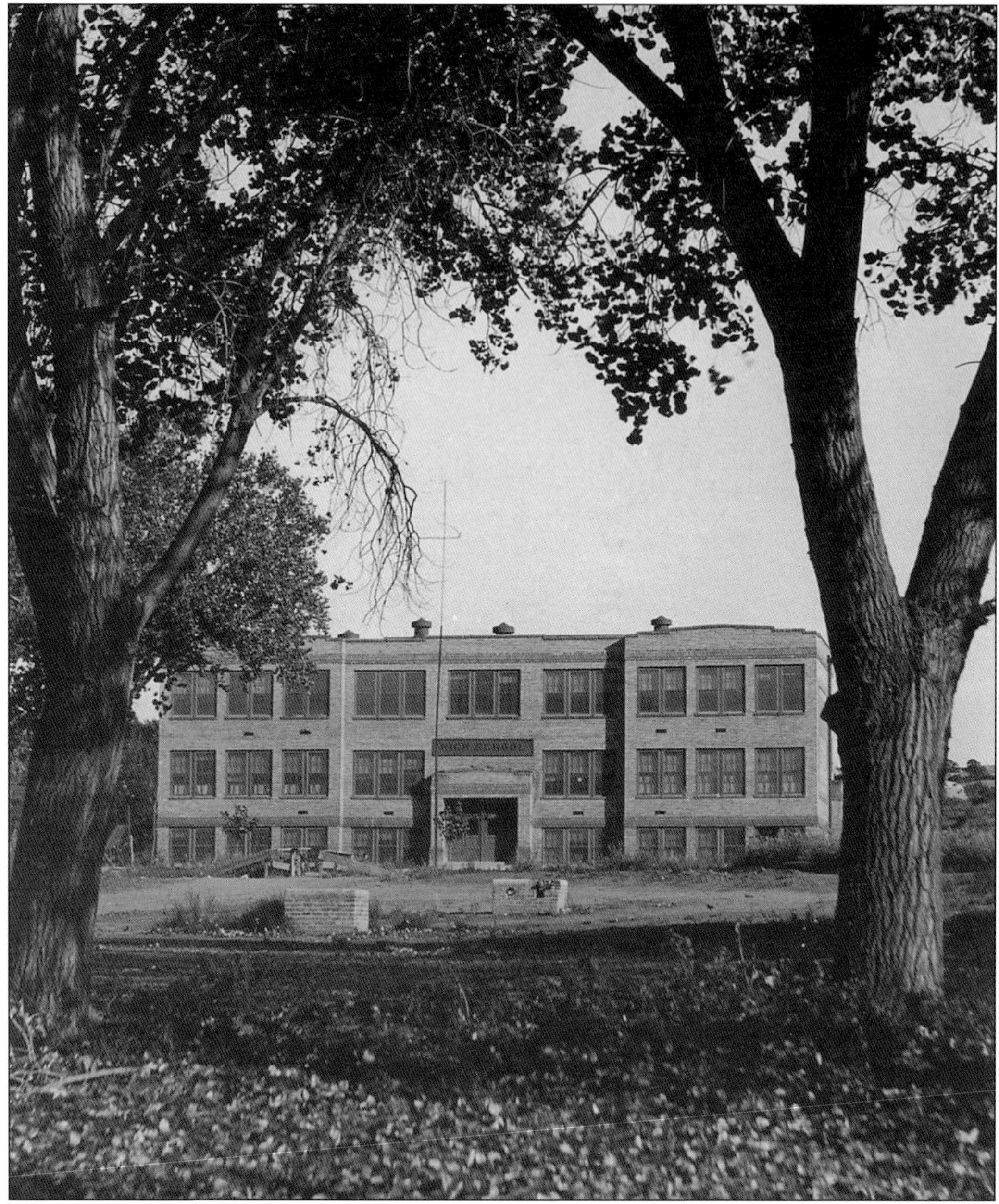

Aztec High School was built in 1922. According to W.K. Noble, "J.A. McWilliams and Joe Thompson made and burned about 300,000 bricks to be used in the new high school building. These bricks were fired by natural gas but the rest of the bricks for this project were burned by wood." This photograph was taken in 1930. (Courtesy Aztec Museum.)

Three

Aztec Ruins

The Aztec Ruins were misnamed because of maps and records dating back to the late 1700s. The area was identified as "First abode of the Azteques from Aztlan" in the early 1800s and then, by 1849, as "Supposed residence of the Aztecs in the 12th Century." In an attempt to correct the record, archeologists today refer to those who dwelled in the ruins as early or ancestral Pueblo people.

On January 24, 1923, the site was set aside as the Aztec Ruin National Monument. A few years later, the boundary was changed, and it was renamed the Aztec Ruins National Monument. It is part of the National Park Service and was listed on the National Register of Historic Places on October 15, 1966.

Further recognition came on December 8, 1987, when the Chaco culture—which includes the Aztec Ruins National Monument—was added to the United Nations Educational, Scientific and Cultural Organization (UNESCO) World Heritage List. UNESCO World Heritage sites are selected because of special cultural or physical significance.

We are indebted to Sherman Howe for early history and exploration information. He and his family were often climbing the ruins and digging up artifacts. As he got older, he continued to search and learn. He wrote about those experiences so others could be aware of the early days at the Aztec Ruins. His booklet, "My Story of the Aztec Ruins," was published in 1955.

Howe's account begins when his family went on a picnic at the ruins in 1880. He describes walls of stone that had to be quarried farther away and transported to the site. Howe states that the dressed stones were laid in mortar and filled between with mud. That mud was so well mixed and tempered that, when dry, it was almost as hard as the rock.

Howe says that people often came for an outing at the ruins and carried artifacts home with them as souvenirs. He wished there was more guidance in the beginning, because untold locations were emptied of relics. He wonders where all those items went and what happened to them, as today's history scholars would know much more about the Chaco culture if they were still here.

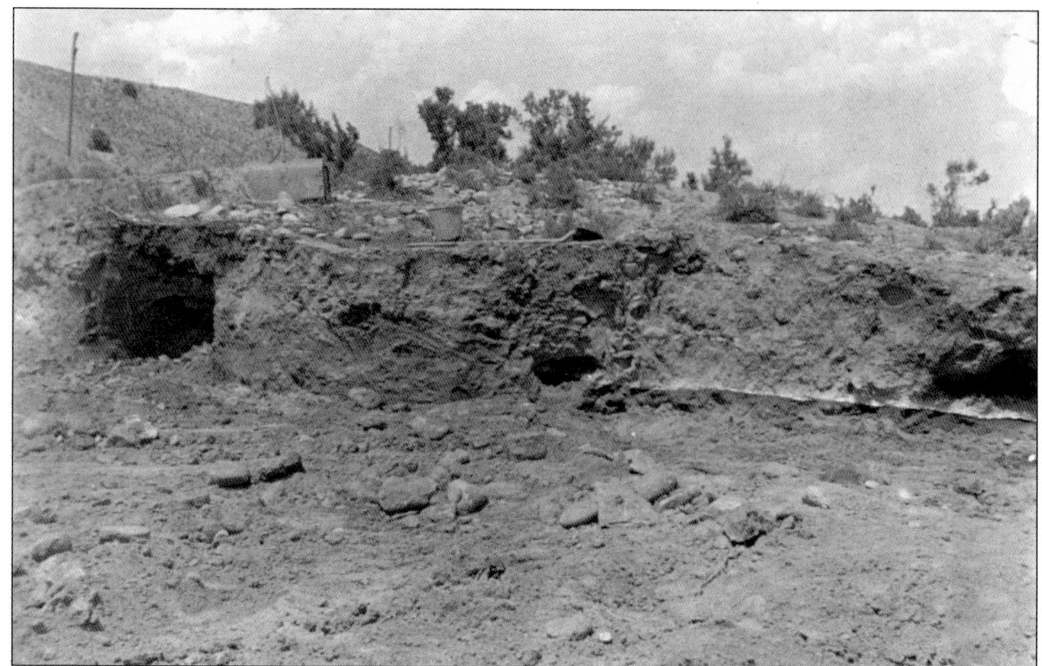

This 1889 photograph of the Aztec Ruins is one of the earliest available and displays the least disturbance to the site. This image shows the west end of the ruins and several holes made for entry. Note the bucket and shovel on the wall. This is the same location in the later picture at the top of page 57. In that photograph, the doorway is in the same place as the large hole at left. (Courtesy Aztec Museum.)

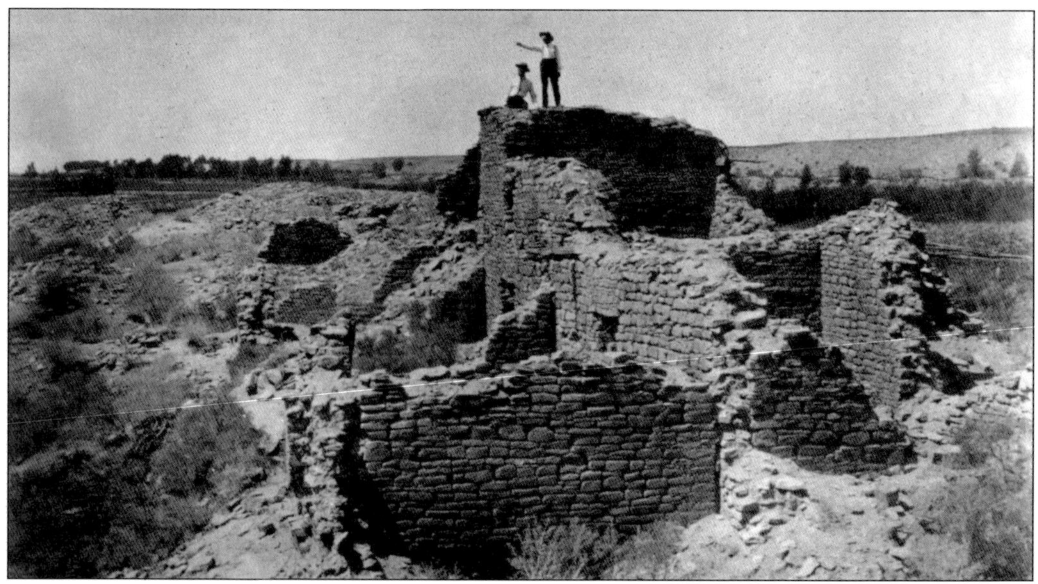

According to historical reports, this complex was constructed about 1100 as an associated community to Chaco Canyon to the south. The ancestral Pueblo people were probably attracted to the area because of available water and fertile soil. By 1300, the village was abandoned. In this image from 1900, multiple walls are uncovered and a lot of excavation has taken place. (Courtesy Aztec Museum.)

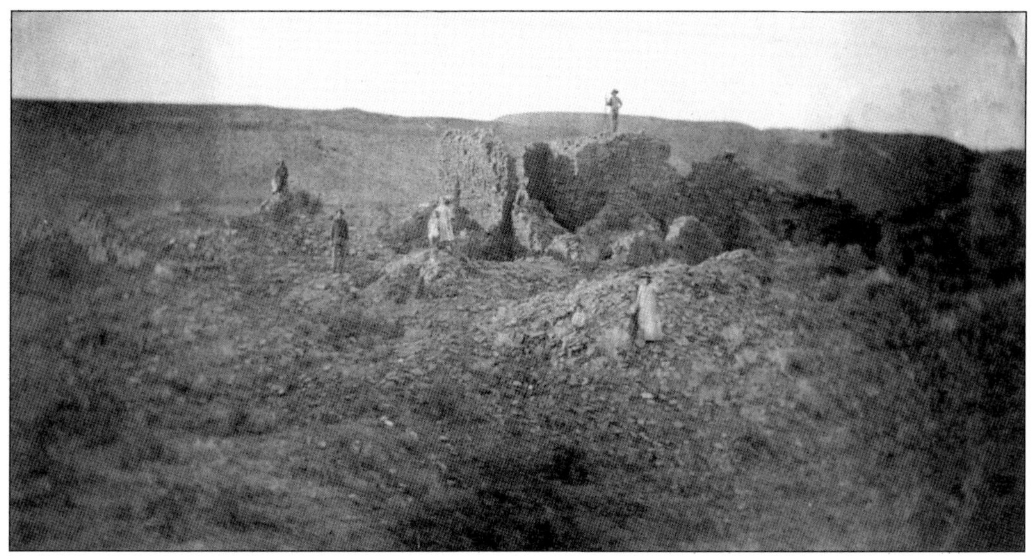

These two pictures show the Faulkner family at the ruins in 1889. The below photograph shows the east ruin. According to various accounts, a day at the ruins was a fascinating form of entertainment for the pioneer families. Children could explore and climb the walls, and families could picnic and, of course, pick up a few relics to display at home. Scott Morris was among several who collected artifacts in the 1890s and then sold them to supplement income. At that time, there were no laws against this activity. Morris's son Earl grew up to be a leading advocate for the Aztec Ruins. (Both courtesy Aztec Museum.)

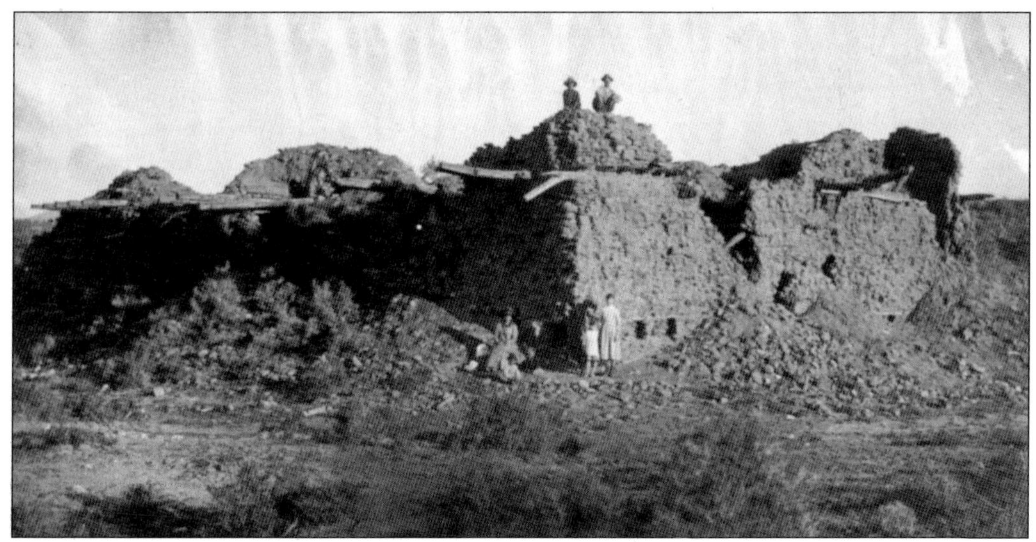

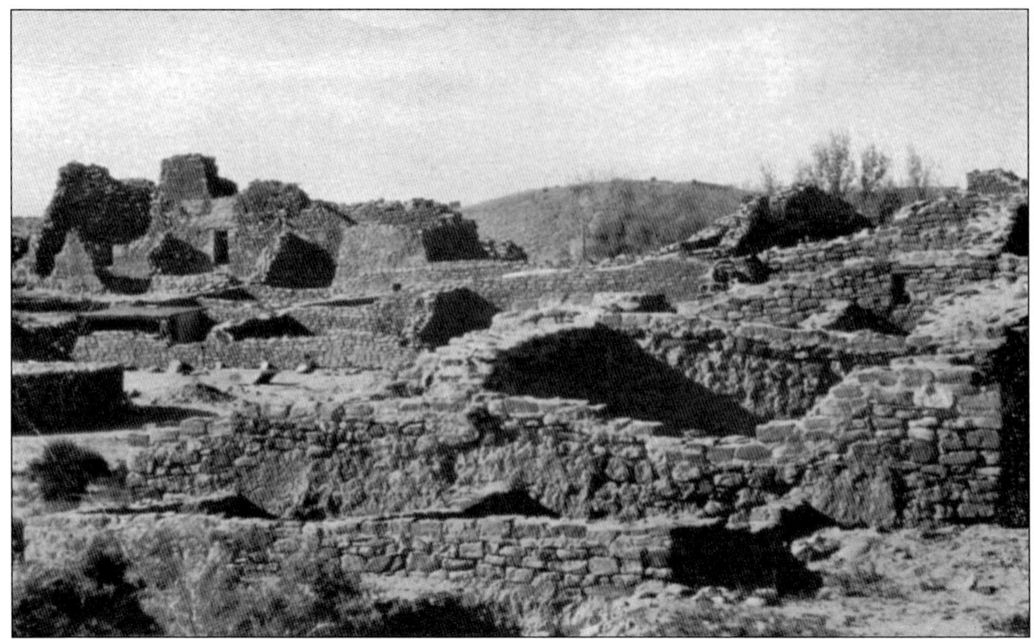

These two photographs exhibit some of the progress of excavation. The above image, from a 1905 postcard, shows a number of walls beginning to emerge. By 1916, Earl Morris was deeply involved with the Aztec Ruins and was living at the site. Morris spent years contacting educational and archeological institutions about excavation and preservation. Finally, the landowner, H.D. Abrams, granted permission for excavation to the American Museum of Natural History of New York. The museum hired Earl Morris as field supervisor. The photograph below is also a postcard. It shows the ruins about 15 years later than the above picture, around 1920; structured excavation and preservation is well underway, and the walls are more defined. Note the line of metatas (grinding stones) leaning against the wall. (Both courtesy Aztec Museum.)

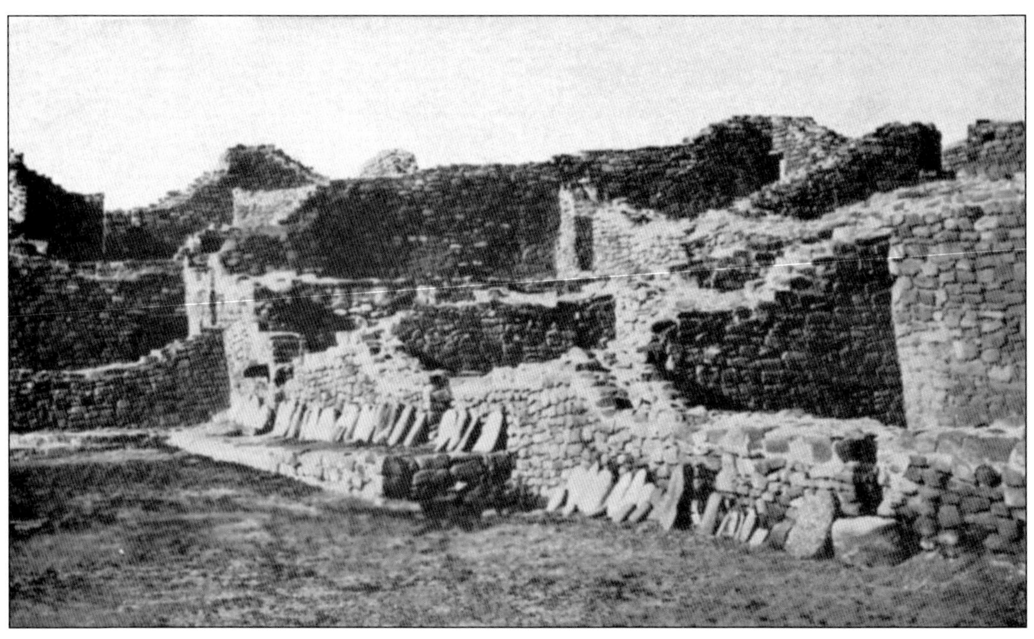

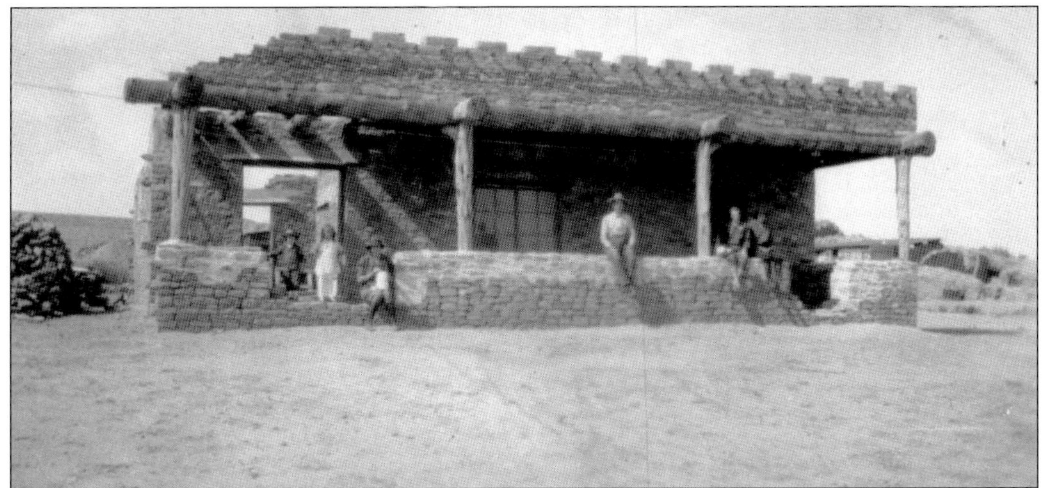

Earl Morris was privileged to live on-site from 1918 to 1933, while excavation and research were happening. This 1923 photograph shows the structure, which was built with stones from the ruins and later plastered. It served as a combined office, residence, and museum and became the nucleus of today's visitor center. (Courtesy Aztec Museum.)

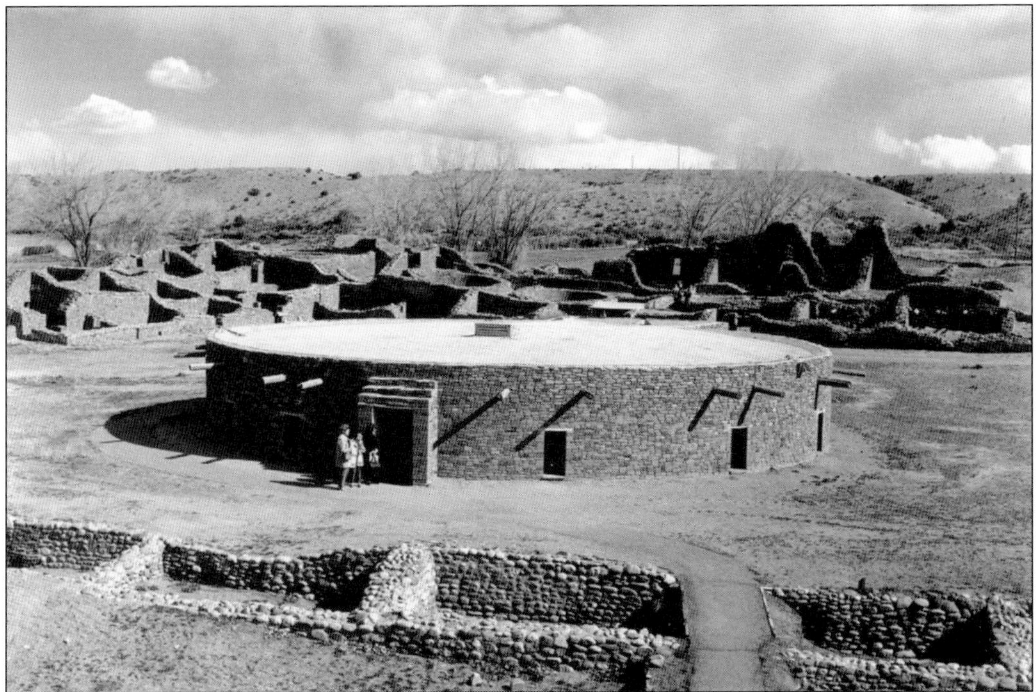

The Great Kiva was excavated in 1921 and restored as a Works Progress Administration (WPA) project in 1935. The kiva remains cool on hot summer days and has been used for Pueblo ceremonial activities, club functions, Easter sunrise services, and other activities. Several weddings have taken place in the kiva. The American Museum of Natural History, which had purchased the site, donated it to the federal government, and on January 24, 1923, the Aztec Ruin National Monument was established. It was deemed an *Anasazi* site, a word borrowed from the Navajo language that translates as both "ancient ones" and "ancient enemy." The descendants of the Pueblo people prefer the term "ancestral Pueblo." (Courtesy Aztec Museum.)

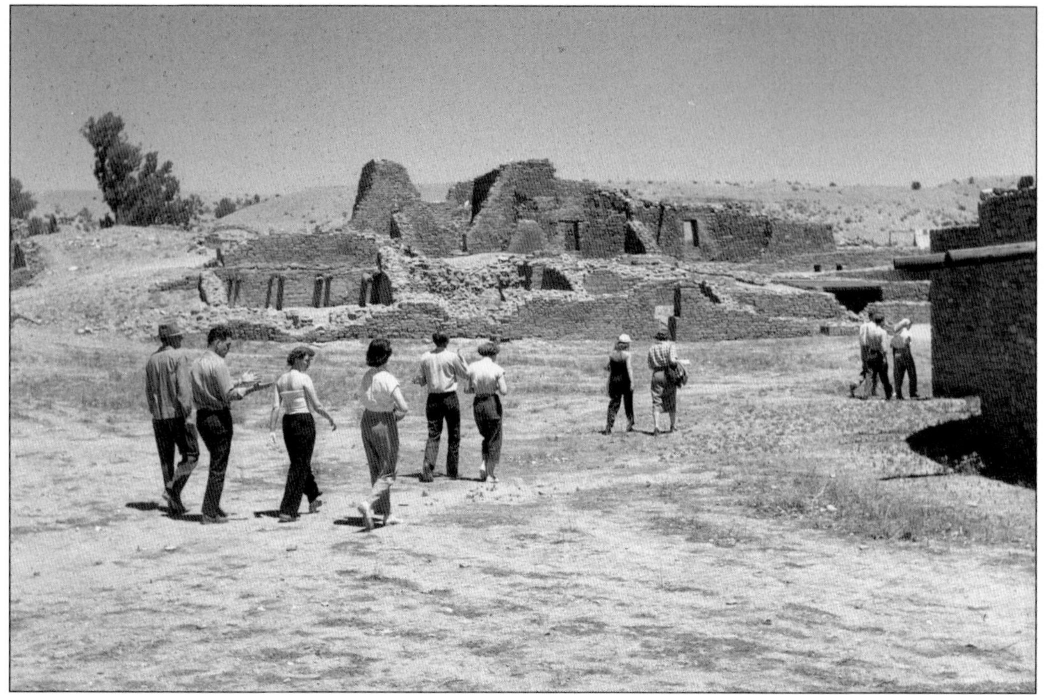

In both 1949 and 1950, a group of airplane enthusiasts called the Cortez Fliers came to Aztec Ruins on an outing. They are shown here on the way to an exploratory tour of the ruins.

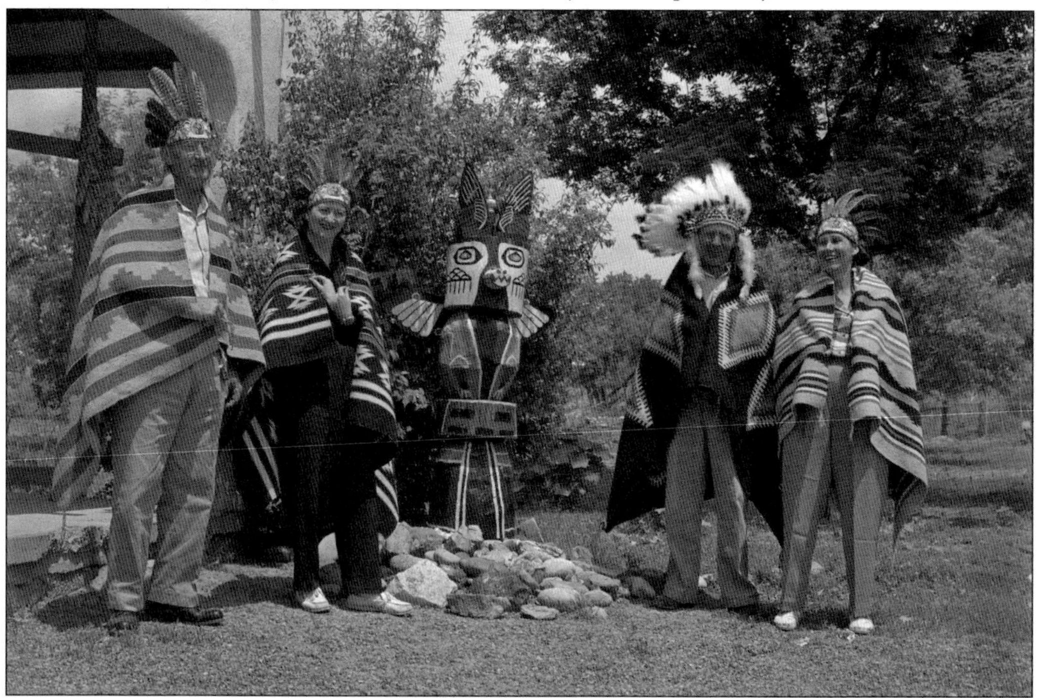

The Cortez Fliers extended their tour with a visit to the Trading Post located just outside the gates of the national monument. Wearing ceremonial headdresses and blankets, they pose by a totem pole. Tours were often the order of the day at the ruins, and that continues today.

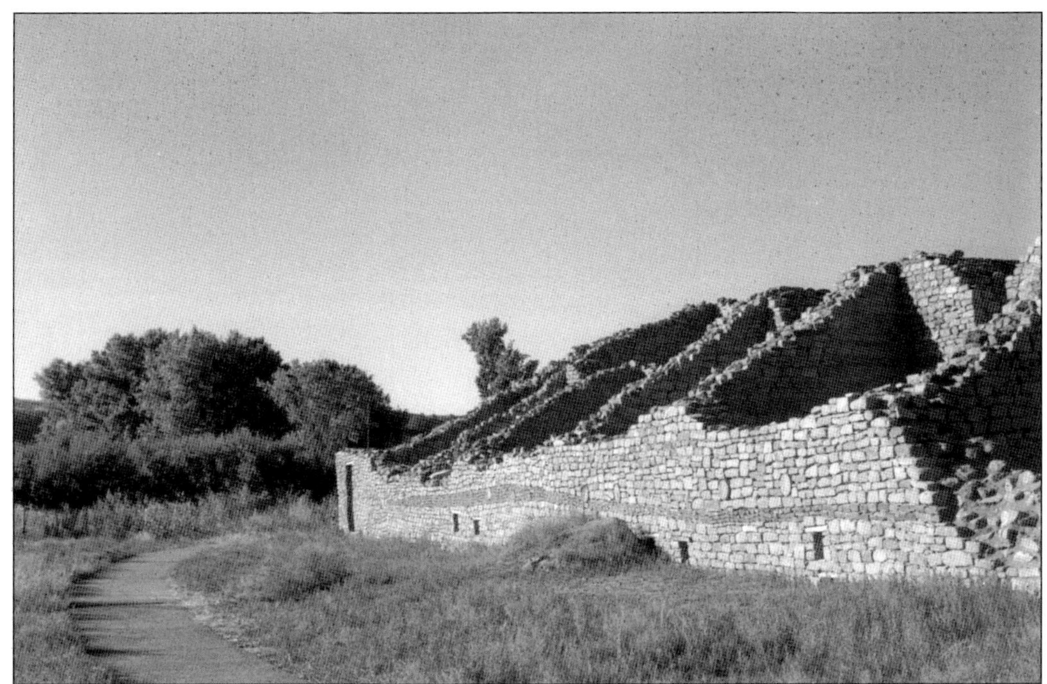

This is the west wall of the ruins, looking north in 1949. The banded area in the middle of the wall is the topmost of three bands of green (greywacke) stones. It is not known why these decorative bands were inserted in the wall, but they run for several yards.

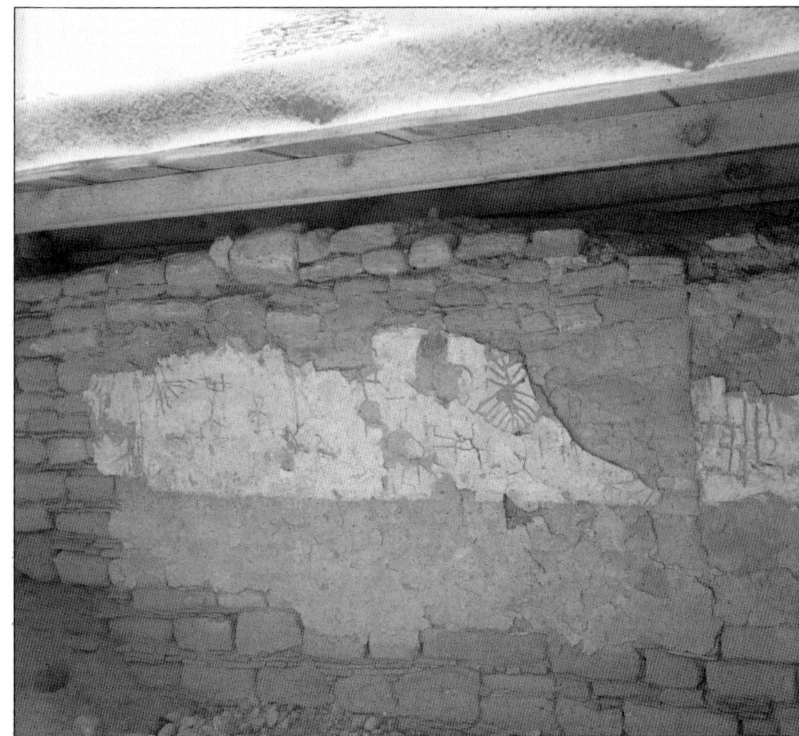

There were several pictographs made with various colors of plaster on the inside walls of the ruins. This 1950 photograph shows one that was protected with chicken wire and sheltered for visitors to view. The area was plastered, and then designs were scratched into the plaster. The scene was a series of human figures. The room has been backfilled to preserve the fragile plaster and is no longer on view.

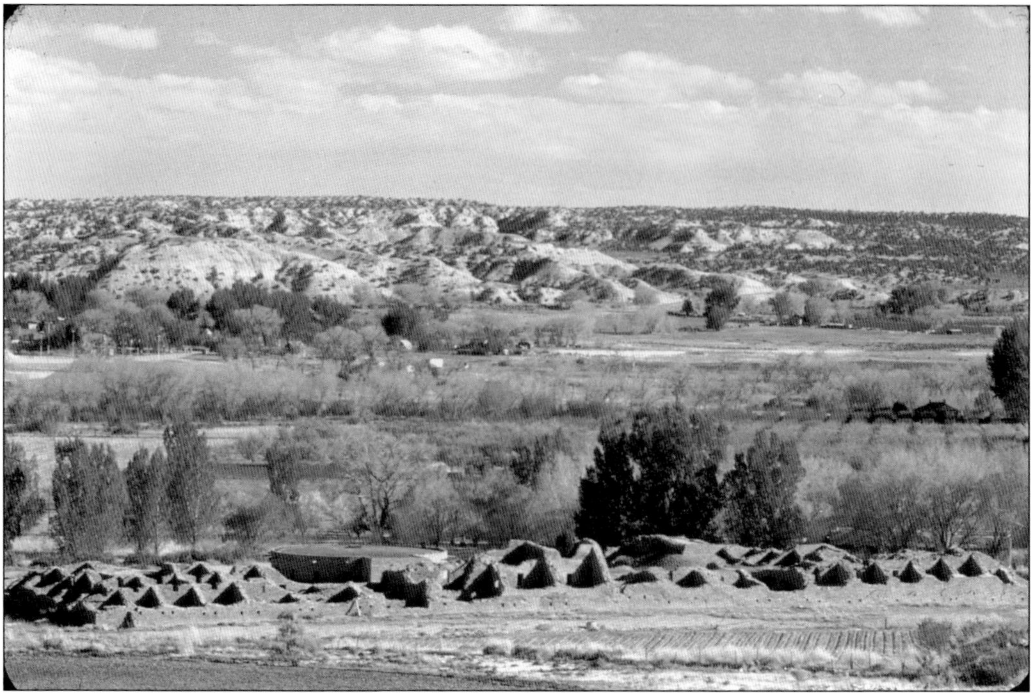

This 1951 view of Aztec Ruins is from the hill north of the site. Note the Great Kiva in the center of the photograph. The Animas River and the hills in the background look much the same today, except there is a lot more habitation on the other side of the river.

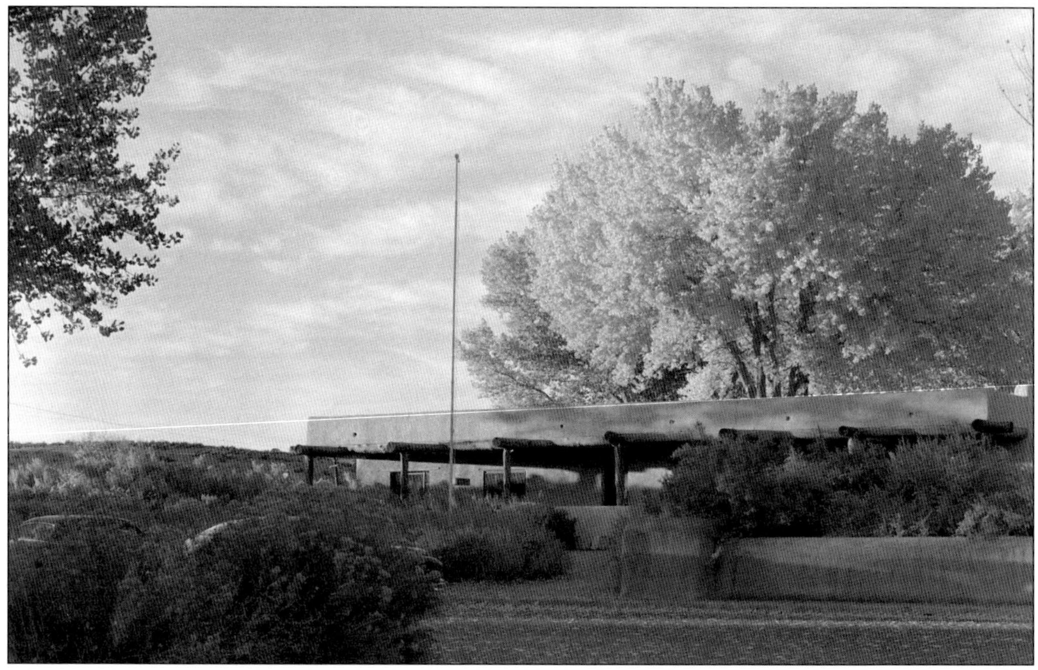

The Aztec Ruins Visitor Center in 1951 looks about the same as it does today, except now there are more walls, steps, and handrails. The visitor center started in 1919—as Earl Morris's house—and has been expanded several times. The current structure was completed in the 1980s.

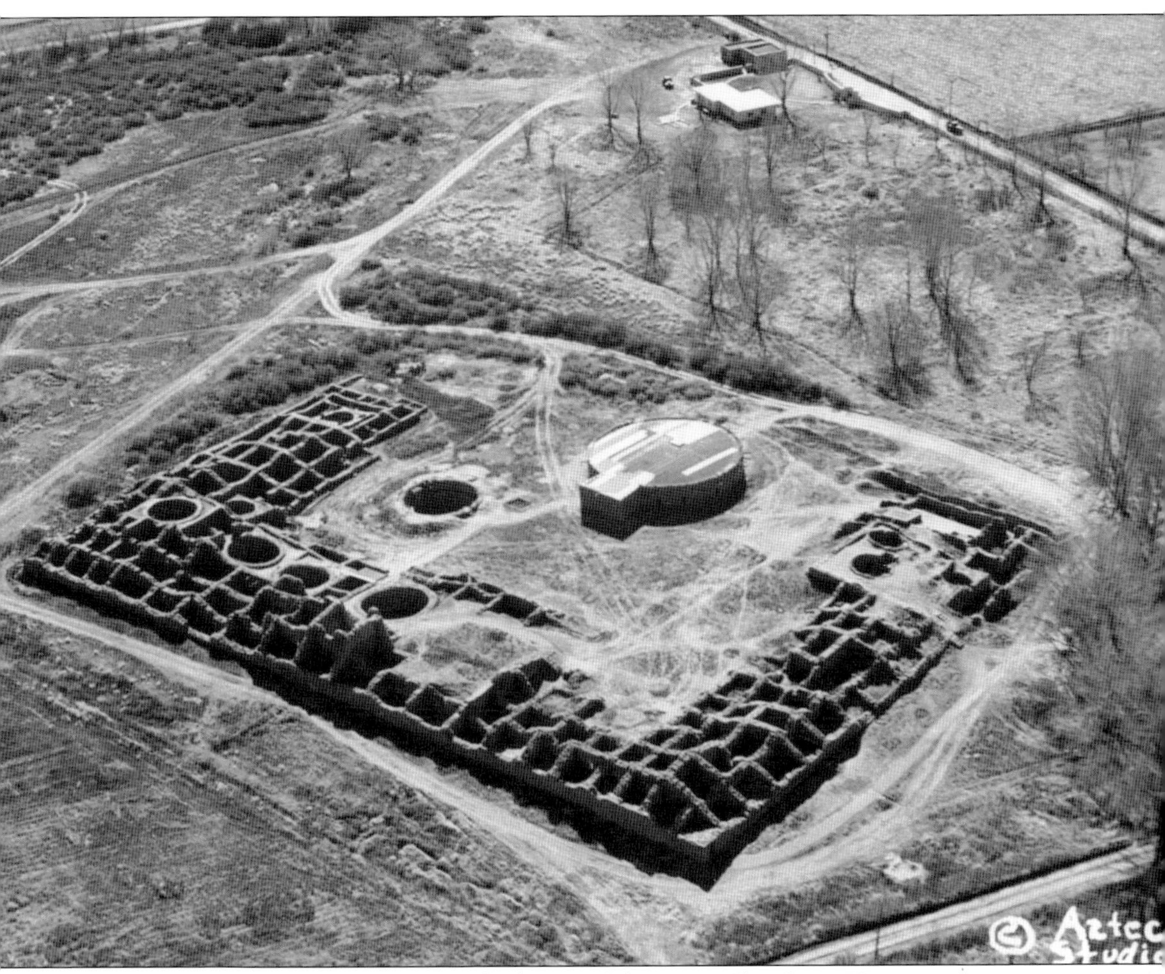

This aerial photograph from 1950 shows the layout of the ruins. The Great Kiva is in the center. The visitor center and the gate on Ruins Road are visible in the upper center. Note the absence of buildings and homes in the area. The roads are not paved.

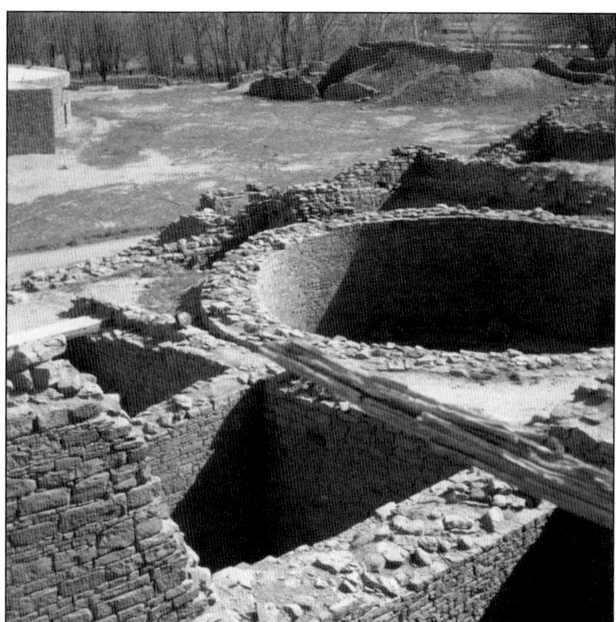

This view of the oldest dated kiva at Aztec Ruins was taken in 1955. The photograph is from the third story overlooking the kiva, which was probably built around 1100.

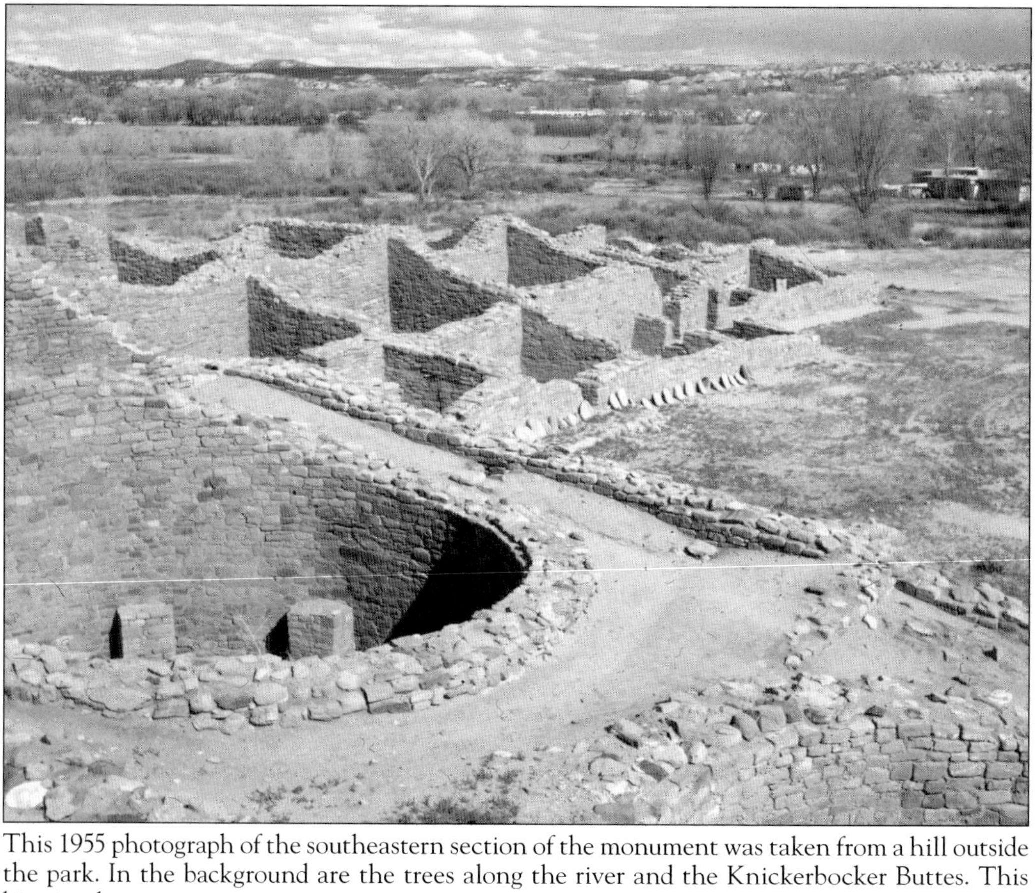

This 1955 photograph of the southeastern section of the monument was taken from a hill outside the park. In the background are the trees along the river and the Knickerbocker Buttes. This kiva is a later one.

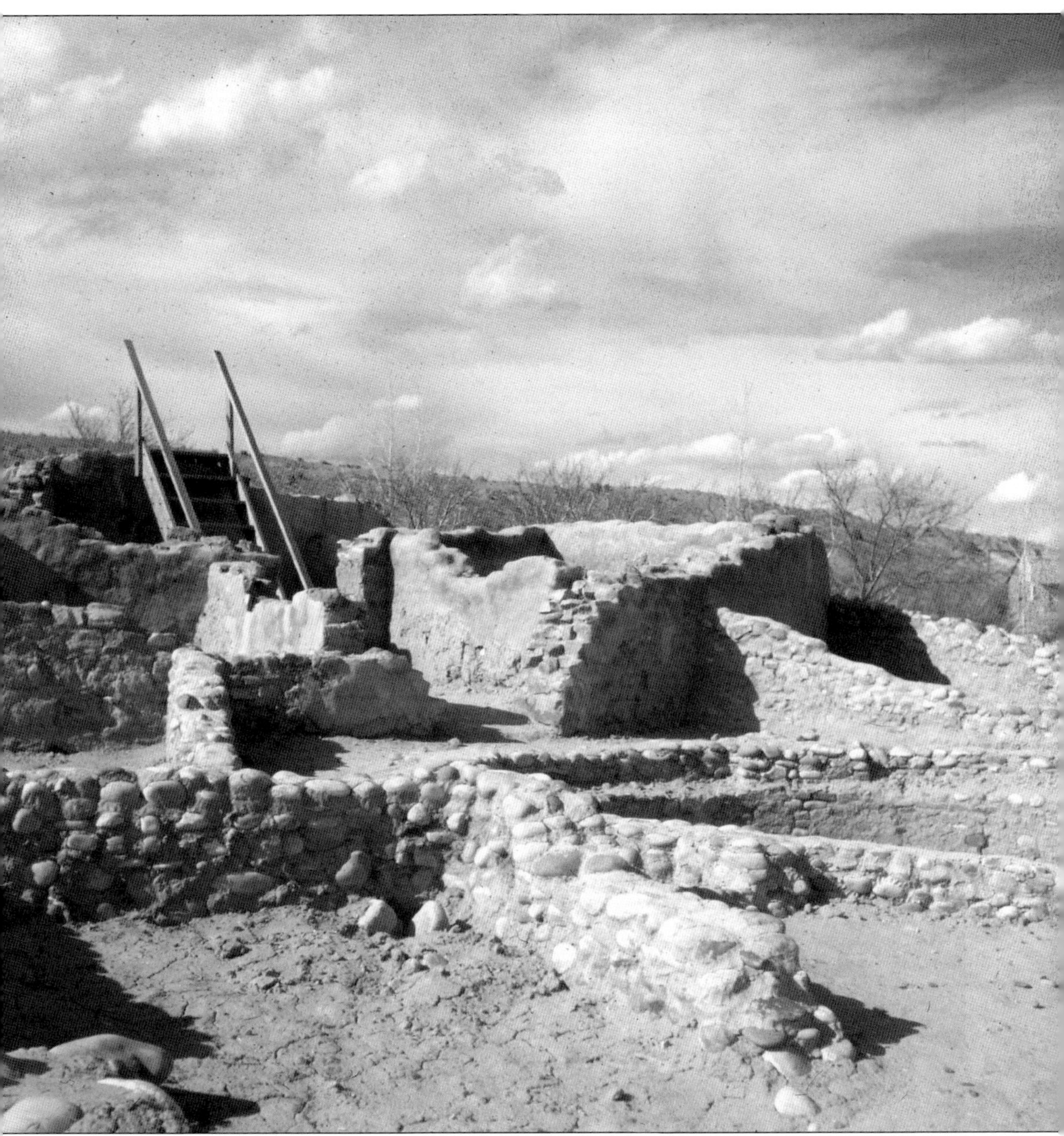

The Hubbard tri-wall structure, also cited as the Hubbard Mound, is northwest of the main ruins. The tri-wall design constituted a unique type of ceremonial building. The ruin was built with river rocks and was excavated in 1923. It was open to visitors for decades, with steps to the bottom of the kiva, but was backfilled in the 1990s to preserve the fragile earthen plaster.

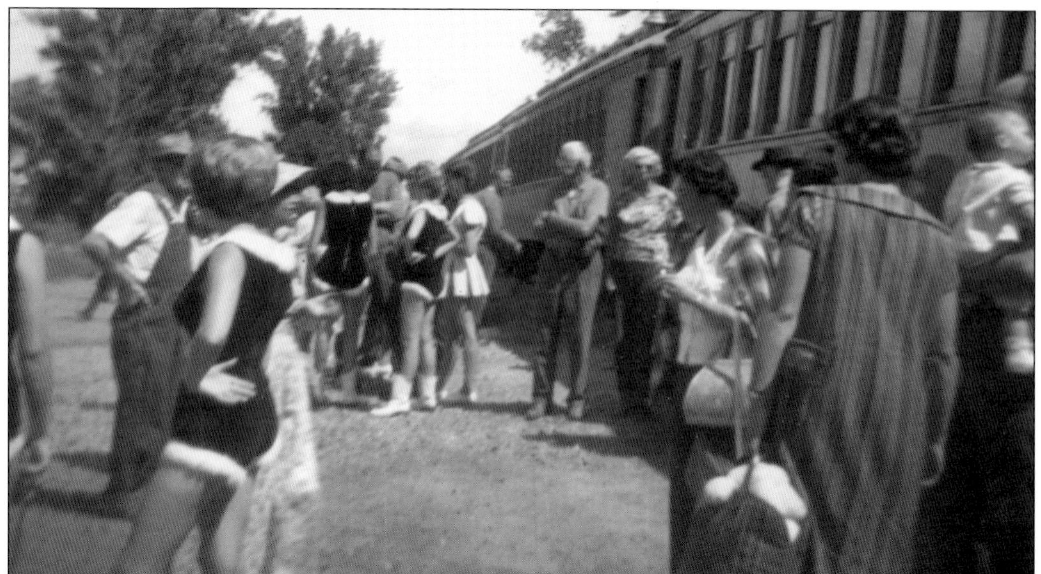

Even though passenger service on the Denver & Rio Grande Western Railroad (D&RGW) to Aztec and Farmington was suspended in 1936, two special passenger trains were assembled in September 1963. The first run had 128 passengers, and the second carried 137. The trains left Durango at 9:00 a.m. and had two stops for taking pictures. They got to Aztec around noon and were greeted by the Aztec High School Band, Indian dancers, and speakers. They were treated to a chuckwagon lunch and went on to Aztec Ruins, where they were privileged to have a special tour with guides. The cost for the outing was $7.50 for adults and $6 for children under 16. (Both courtesy Aztec Museum.)

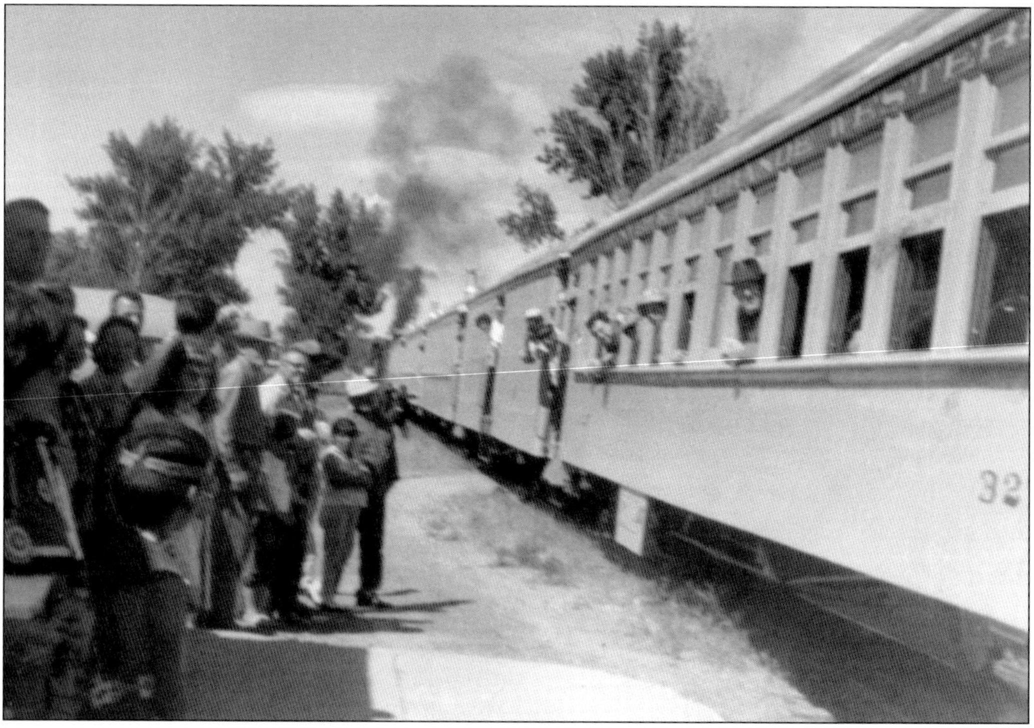

Four

Aztec Expands

Aztec, along with the rest of the country, felt the impact of the Great Depression in the 1930s. However, things were not so bad in Aztec, an agricultural area, as in the cities. Neighbors helped neighbors, gardens were grown, and bartering became the order of the day. One of the major changes was the end of passenger service to Aztec and Farmington by the Denver & Rio Grande Western Railroad. Often, one passenger car was attached to the end of a freight train. In 1936, this service was stopped, and the only time passenger cars came through Aztec were by special arrangement for a particular purpose.

In 1941, the town went on to face World War II and watched most of the young men of the community go to war. Newspapers of the time carried as much as could be learned about the local service persons. Many of the soldiers never returned, but people carried on—holding onto the memories and moving forward.

Aztec's population did not change much for several decades. In 1920, it was 489, and it increased to 740 in 1930. By 1950, the number was 885, and the town was growing quickly. In spite of the small population, Aztec was a busy community, serving as a trade center for settlers in Gobernador Canyon, Center Point, and Cedar Hill. Saturday was shopping day, and the community was always bustling with people, cars, and wagons.

The Aztec Museum is fortunate to have a collection of pictures taken by local photographer Henry Jackson, who came to Aztec in 1947 with Magnolia Petroleum. In April 1949, he opened a photography studio, sold photography equipment, and did photo processing. From 1948 to 1996, Jackson was diligent about snapping pictures of local people and events, taking care to get names and places recorded correctly. Jackson donated his works to the Aztec Museum and the San Juan County Historical Society; thanks to him, the town has a chronicle of activities in Aztec throughout those years, and one can follow the growth through his eyes.

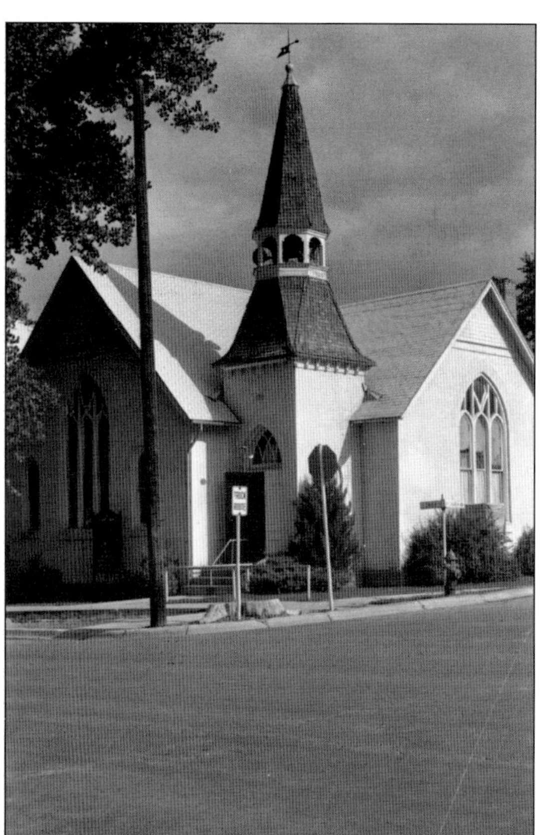

The First United Methodist Church of Aztec was built in 1906 with brick fired nearby. It was enlarged in 1928 with a rear addition. From this angle in this 1950s photograph, the church looks much as it did in the beginning. It is one of Aztec's registered historic buildings.

The interior of the Citizens Bank is shown here in 1930. In the photograph are Ellis Hamption (left) and Everett Brewer. When the bank moved to its present location, the interior fixtures were purchased by C.V. Koogler and stored. Forty years later, these items were donated to the Aztec Museum for the bank replica in the Pioneer Village. (Courtesy Aztec Museum.)

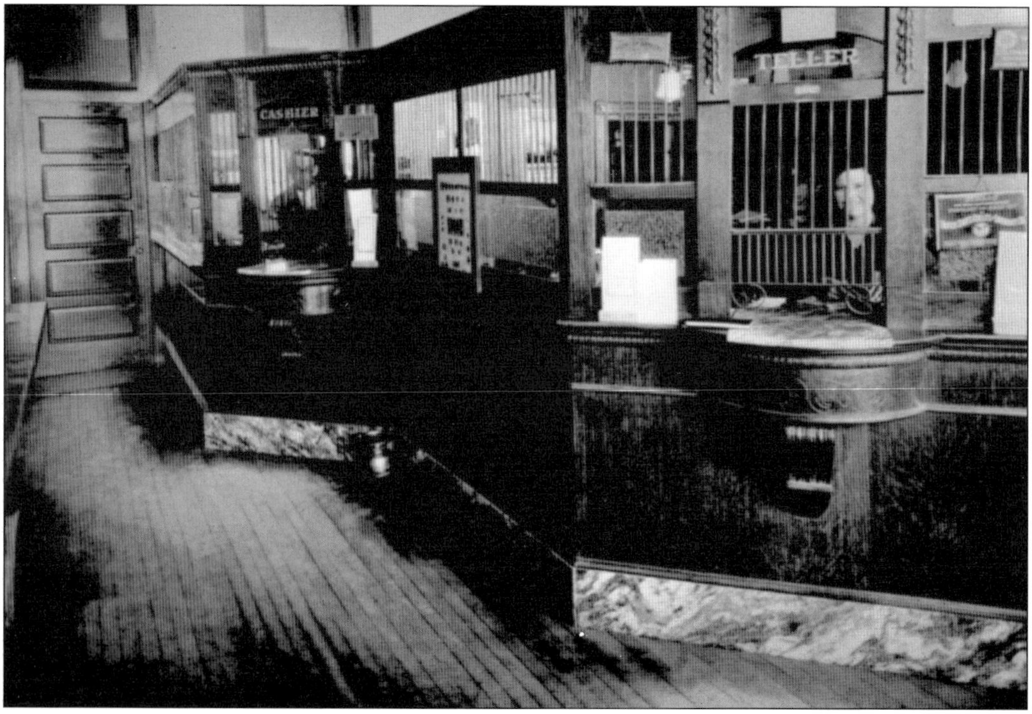

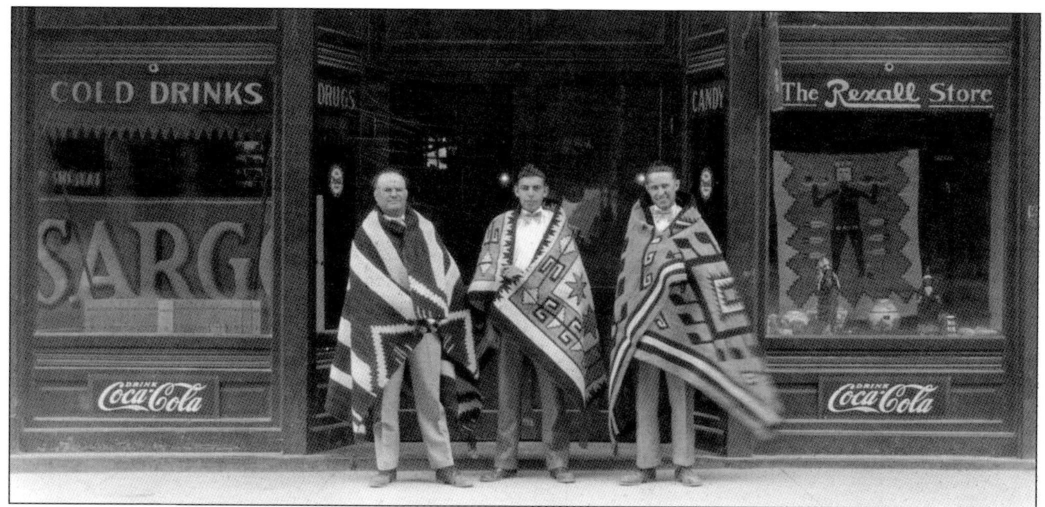

James F. Eubanks (left), Bill Deason (center), and Don Gay stand in front of the Aztec Drug Store at 121 South Main Avenue in 1922. For some reason, they are wrapped in Navajo rugs, and another rug is on display in the window. Eubanks opened the drugstore in 1921, and the family lived upstairs. In the 1930s, tradition allowed for children to come by on the last day of school and be treated to a free ice cream cone. (Courtesy Aztec Museum.)

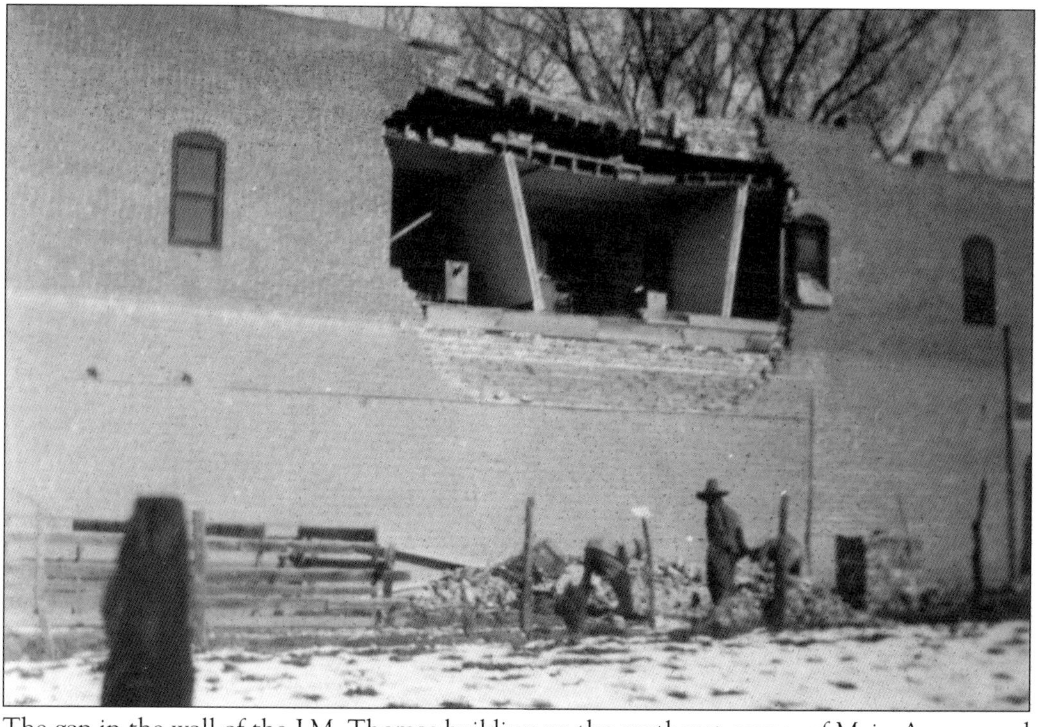

The gap in the wall of the J.M. Thomas building on the southeast corner of Main Avenue and Chuska Street was an unfortunate accident. On a cold day in 1930, Mr. Mosley of La Plata came to town, and Thomas rented him a room above the post office. When Mosley—who knew little about the dangers of natural gas—attempted to light the newfangled gas heater in the room, in an instant he was outside on top of a pile of bricks. Mosley recovered after a stint in the hospital, and Thomas had a sizeable repair bill. (Courtesy Aztec Museum.)

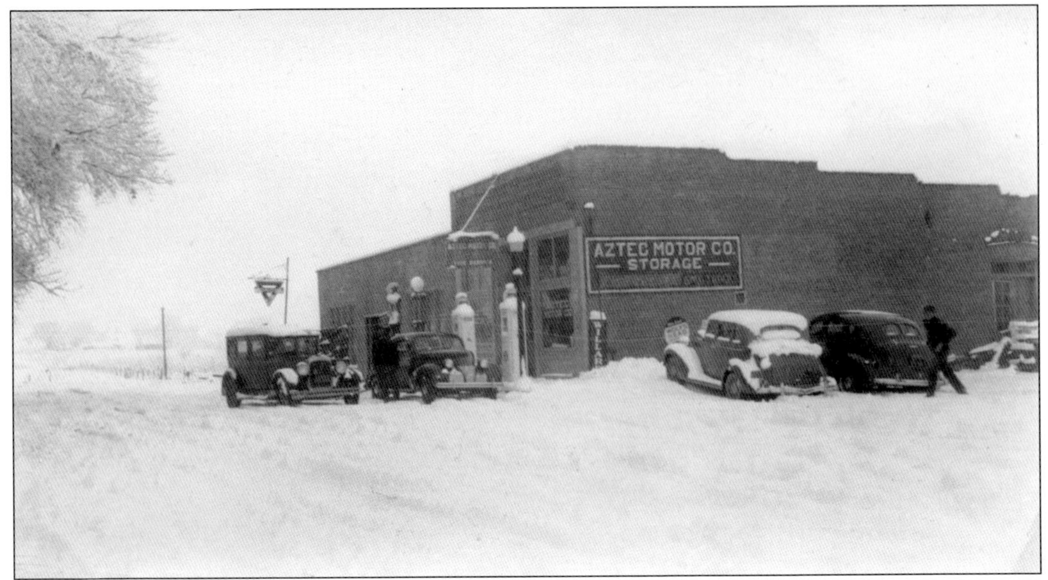

Brothers Floyd and Maurice Rhodes bought the Aztec Motor Company in 1932. The day they opened the business, they pooled their funds and, according to Floyd, had 85¢ between them. They went on to become well established and respected. Located on the southwest corner of Main Avenue and Zia Street, the place is seen here after a winter snowstorm. There was nothing south of it then, but that area is filled with businesses today. (Courtesy Audrey Glazebrook.)

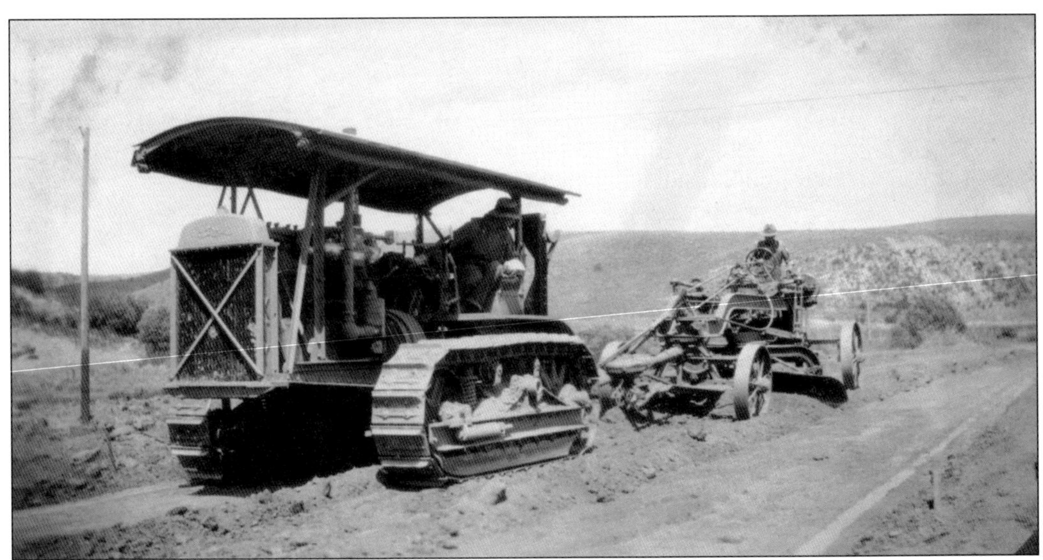

Ray Atchison made his first trip into Aztec in style when he rode this Caterpillar tractor from Bayfield to Aztec in 1931. At that time, he was towing a grader and five wagons on a gravel road. He said that during the two-day trek, he didn't see over 25 cars on the entire 50-mile trip. (Courtesy Atchison family.)

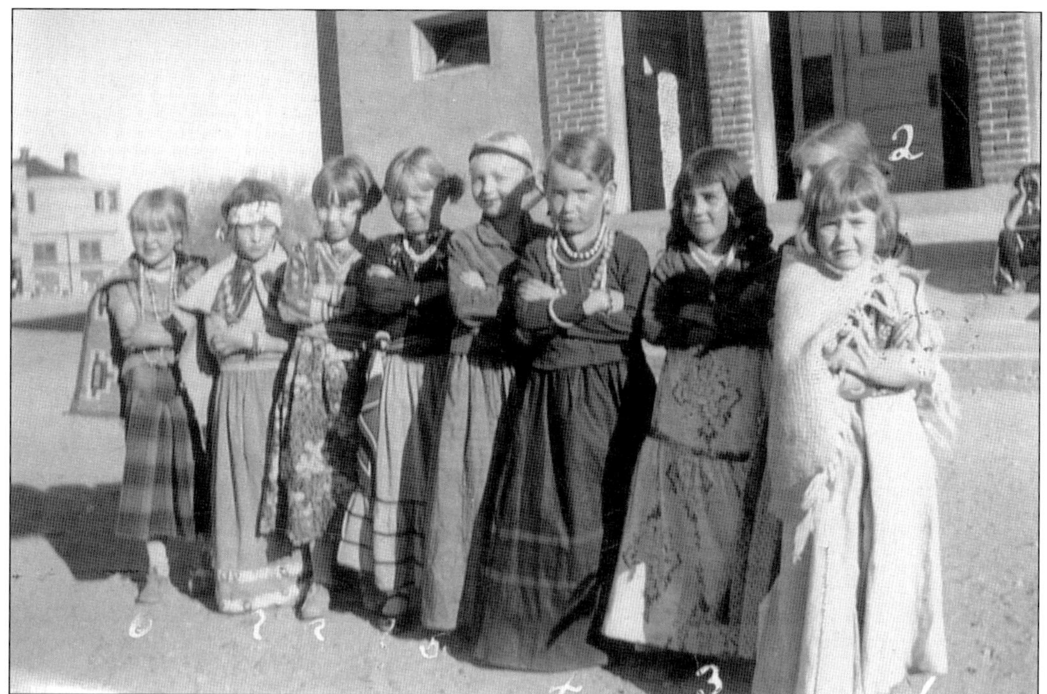

Students in the Aztec Elementary School third-grade class pose in their International Day outfits in 1935. Marked number three is Esther Jacquez (Smith). The group stands in front of the elementary school that was previously the high school building. (Courtesy Esther Smith.)

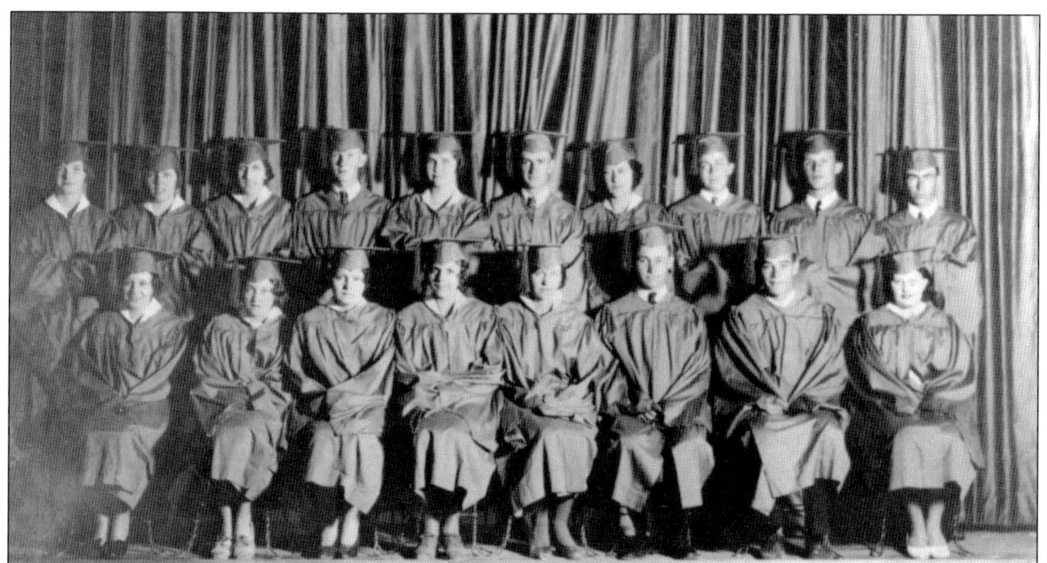

The Aztec High School graduating class of 1933 poses in caps and gowns. Although the exact order of the names written around the photograph was unclear, the students pictured here are Dephina Passerin, Sylvia Sategna, Lorene Pawley, Doris Dufur, Mamie Howe, Harland Polk, Evan Solomon, Blanche Taylor, Beulah Bell, Juanita Townsend, Juanita Burton, Clifton Anderson, Mary C. Johnson, Hubert Breshears, Helen Shetz, Lyle McWilliams, Bob Hubbard, and Ariel Johnson. (Courtesy Judy Hollar.)

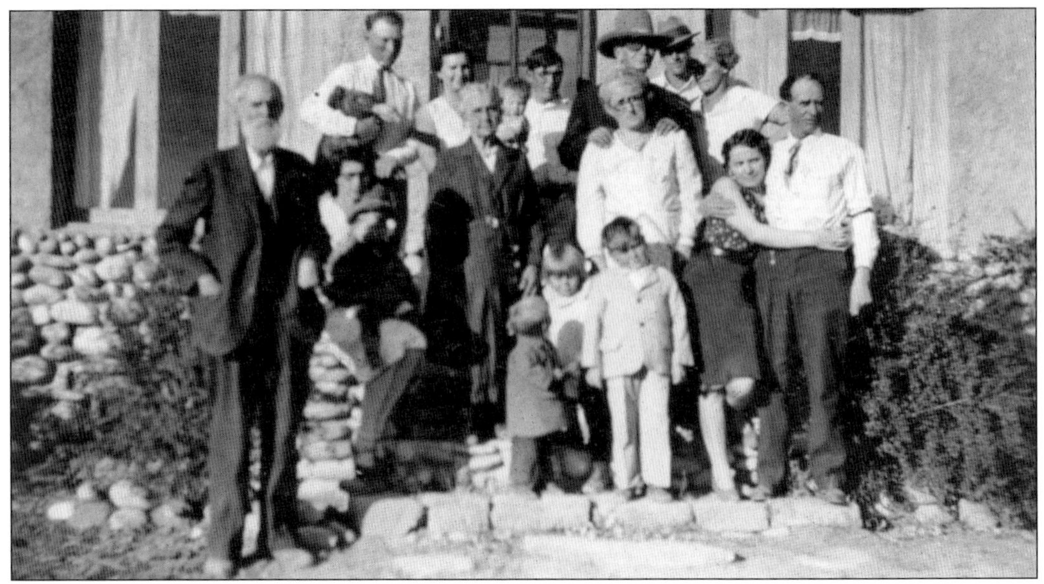

A pioneer family poses in front of the house on the rise above Ruins Road and Estes Arroyo about 1933. The man in the large hat near the center of the photograph is Robert Ellis Pawley, with his wife, Pearl, in front of him. Next to Robert, on the right, are Bud Randall and his mother, Bessie Austin Randall. The house, built by Oren Randall, later became a popular restaurant called the Riverview Steakhouse. (Courtesy Pawley family.)

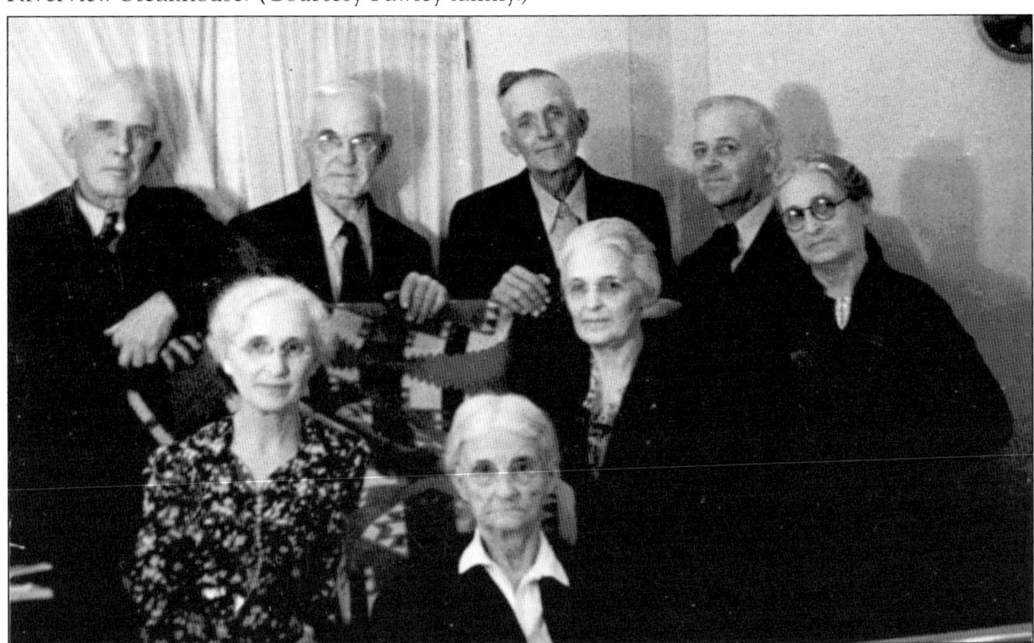

The Wood family—four brothers, three sisters, and their mother—is shown here in 1937. In the first row are, from left to right, Texanna, Cammie Carolyn Meek Wood (mother), Della, and Desda. Standing behind them are, from left to right, James Franklin Jr., Cave Johnson, Will, and Aubrey. The Wood family migrated here in 1906 via the Largo Canyon Road and crossed the San Juan River on the ferry at Blanco. James Franklin Wood Jr. bought the Fred Bunker house on Lovers Lane and settled into life in Aztec. (Courtesy Aztec Museum.)

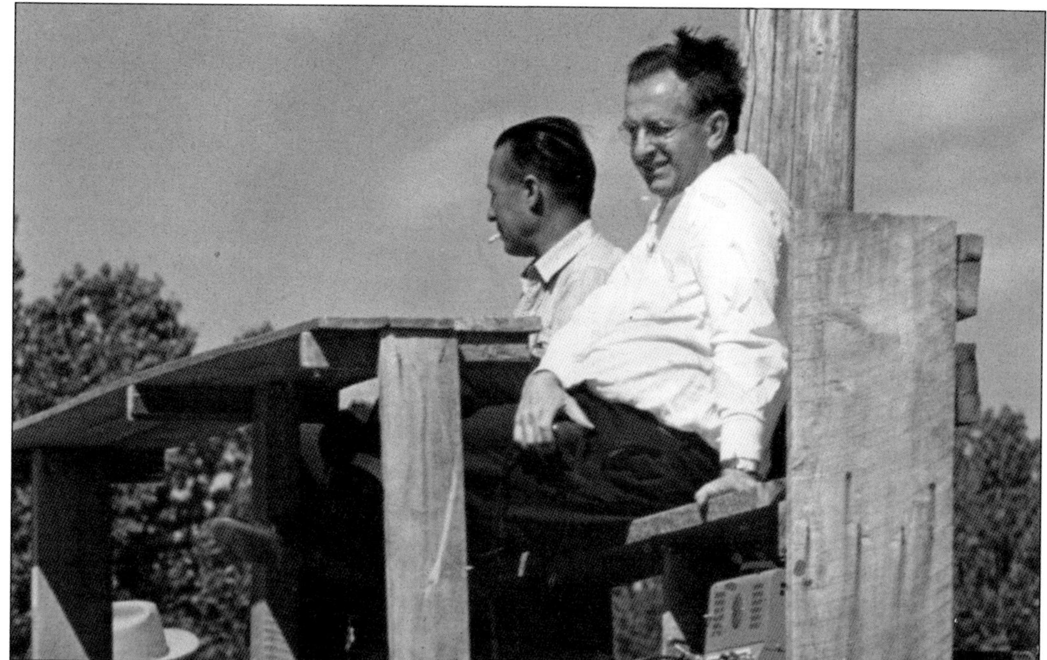

Sports were an integral part of life in Aztec. Here, Don Gay (left) and Charles Utton sit in the announcer's booth to call the plays in a 1939 baseball game. They seem to have quite a precarious perch compared to announcer's booths of today. (Courtesy Aztec Museum.)

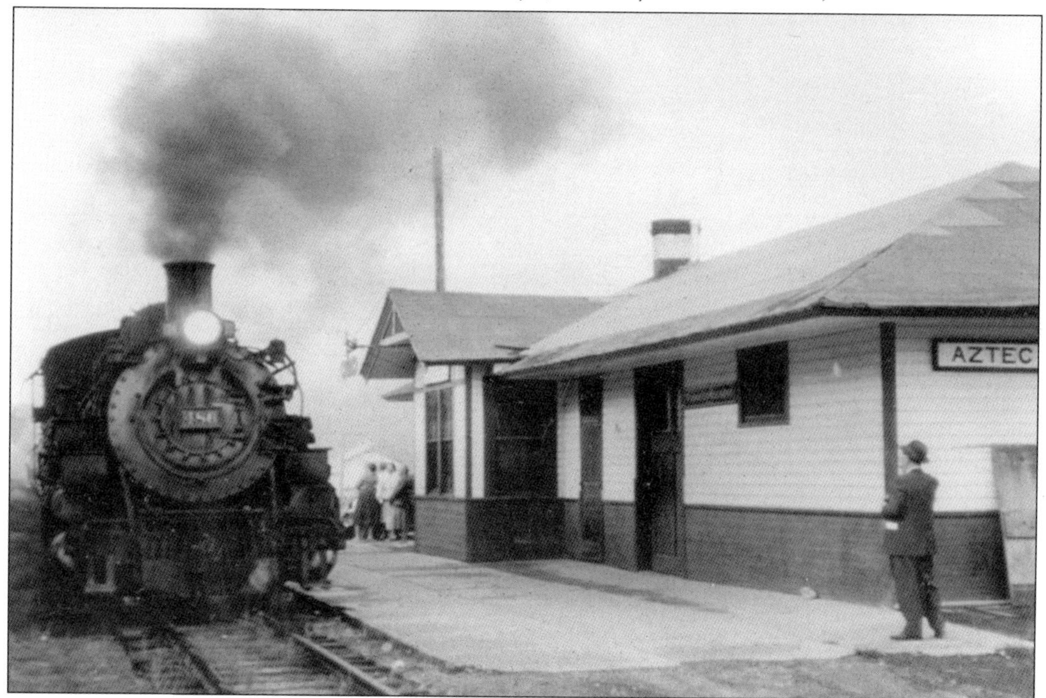

Passenger service on the D&RGW railroad ended in 1936. It appears these folks are waiting for someone to embark or board. There are many stories of people going back and forth to Durango by train for business, shopping, and visiting. (Courtesy Ron Nott.)

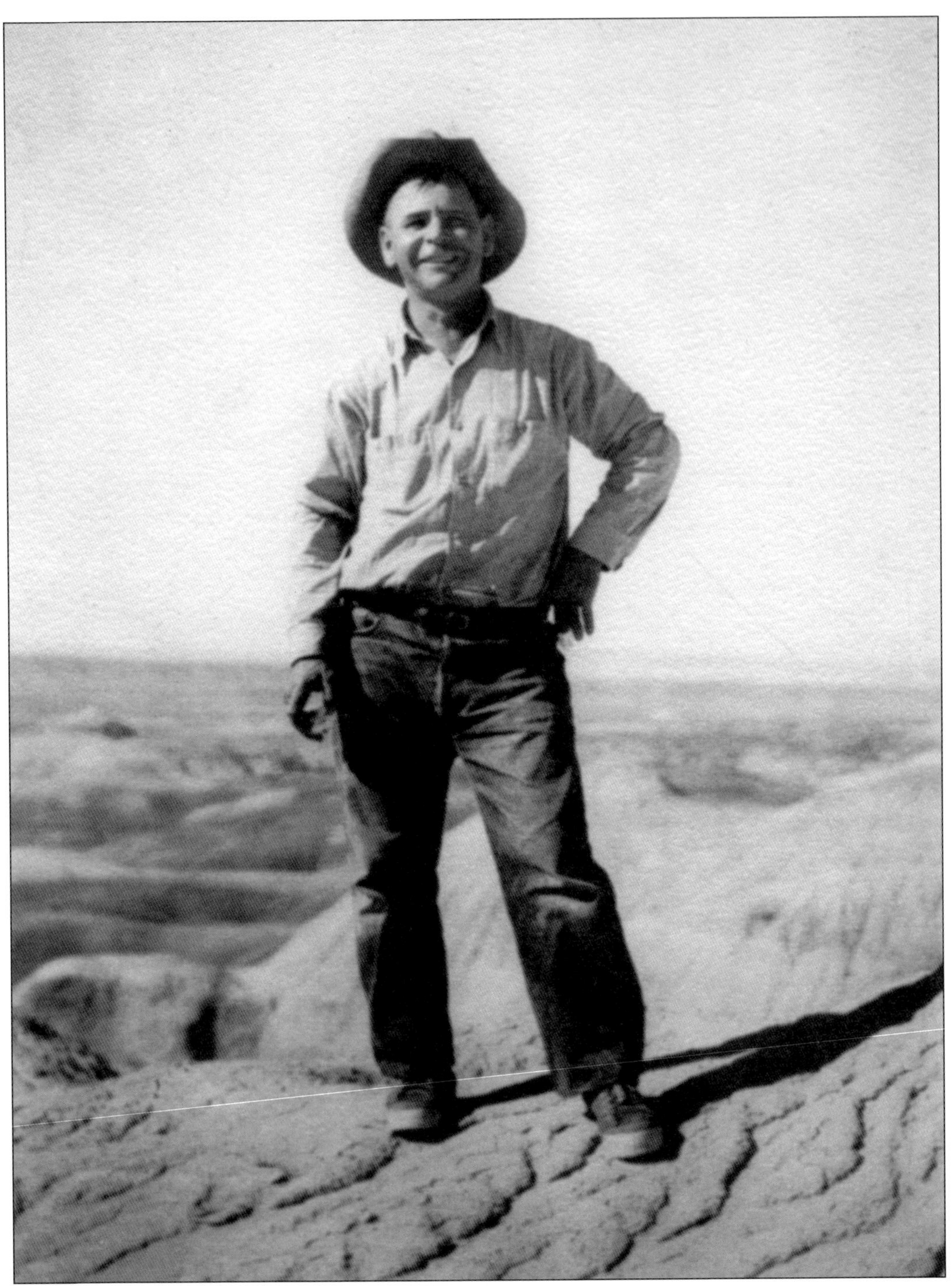

Guillermo (Willie) Lobato and his wife, Jane, were major contributors to the Aztec Museum. The museum's extensive rock, shell, and mineral collection was a gift from the Lobatos, and Willie's cowboy hat, boots and American Legion mementos are on display. Willie was a World War I veteran, and some items from his tour of duty are on exhibit. This 1940s photograph is probably at his ranch east of Aztec. (Courtesy Aztec Museum.)

This special movie was presented as a memorial to local boy Bill Bowra at the Aztec Theatre in 1945. Bowra was serving in the Philippines during World War II when he was taken prisoner by the Japanese. A Bloomfield soldier saw Bowra being put on a ship with other prisoners, and he was never heard from again. Bowra was declared deceased about the time of this tribute. (Courtesy James Bowra.)

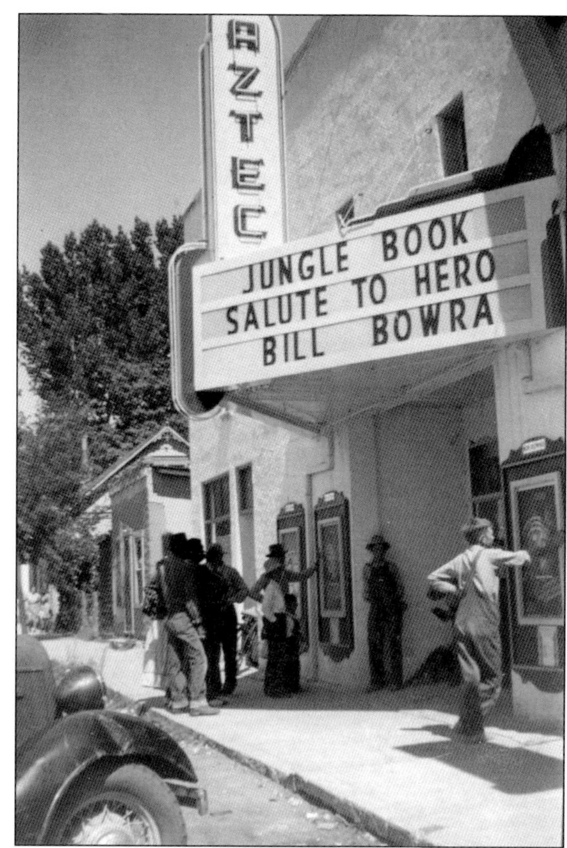

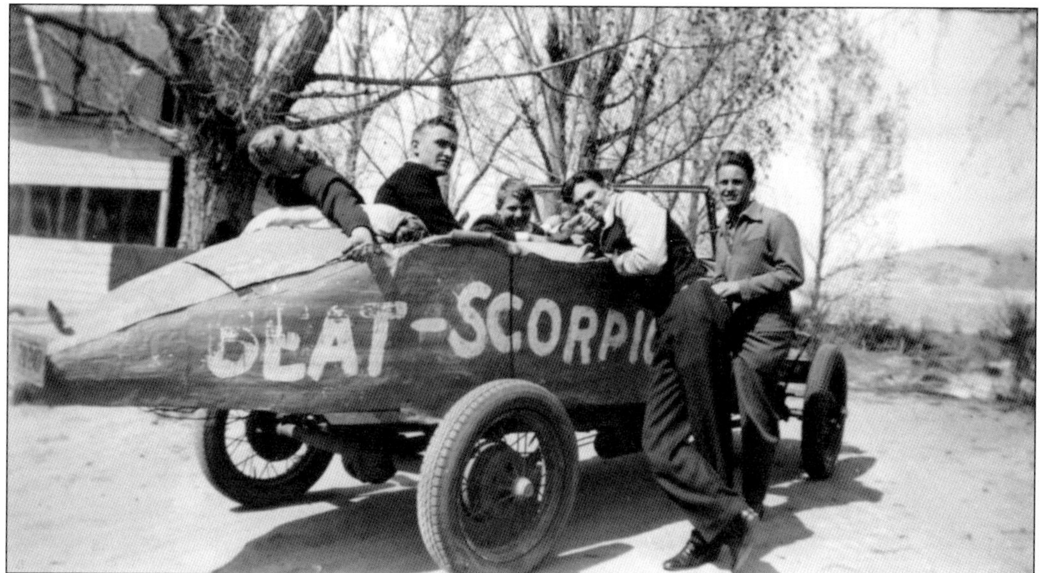

Homecoming games were a big event, and rivalry between the Aztec Tigers and the Farmington Scorpions was usually on the top burner. In 1941, these young men decorated their vehicle for the parade. Pictured from left to right are Wayne Harris, Lewis Townsend, Bruce Hare, Bob Ridenour, and Kenneth Townsend. (Courtesy Lewis and Bobbie Townsend.)

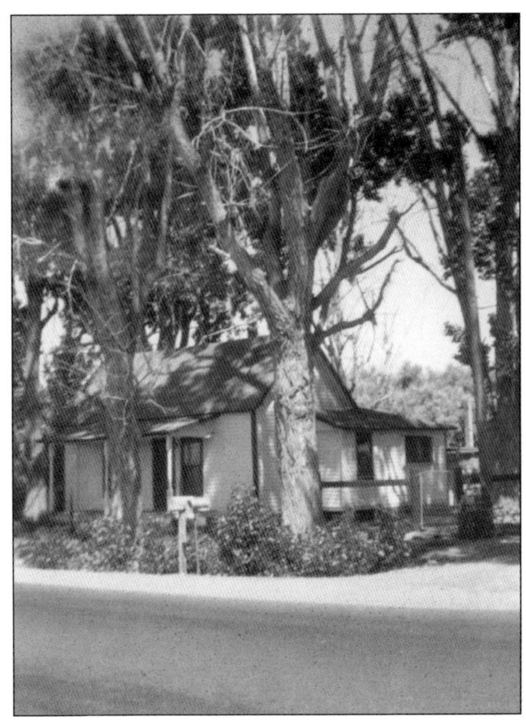

This house was the first one spotted on the left as a driver came into Aztec from Farmington. In 1948, it belonged to Ed and Lenore Jones. It was quiet and cozy until the four-lane highway came; then it was noisy, and the eastbound lane came right up to their fence. The steps had to be moved around to the side. The Jones family moved the house to the top of the hill behind the original location, and it remains there today. Ed and Lenore Jones are pictured below in 1962. (Both courtesy Art Jones.)

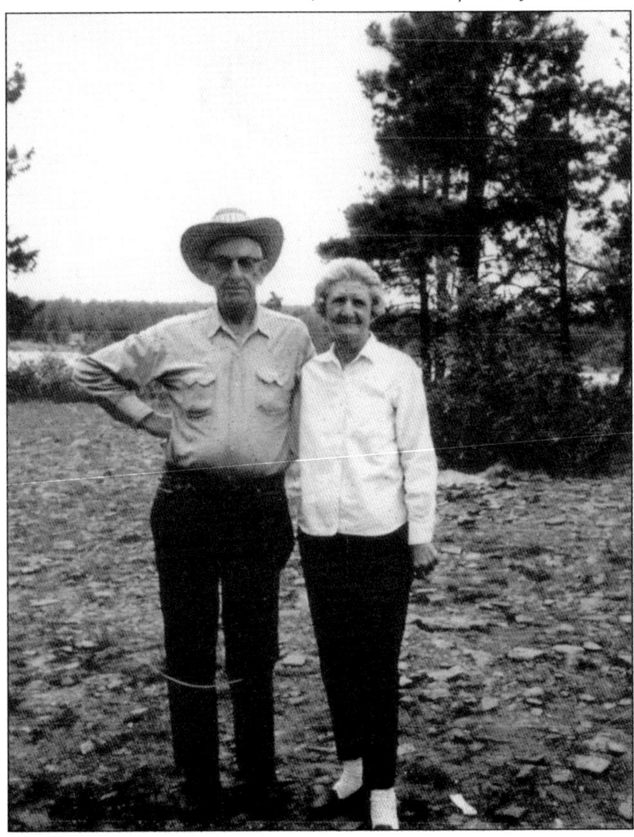

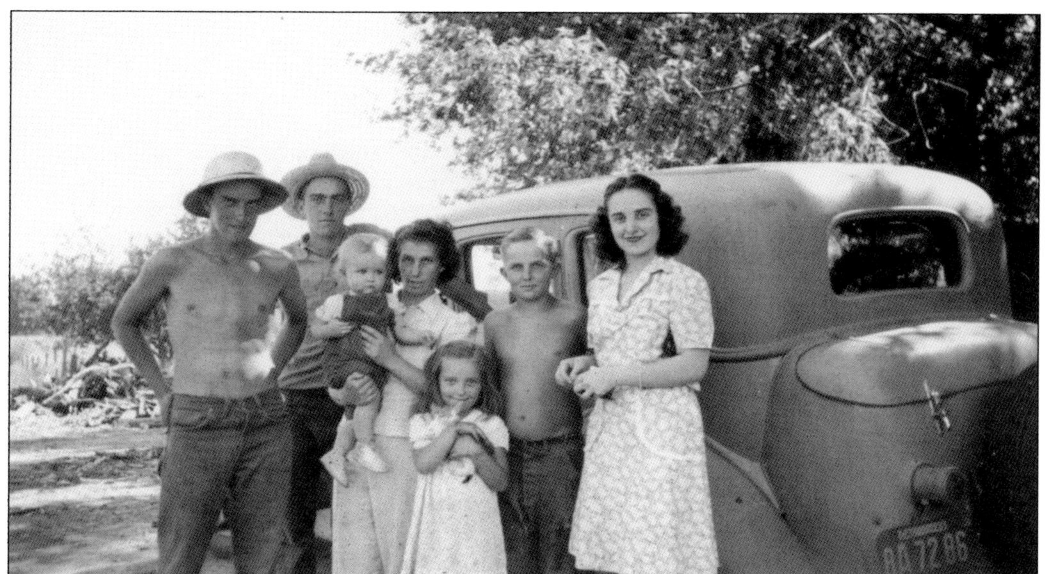

The Irven Morrison family is shown here in 1945. They are, from left to right, Joe, Johnny, Deanna (baby), Nellie, Marilyn, Lynn, and Evelyn. Nellie was widowed before Deanna was born and is an example of a woman forging ahead, as she and her six children kept a large farm going. In 1949, Nellie married Irvin Randlemon, and the pair became very active in church and community projects. (Courtesy Deanna Morrison Blythe.)

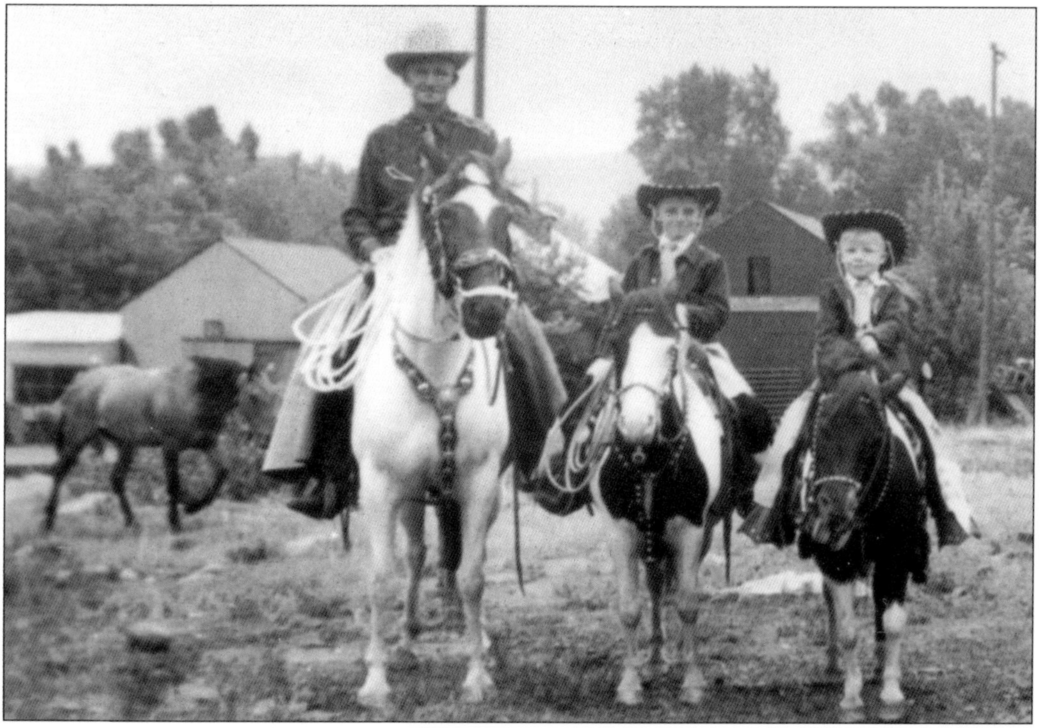

In this c. 1946 image, Dick Thurston and sons Jim (center) and Robbie are dressed up and ready to ride in a parade. Thurston raised some good horses—he once sold a paint horse to well-known rodeo cowboy, movie star, and trick rider Monty Montana. (Courtesy Judy Hollar.)

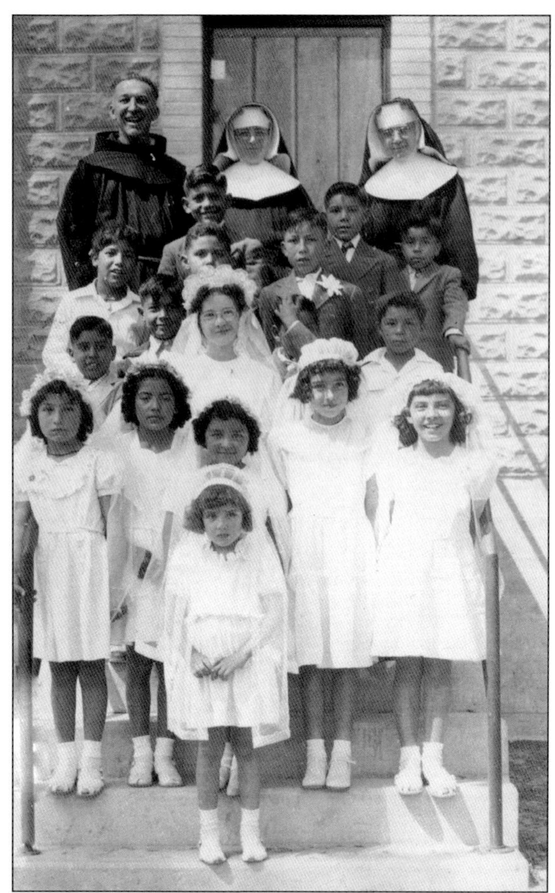

A first communion class stands outside St. Joseph's Catholic Church on May 4, 1947. Pictured here are, from left to right, Connie Griego (on the lowest step); (second row) Berla Jaquez, Cordy Jaquez, Annie Esquibel, Sylvia Griego, and Cleofas Jaquez; (third row) Eddie Ortega, Sephie Martinez, Mary Jane Farmer, Ernest Martinez, and Donald Selph; (fourth row) Vernon Selph, Gilbert Jaquez, and Eddie Jaquez; (fifth row) Alberto Martinez, Louie Martinez, and Oliver Tujillo; (sixth row) Fr. Eugene Rousseau, OFM, and Sisters Cecilia and Benedict Joseph. (Courtesy Cleofas Montoya.)

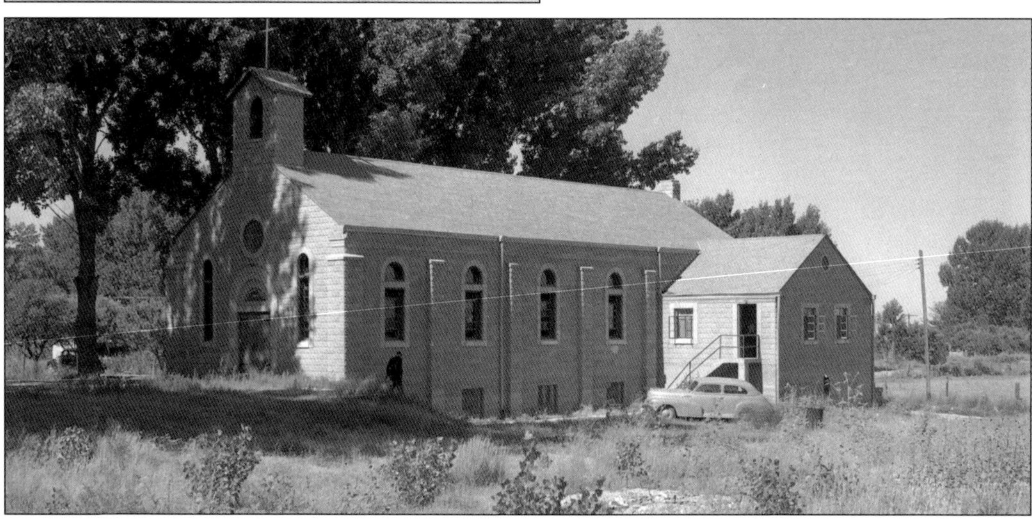

St. Joseph's Catholic Church was built in 1946 on North Mesa Verde Street. The main highway through Aztec went right in front of the church. Before this building was erected, the congregation met at the Funeral Home on Sutton and Rio Grande Streets. One of the children in the communion class said she remembers meeting in the funeral home and having to kneel on very hard, bare wooden floors.

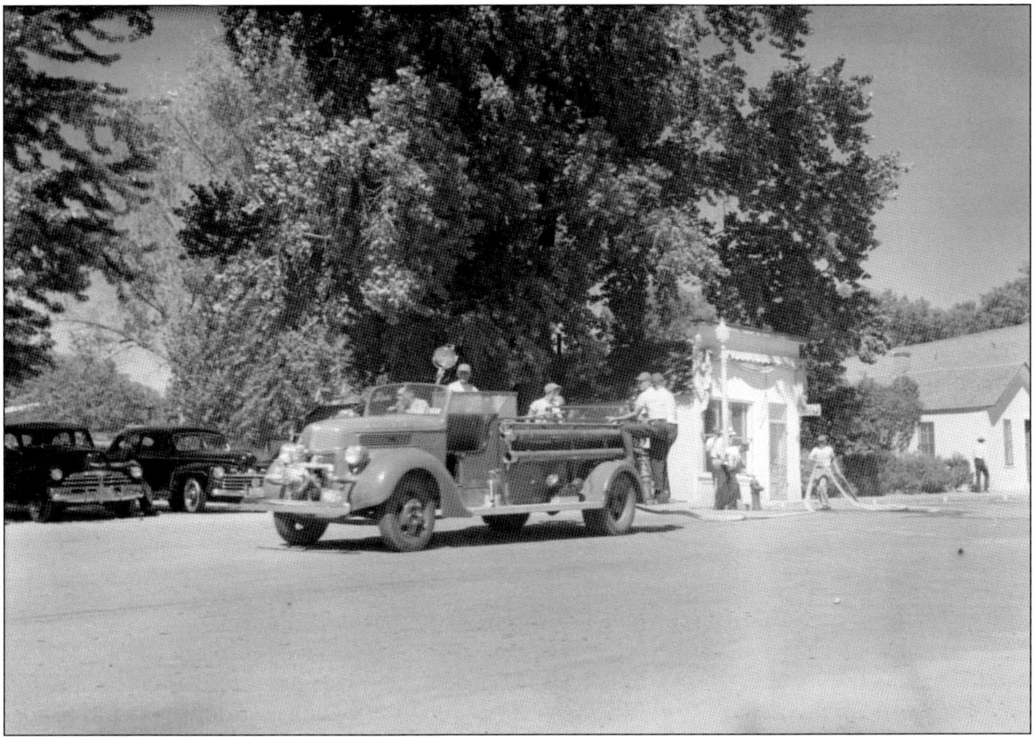

Aztec was host to a firemen's convention in 1948. There were several types of competitions among firefighters during the event. Here, the men hook up a fire hose.

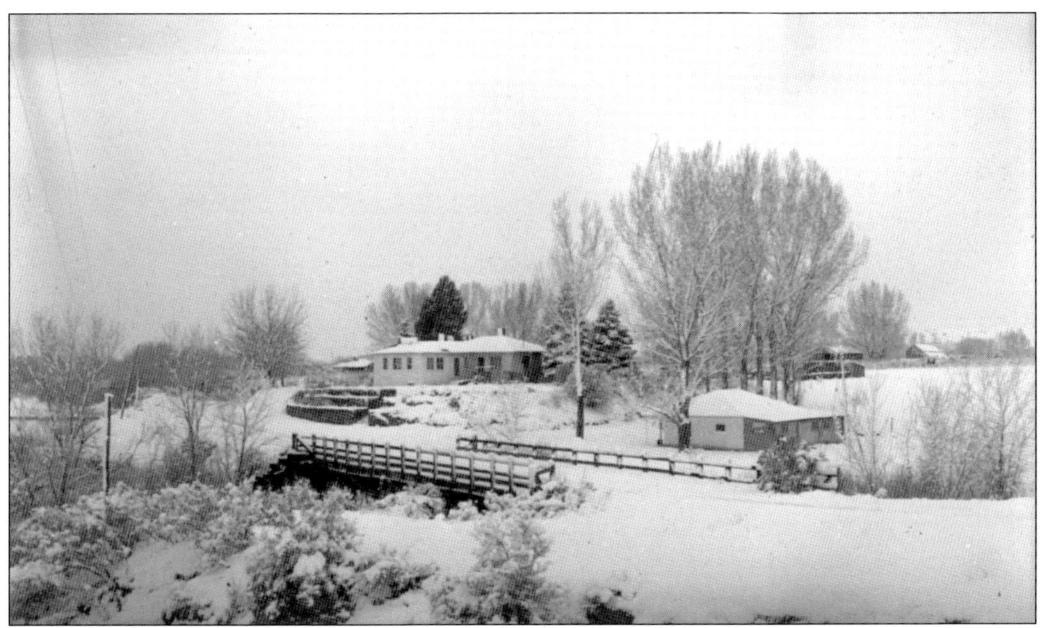

Yes, it does snow in Aztec. This 1948 winter scene is of the Riverview Steakhouse on the hill above the mouth of the Estes Arroyo and the Animas River. It was a popular restaurant for several years until it was destroyed by fire. The bridge crosses the Estes Arroyo.

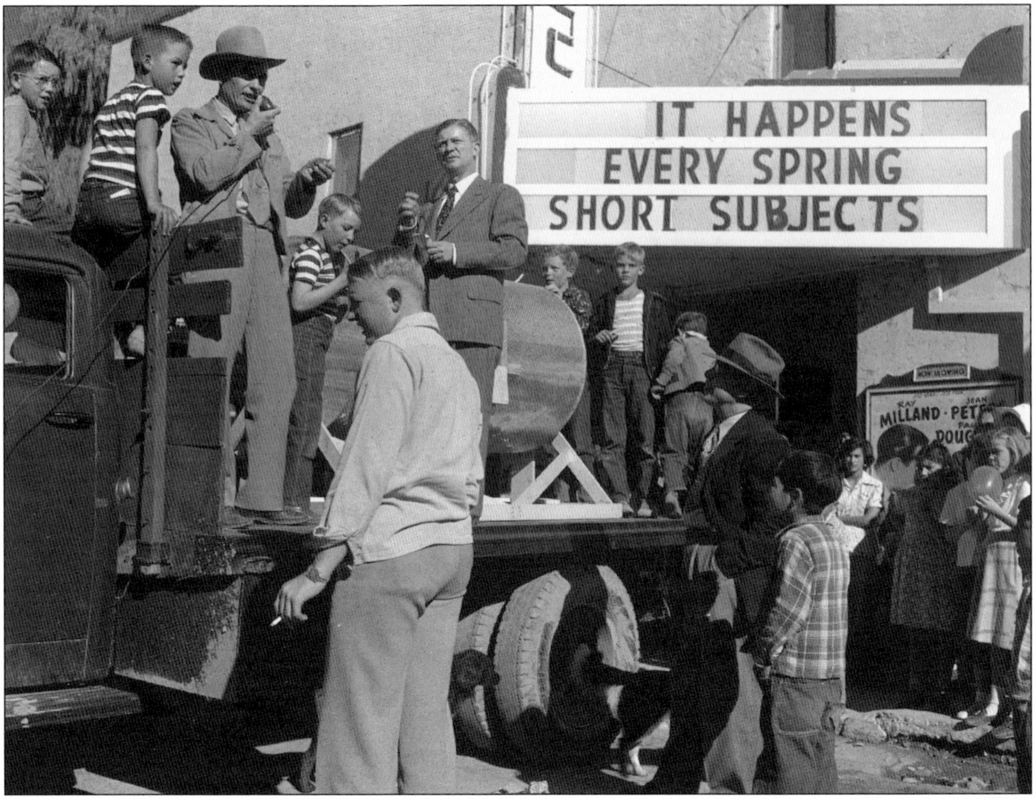

Appreciation Day was celebrated on September 28, 1949. A search through old newspapers yielded no information about the event, but several pictures show this truck moving around to different locations. The above photograph shows the group in front of the Aztec Theatre. Below, a group gathers across the street from the feed store at the Hotpoint Appliance Store. There must have been a drawing associated with the event, as a boy is being blindfolded to pull a lucky number out of the mix.

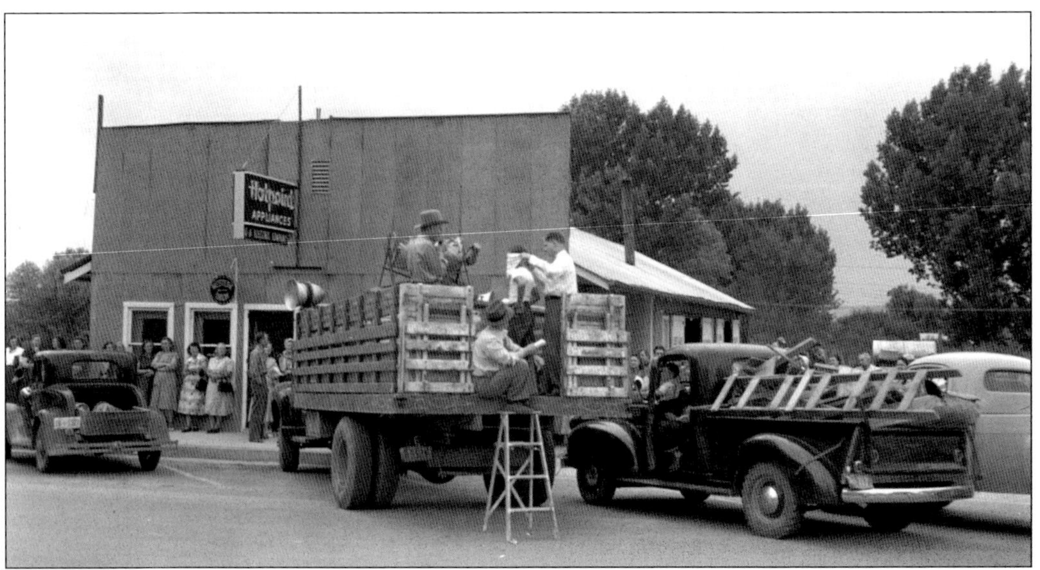

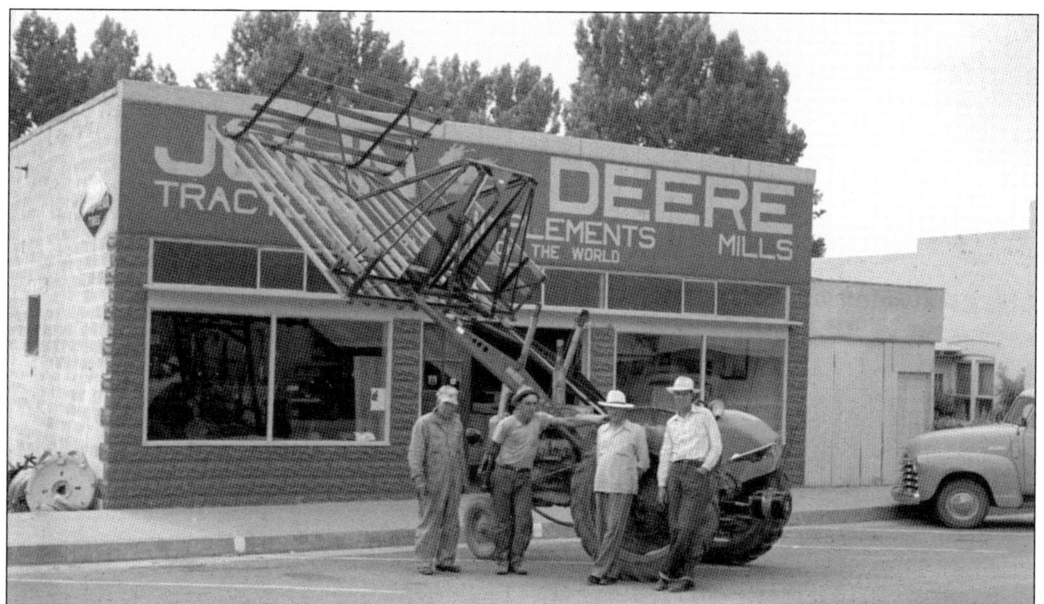

Bill Baird (second from left) shows off his new hay lifter in front of the John Deere outlet in 1949. The building was torn down to make way for the Citizens Bank's parking lot. Farming was a major industry in Aztec and continues to be a staple in the economy of the community today.

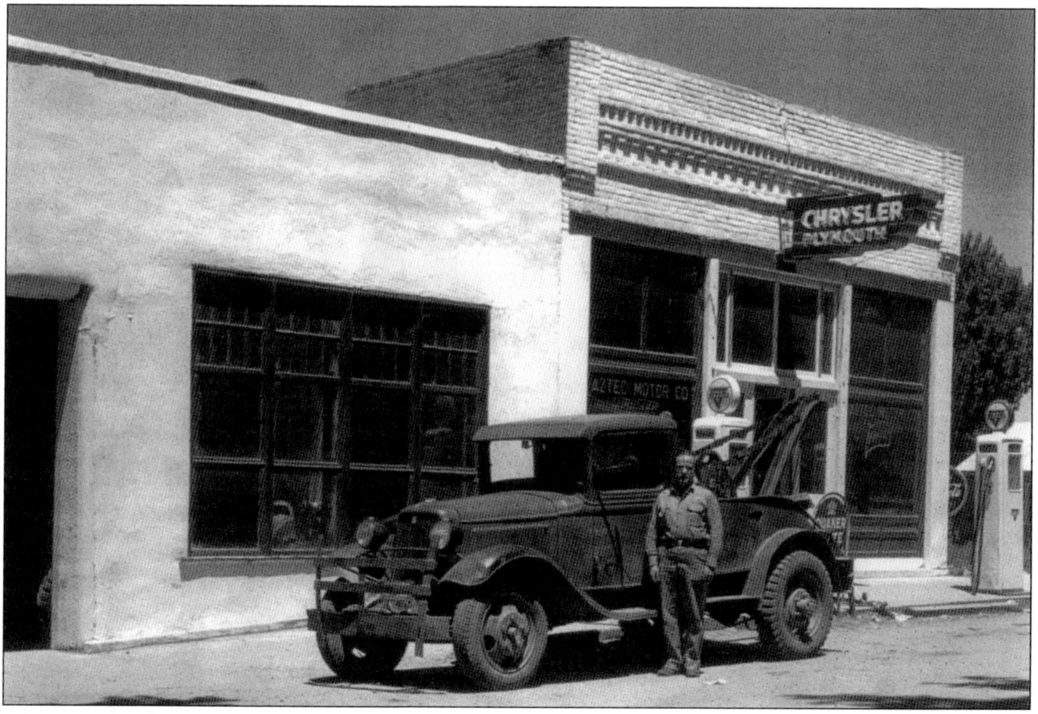

Maurice Rhodes poses with the wrecker at Aztec Motor, his place of business, in 1949. The wrecker is a 1932 or 1933 model. Maurice and his brother Floyd ran Aztec Motor together. Reportedly, they sometimes brought in a wrecked vehicle and parked it nearby for folks to examine. (Courtesy Audrey Glazebrook.)

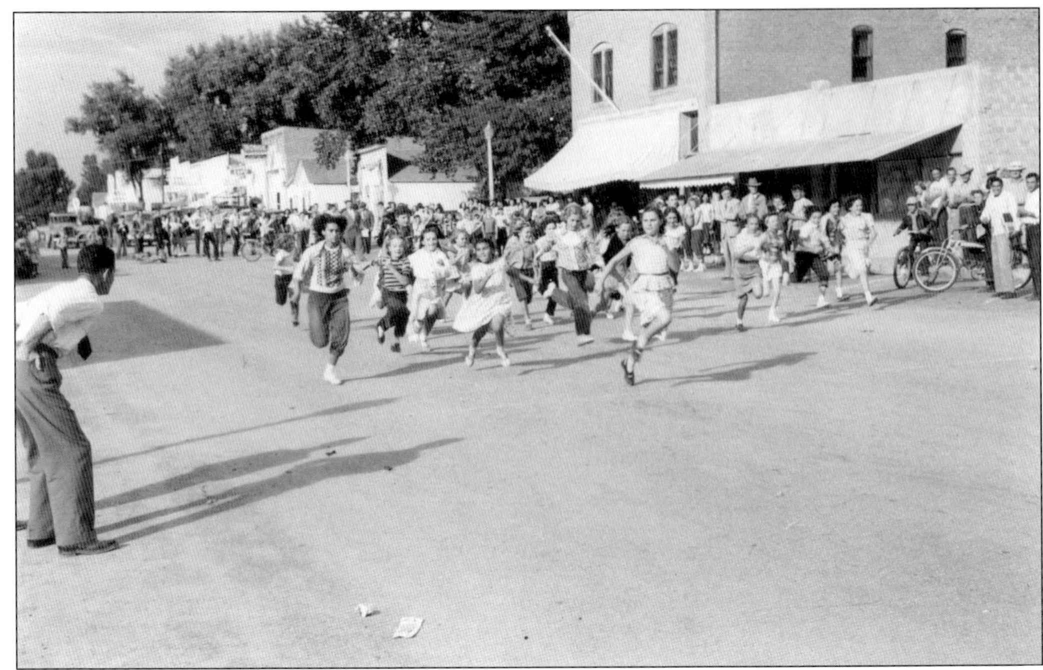

Aztec is well known around the county for its parades. The above image, from September 13, 1949, is dubbed "Aztec Schools Parade." A portion of the above photograph—showing a girls' 50-yard footrace—is featured on the cover of this book. The photograph below shows students of all ages walking down Main Avenue. Notice how this section of Aztec's Main Avenue has changed little through the years.

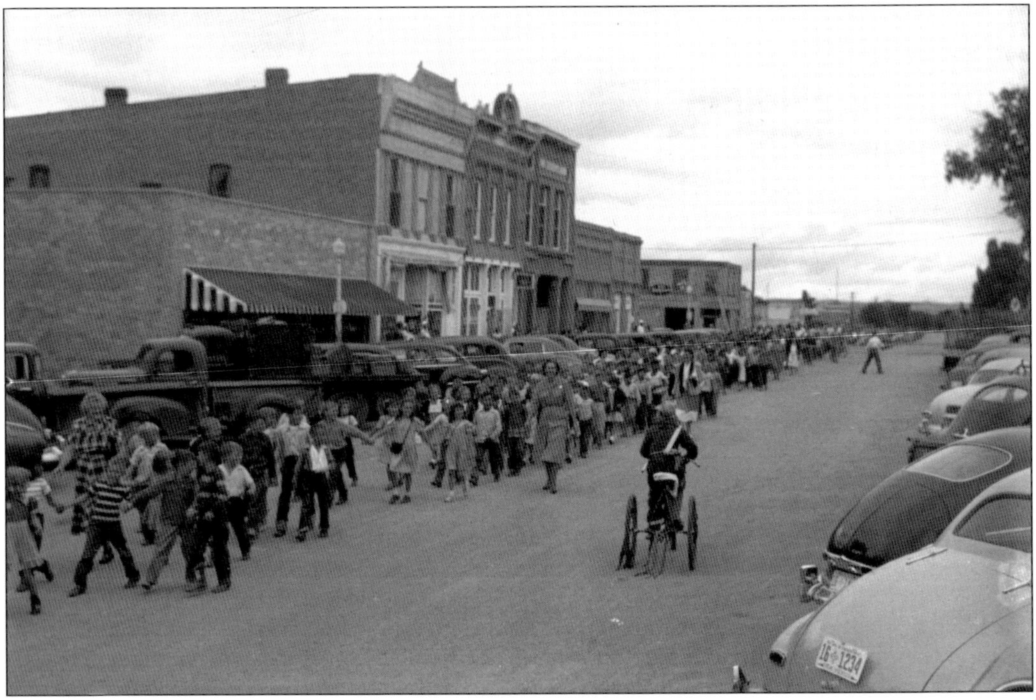

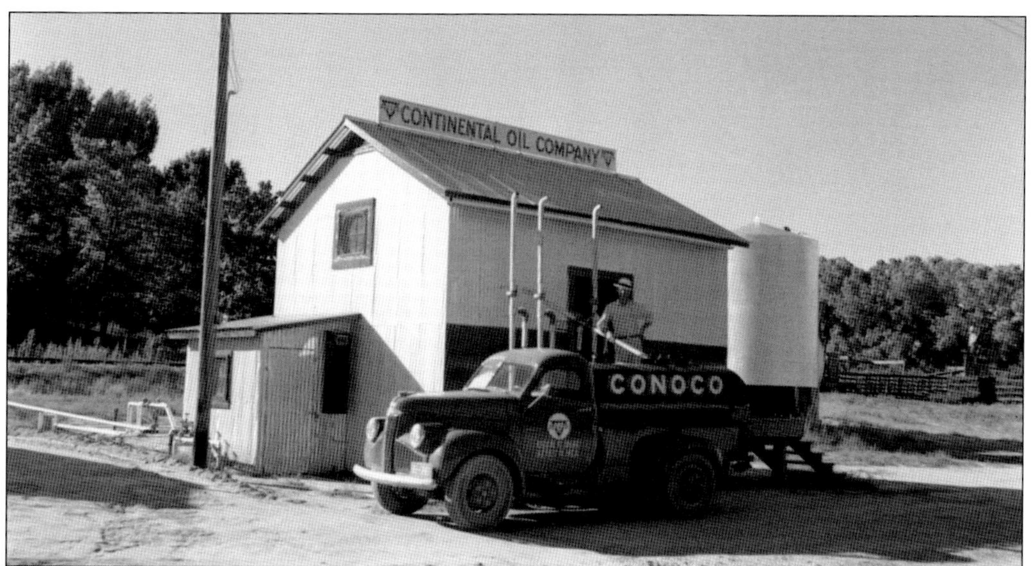

Cecil Dial is shown here in 1949 at his Continental Oil Company bulk plant on the southeast corner of Rio Grande Avenue and Lovers Lane. The next few years brought major expansion to Dial Oil Company, and the vacant area around this first structure soon filled up. Note the railroad tracks behind the building.

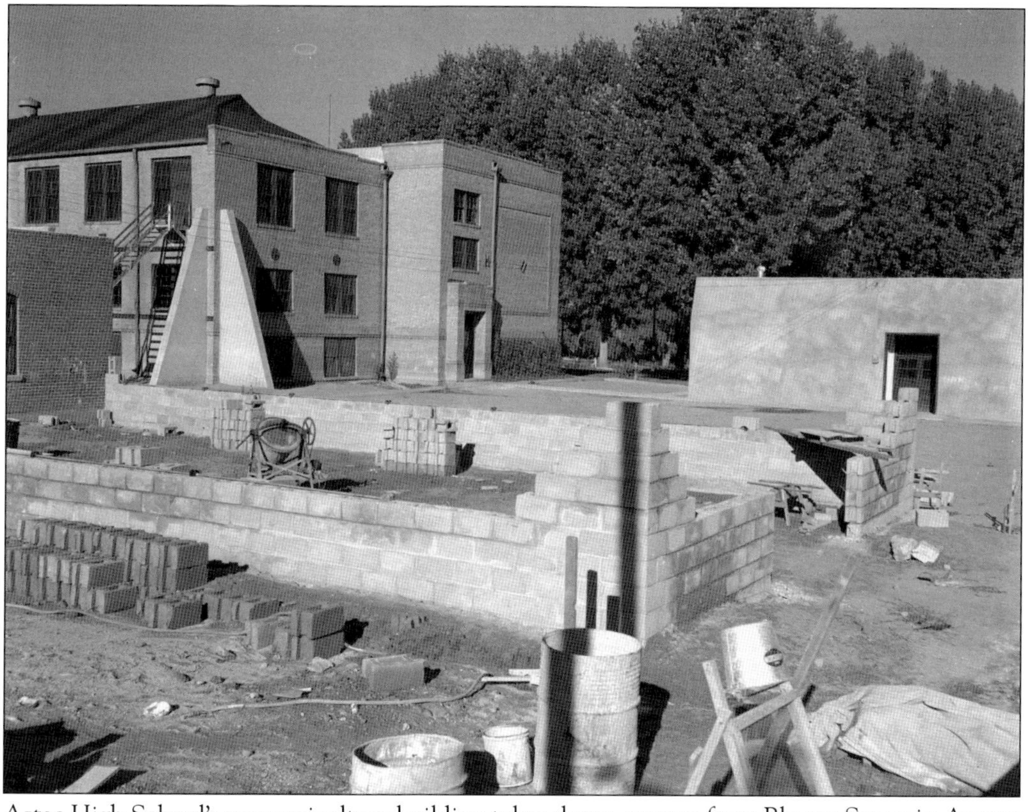

Aztec High School's new agriculture building takes shape, as seen from Blanco Street in August 1949. The high school is in the background, and the WPA building is to the right.

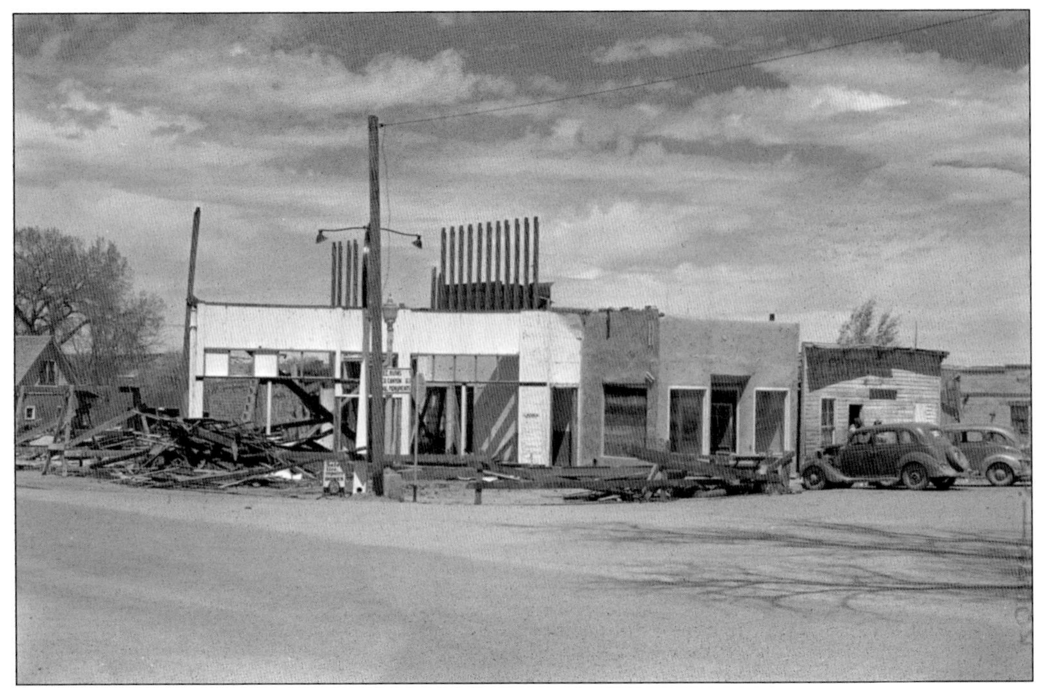

In 1949, Chaco Street was still the main highway through Aztec. The image above shows a gas station on the northwest corner of Main Avenue coming down to make way for a new building. The highway sign says "Aztec Ruins 1, Chaco Canyon 63, National Monuments." Below is the almost finished structure, dubbed the Walters building, that replaced the gas station.

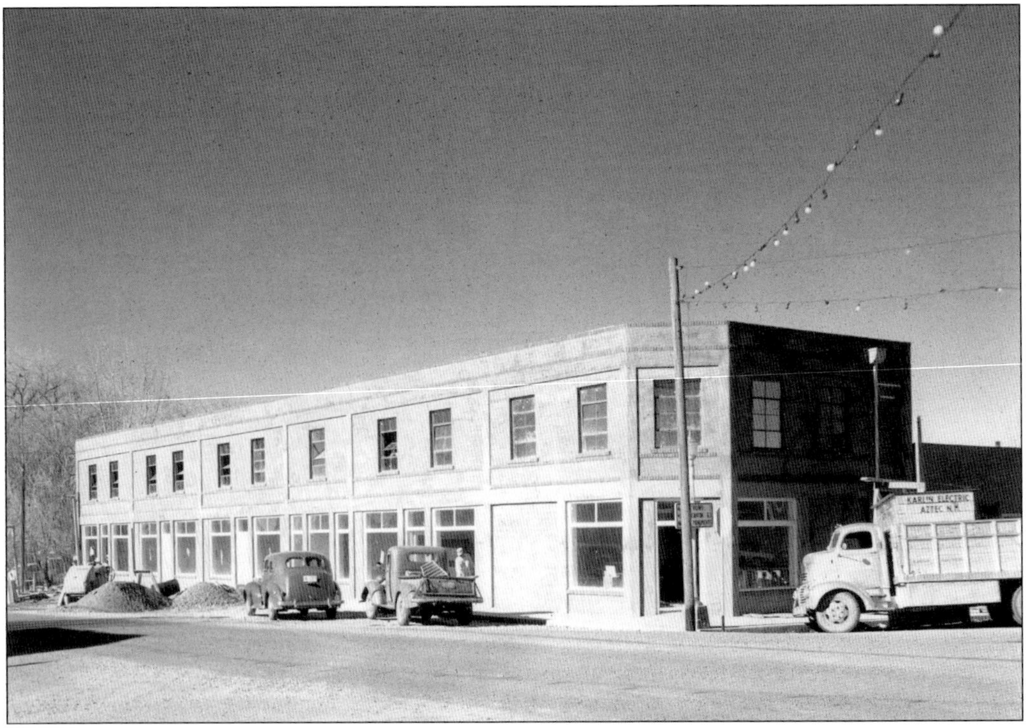

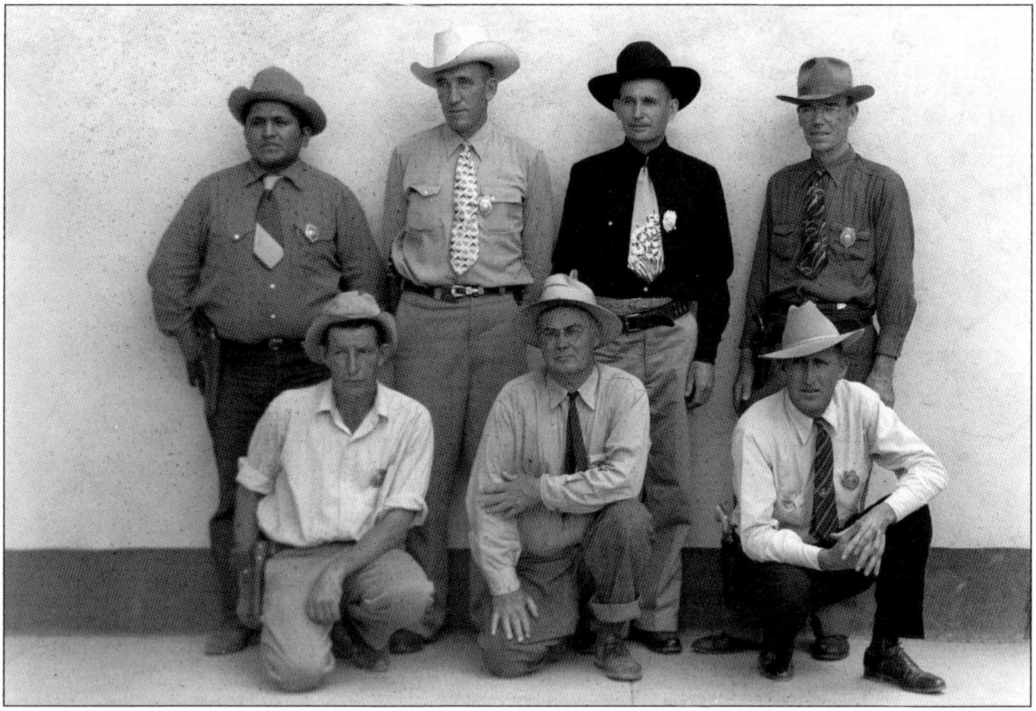

Sheriff Bill Noland (second row, in black) and his deputies pose for a photograph in 1949. Noland served from 1948 to 1952. Pictured here are, from left to right, (first row) Jim Farmer, unidentified, and Roy Sullivan; (second row) unidentified, Dan Sullivan, Noland, and unidentified.

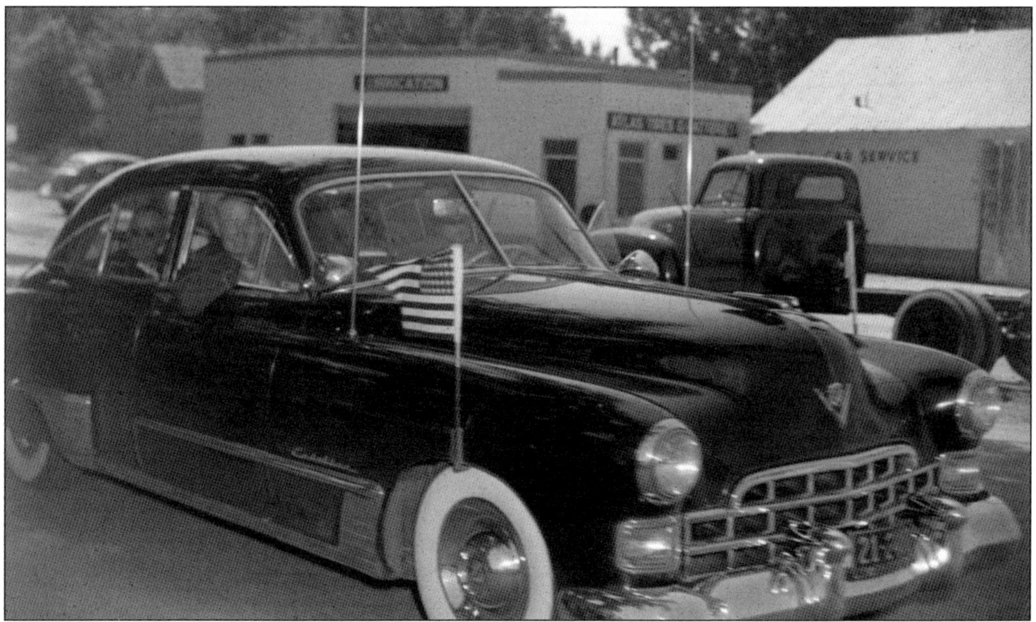

Colorado governor William Lee Knous passed through Aztec on the way to the Four Corners Monument on July 4, 1949, when governors of all the Four Corner states met for lunch. At the time, the monument was just a short concrete pillar, so a table was placed over the monument, and each governor ate in his own state.

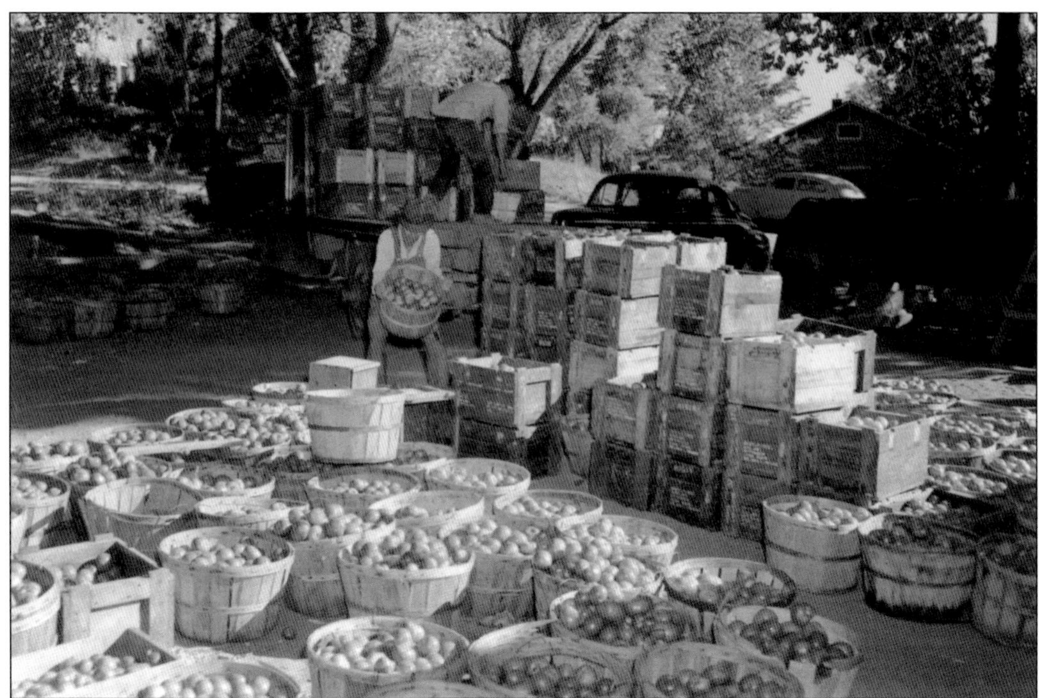

The Lawson Cannery was a thriving business near the corner of Blanco Street and Pollard Avenue. Above, crates of tomatoes are unloaded and stacked for processing in September 1949. In the image below, workers sort the tomatoes and ready them for canning. In 1951, Fred L. Lawson announced that he was closing the cannery and had leased the buildings to the Utah Mud Company.

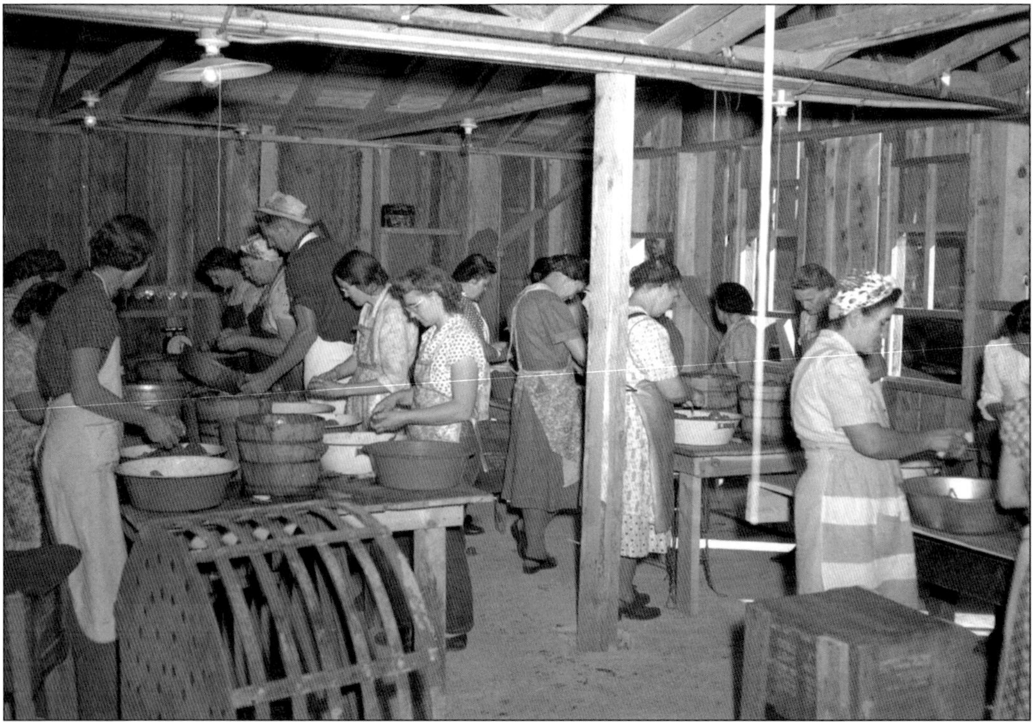

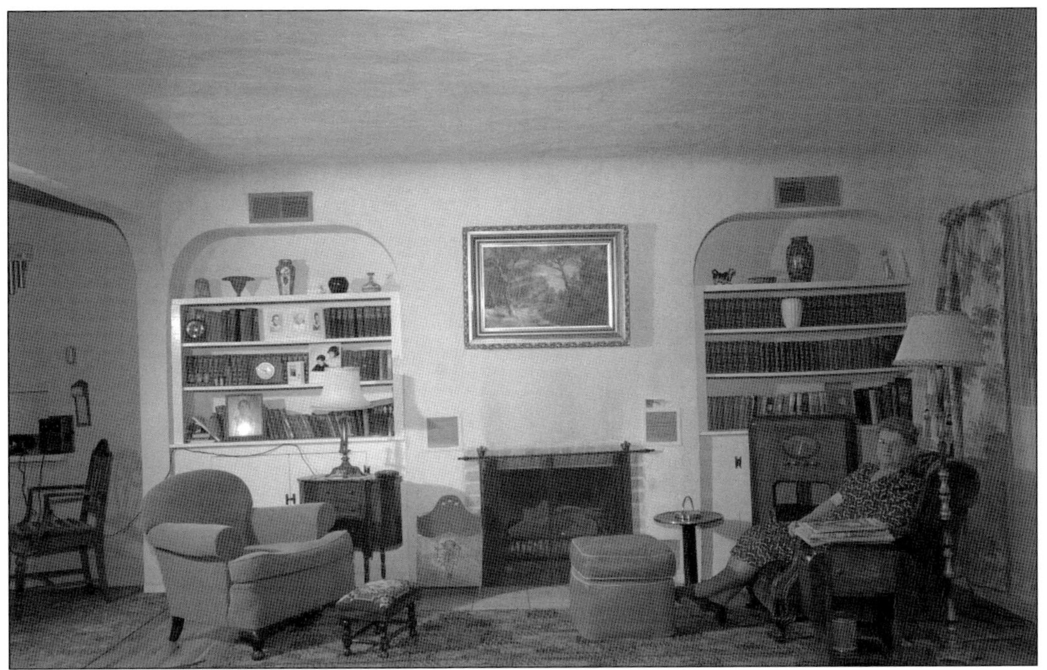

Grace Bruington relaxes in her living room in 1949. Her husband, George, was a local attorney. Notice the crank telephone at far left and the radio to her right. These were standard fixtures in nearly every home at this time.

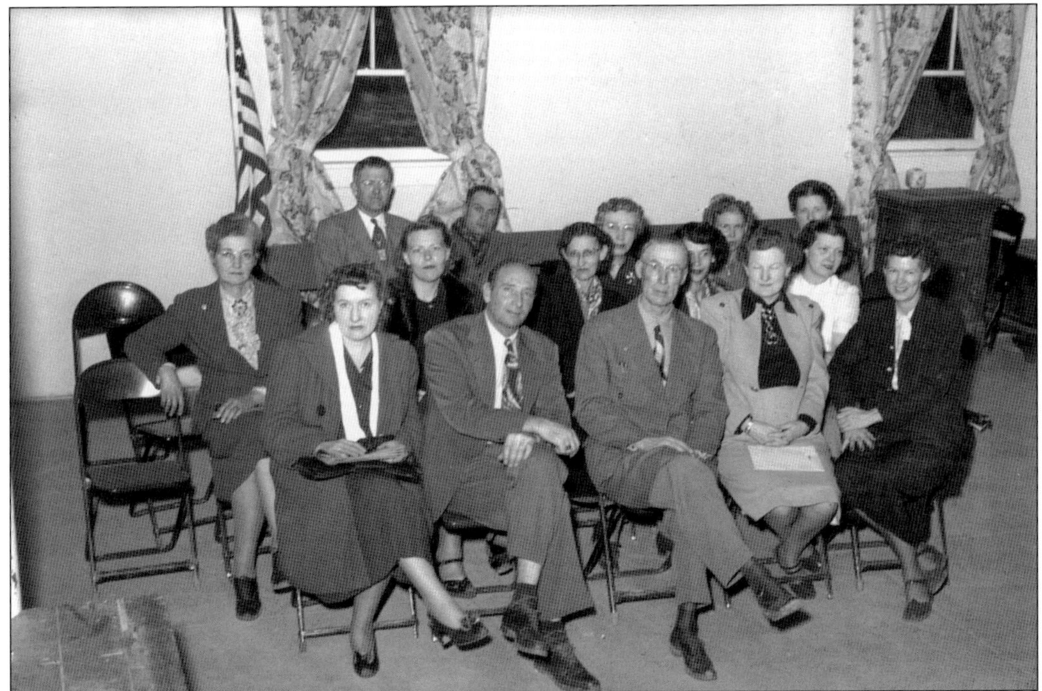

In February 1949, World War II was over, but there was still plenty of work for the Red Cross. These workers gathered in the Methodist church basement were on standby to help in case of fires, floods, or other emergencies.

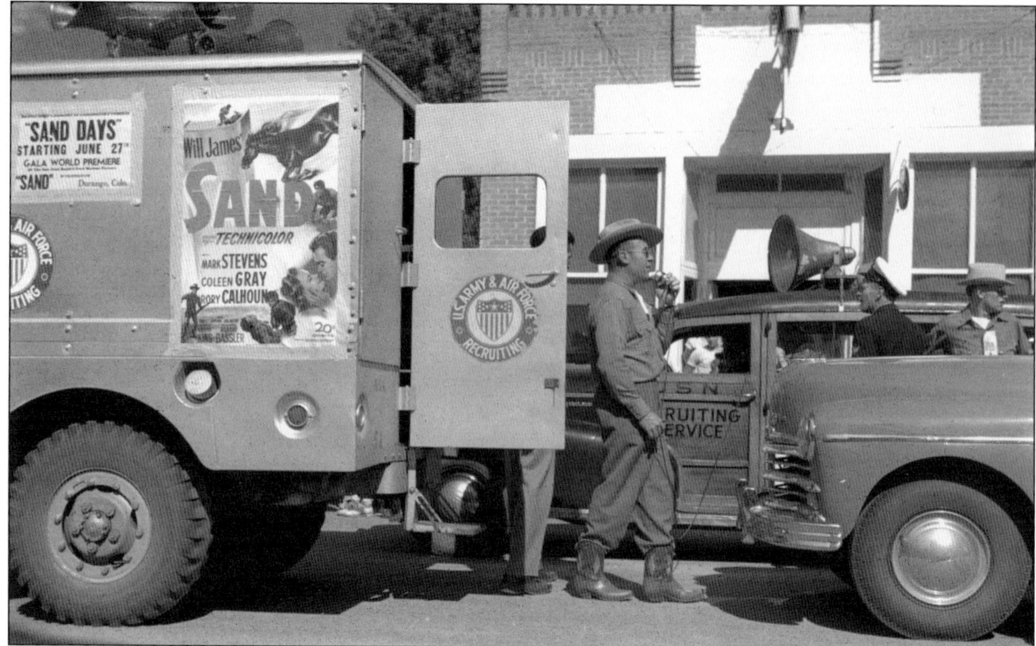

Many western movies were filmed around the Four Corners during the 1940s and 1950s. One of them was *Sand*, starring Rory Calhoun. The premiere was in Durango, and that city brought the parade to Aztec and hosted Sand Days on June 23, 1949. After the Sand Days parade, the crowd was treated to music, food, and other entertainment. The movie was also shown in Aztec and Farmington later that summer. There were a couple of movies filmed nearly exclusively in and around Aztec, and scores of locals found temporary employment as extras.

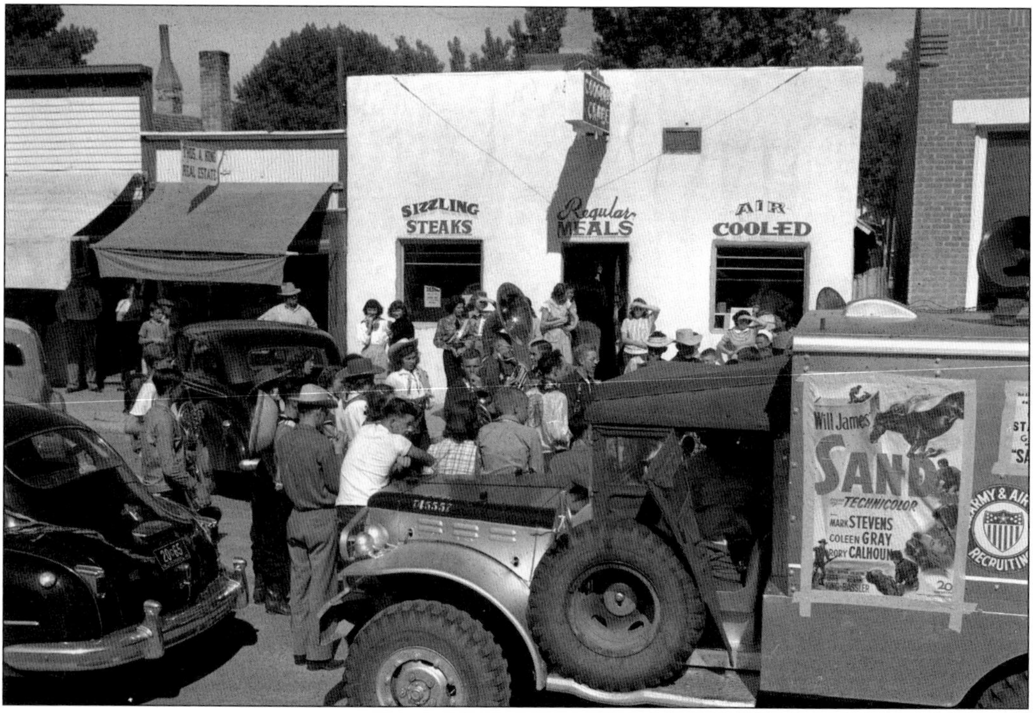

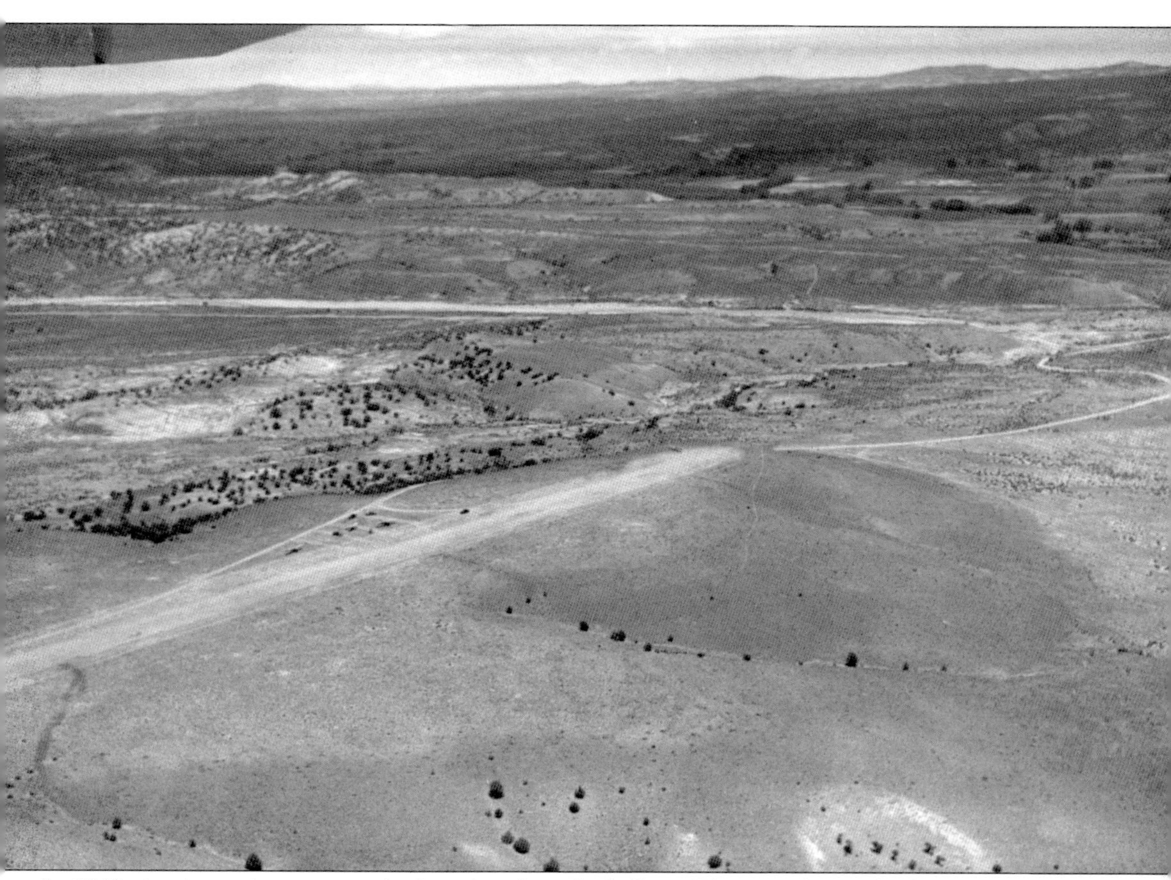

In 1949, the Aztec Airport was fairly isolated on the hilltop. This aerial view, looking north and a little east, shows the runway in the foreground. There are three airplanes and four vehicles parked nearby, but no buildings. The white line across the center is the Estes Arroyo, with the Aztec to La Plata highway (now NM 574) running alongside it.

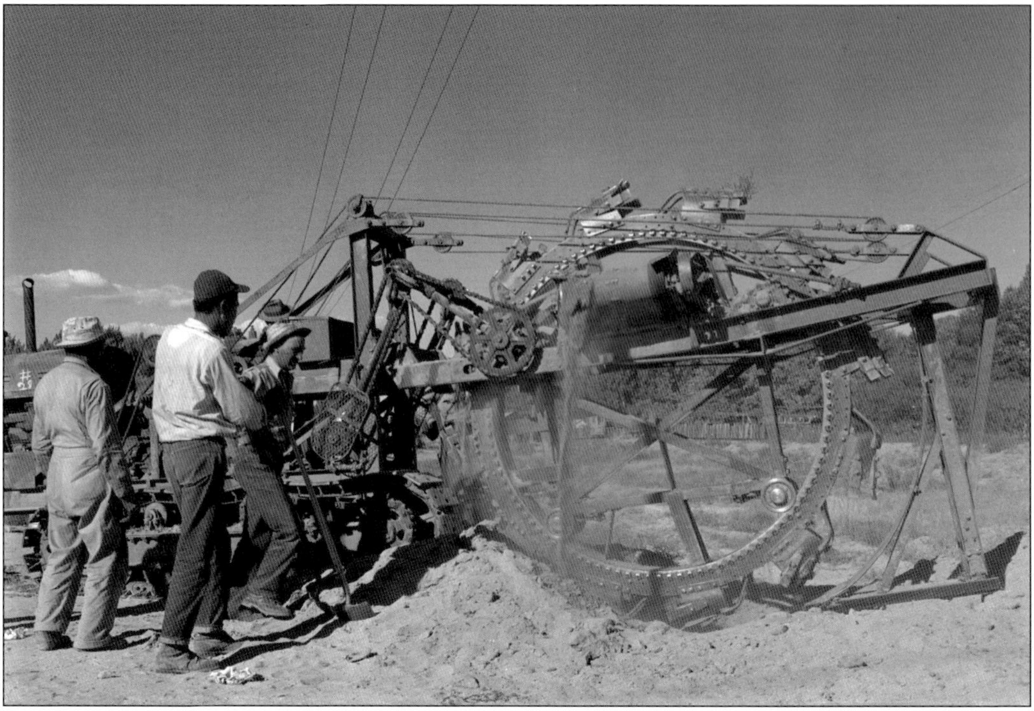

Southern Union Gas Company crews were kept busy as the community continued to grow. This group works a ditcher north of Aztec High School in September 1949.

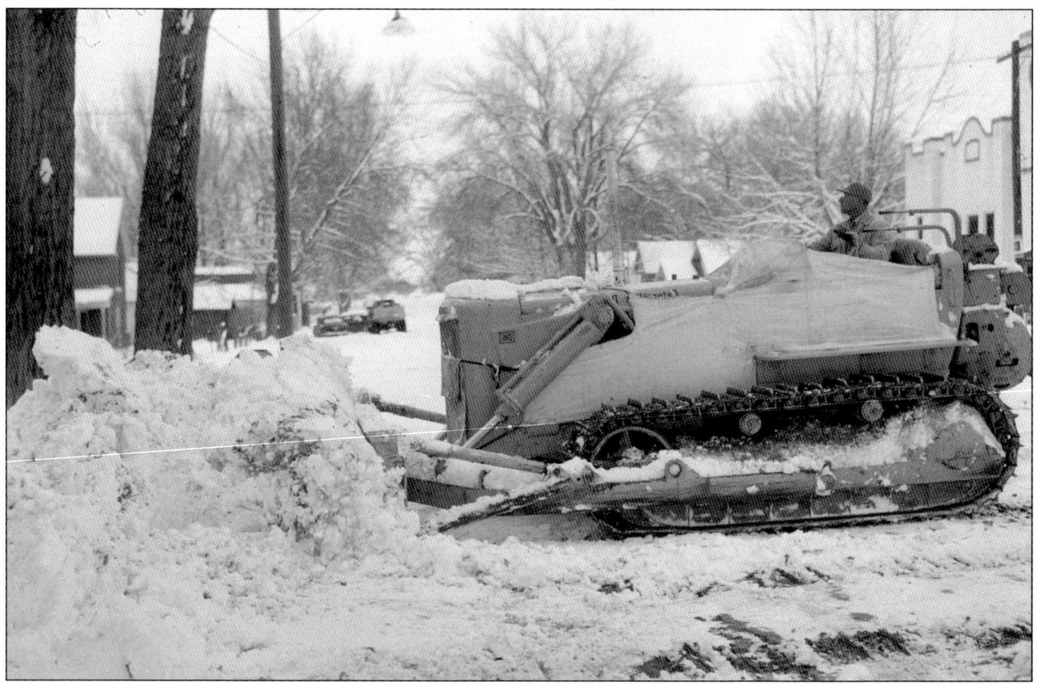

February 1949 brought a big snowstorm to Aztec. Here, Mr. Trosper tries to clear the snow off Chaco Street, which was part of the main highway from Farmington to Durango. The First Baptist Church is on the right at the southeast corner of Chaco Street and Church Avenue.

Five

Aztec Is Booming

The 1950s and 1960s were a dynamic time for Aztec. Emery Arnold wrote an essay for the 1997 *Pioneer Bulletin*, volume 8, issue 1, entitled "Construction of the Navajo Dam Road." He was the Oil & Gas Conservation Commission supervisor and ably walks the reader through this time. He writes in detail, and the following are excerpts from that essay: "In 1950 there were about 300 oil and gas wells in the San Juan Basin. By 1960 there were over 5,000 wells. The population of Aztec in 1950 was 885 and it grew to 4,137 in 1960. In that decade the infrastructure of the community was stressed. Aztec schools held classes in gyms and churches."

Then, things changed. By the early 1960s, employment in the drilling business dropped sharply, and suddenly there was an oversupply of housing. Arnold pointed out these facts to lay the foundation for what happened next.

Navajo Dam was completed in the fall of 1962 and was expected to enhance the tourist industry. Aztec had no direct route to the dam; Highway 64 was slated to go through Bloomfield and bypass Aztec.

The Chamber of Commerce discussed the situation at length, and someone said, "Let's build a road." After a big laugh, reality set in, and the discussion started in earnest—why not?

Committees were appointed, right-of-way acquired, and financing would be through donations and volunteer labor. It was expected to take a year to complete the project. Arnold concludes, "It helped that there was a lot of industrial equipment idle due to a downturn in the economy and the winter was milder than usual."

Ground was broken on January 6, 1963, and the Navajo Dam Road was finished in a little over three months. The dedication of the completed road was held on April 19, 1963. The Navajo Dam Road cut a trip of 35 miles down to about 19. Now Aztec folks could enjoy the lake, the fishing, or camping without the roundabout jaunt.

The road brought an additional honor to Aztec when the community was nominated for an "All America City" award given by the National Municipal League and *Look* magazine. In 1963, Aztec beat out other nominees and became the third city in New Mexico to receive this award.

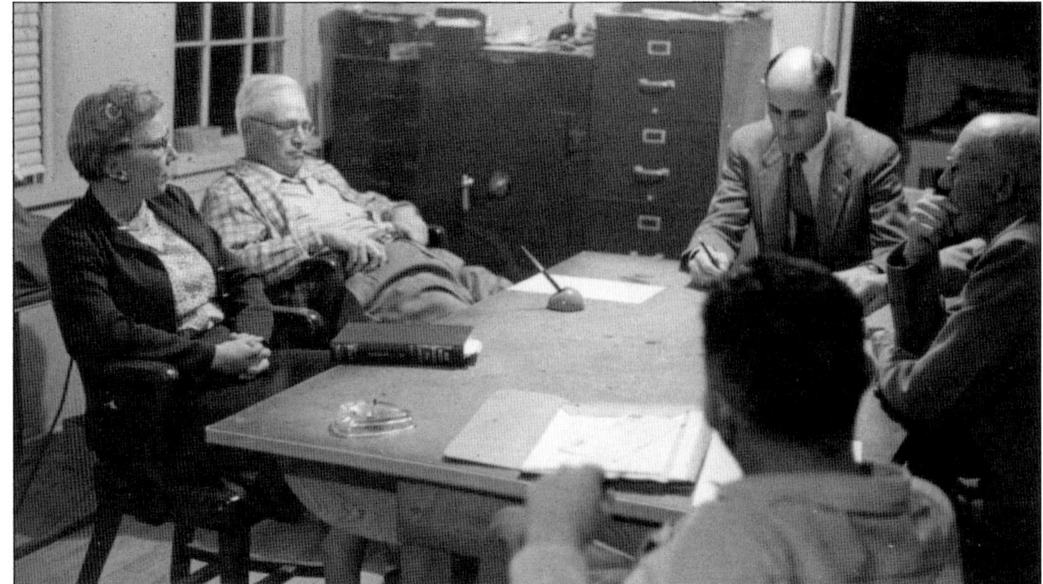

Aztec's Town Board is shown here around 1953. Going around the table from left to right, they are Esther Crane, Joseph S. Hartman, Mayor Harold Lavender, Charles Maddox, and Minehart Brutlag. Lavender was mayor from 1952 to 1956 and later served as city manager. (Courtesy Aztec Museum.)

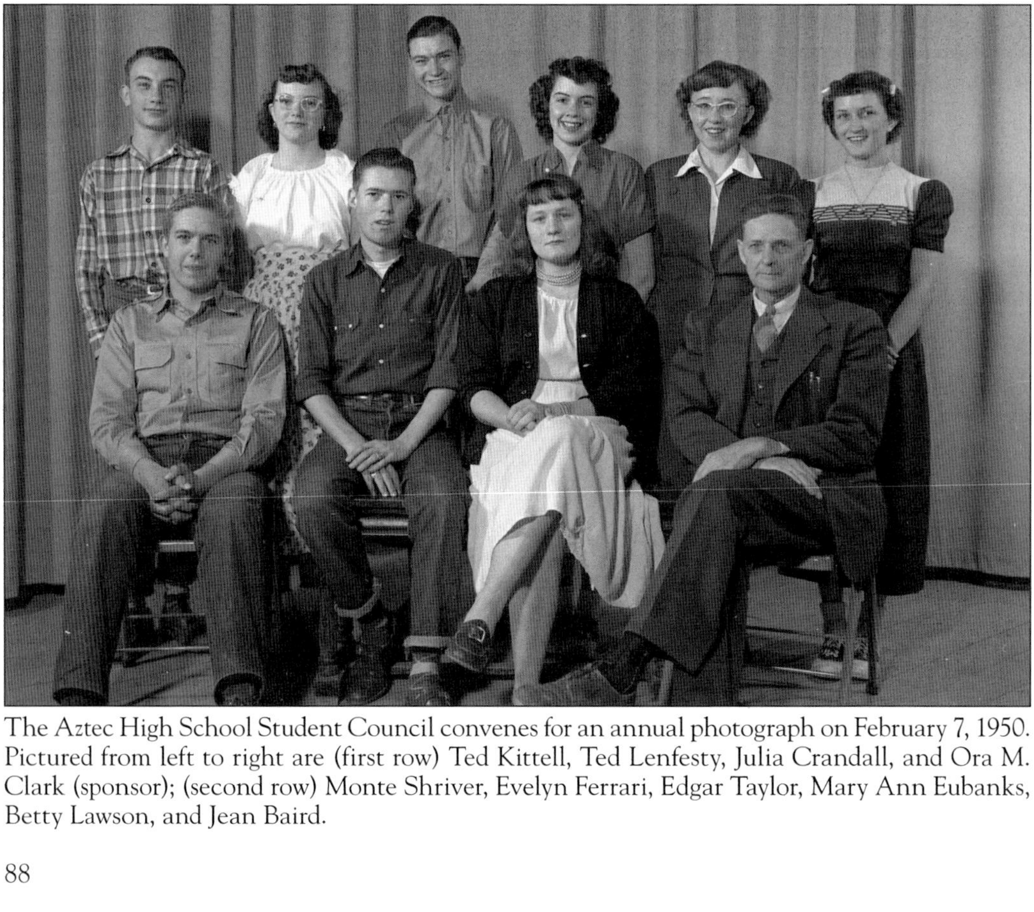

The Aztec High School Student Council convenes for an annual photograph on February 7, 1950. Pictured from left to right are (first row) Ted Kittell, Ted Lenfesty, Julia Crandall, and Ora M. Clark (sponsor); (second row) Monte Shriver, Evelyn Ferrari, Edgar Taylor, Mary Ann Eubanks, Betty Lawson, and Jean Baird.

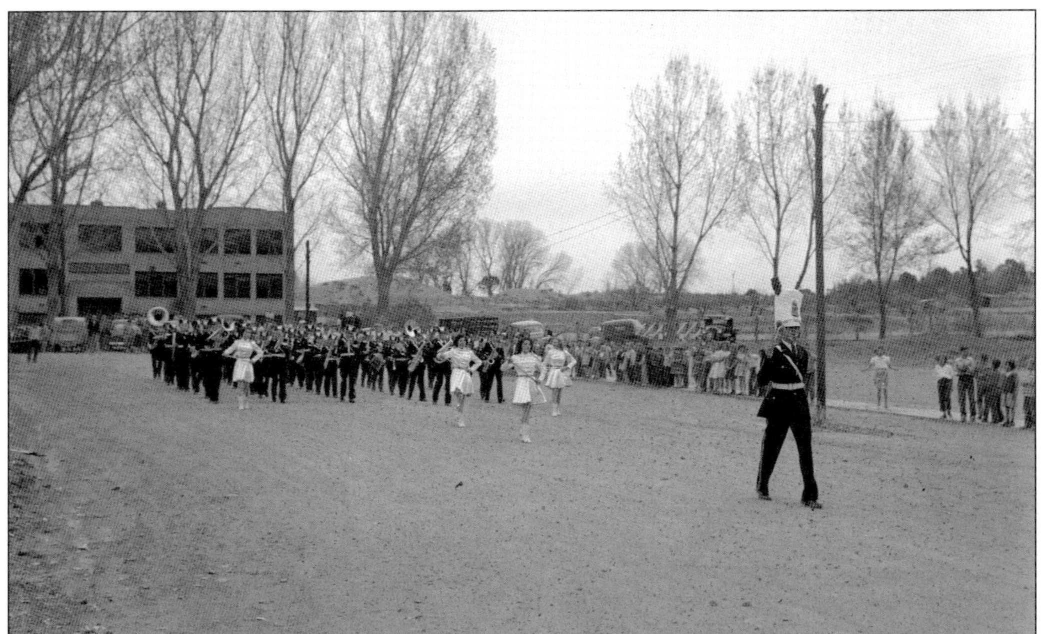

The Aztec High School band shows off their new uniforms in April 1950. Notice how empty the area around the high school building was at this time. Today, the area is built up all around.

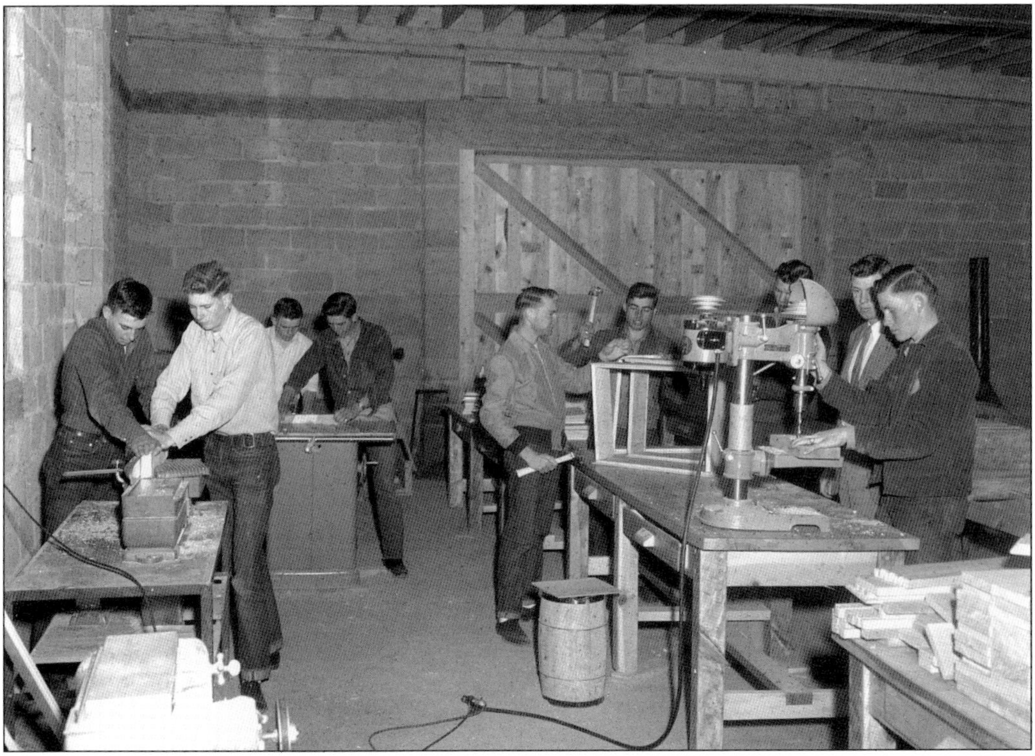

The boys in the Aztec High School shop class are busy working on projects. The agriculture building was erected east of the WPA building on Blanco Street in the summer of 1949. This March 1950 class was probably among the first groups to use the new building.

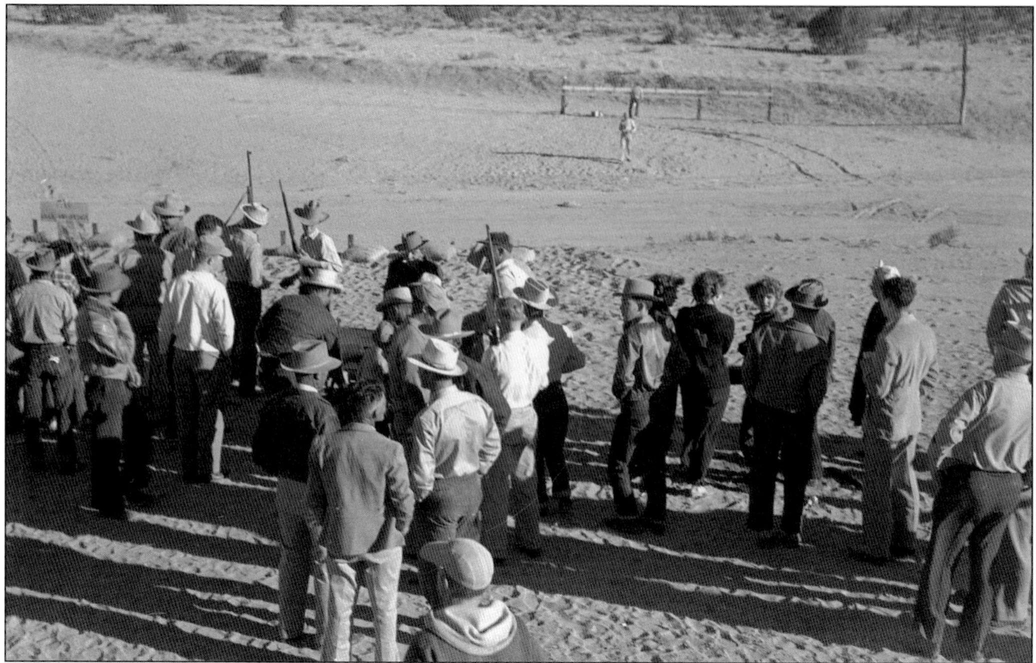

Most Aztec families owned guns for sport and hunting. Any opportunity to use those guns was relished. This group gathered at an arroyo on Veterans Day 1950 for a turkey shoot. Were the targets real turkeys or fake ones? Regardless, it was a good way to spend a fall day.

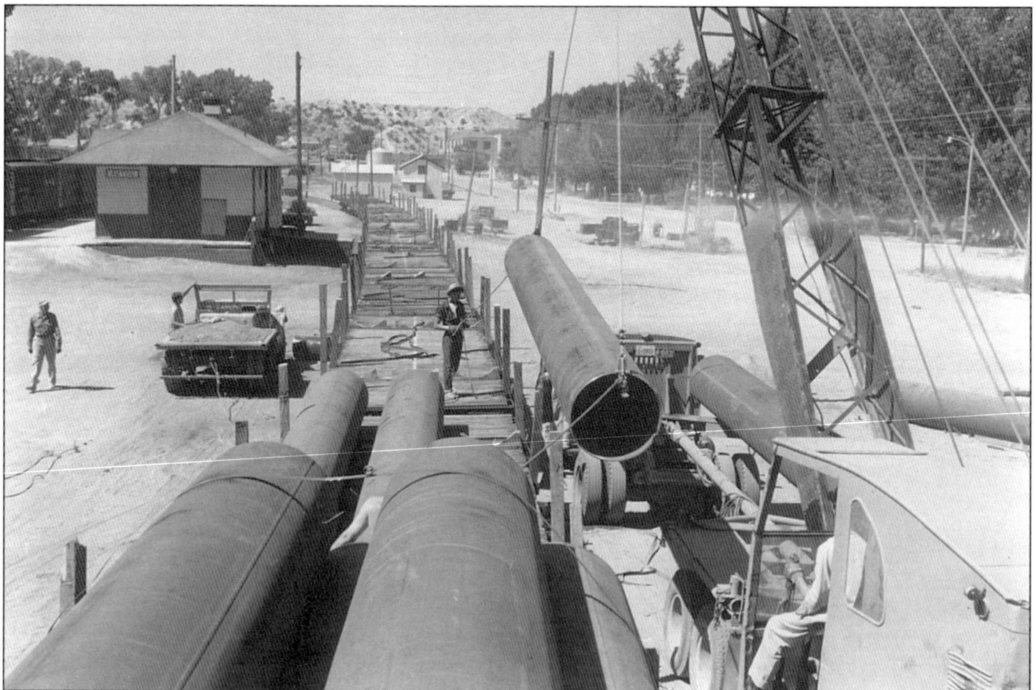

Aztec benefited from the natural gas boom of the 1950s, and the train and depot were busy. This crane is unloading 24-inch pipe. The half-track spots the cars so that the crane doesn't have to move. During the peak of the boom, there were sometimes three trains per day.

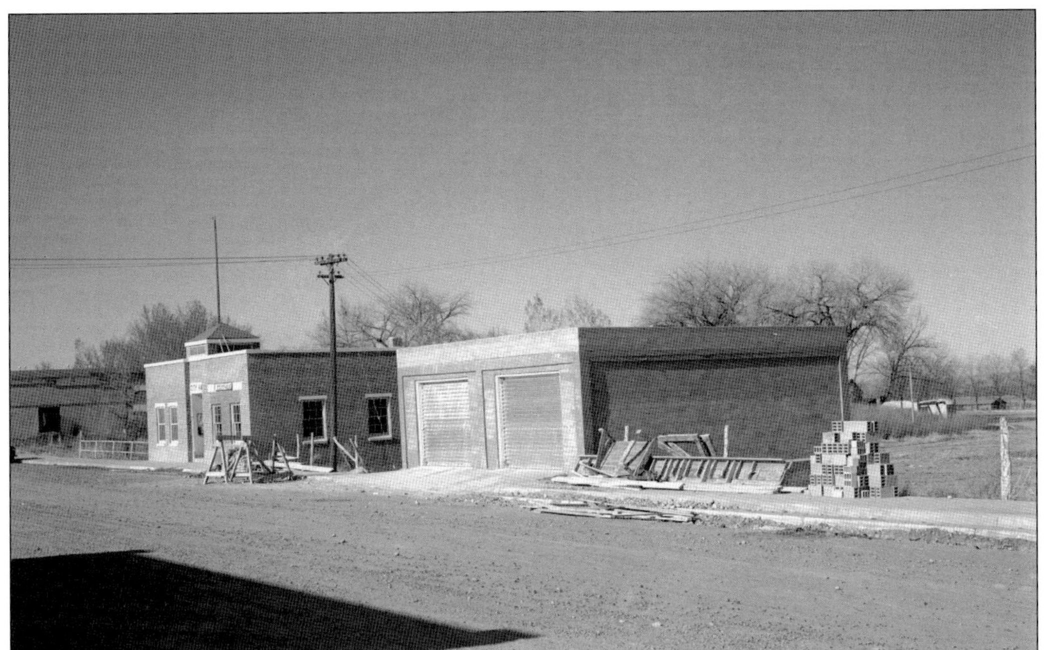

Spring 1950 brought the addition of a new fire station to Aztec. Beyond it is the city hall and courthouse building, which was built in 1939 with WPA funds. The city hall later became the chamber of commerce. Today, both buildings are part of the Aztec Museum complex.

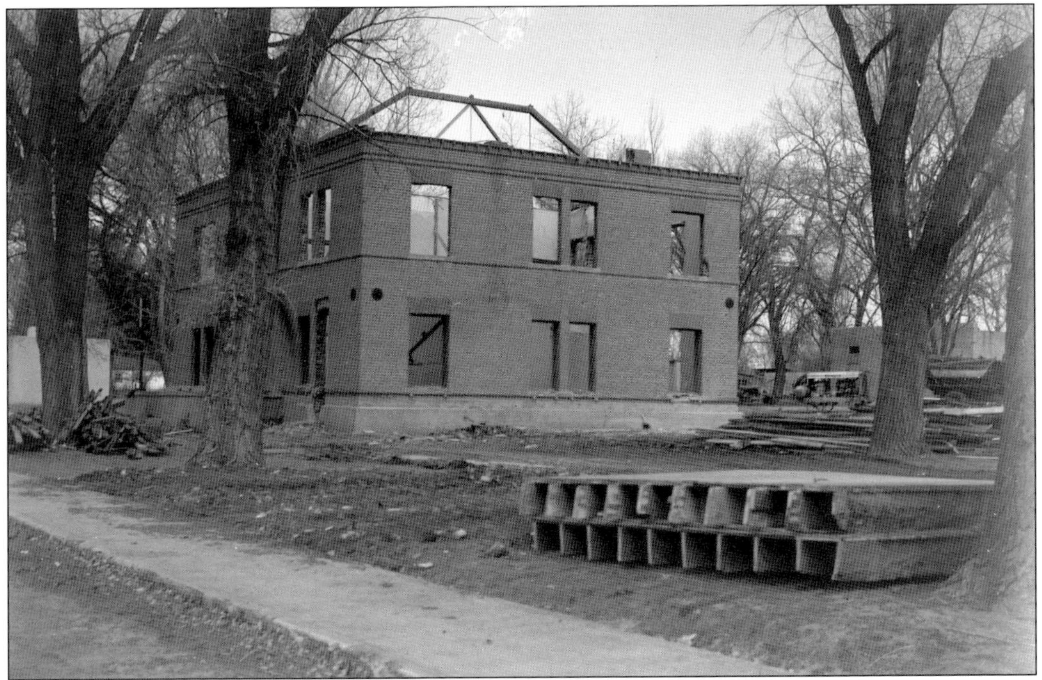

The old San Juan County courthouse, built in 1898, was demolished in March 1950 after years of service. Some folks salvaged a brick or two to keep as souvenirs. As soon as this building came down and the area was cleared, a new courthouse was constructed on the same Mesa Verde Avenue site.

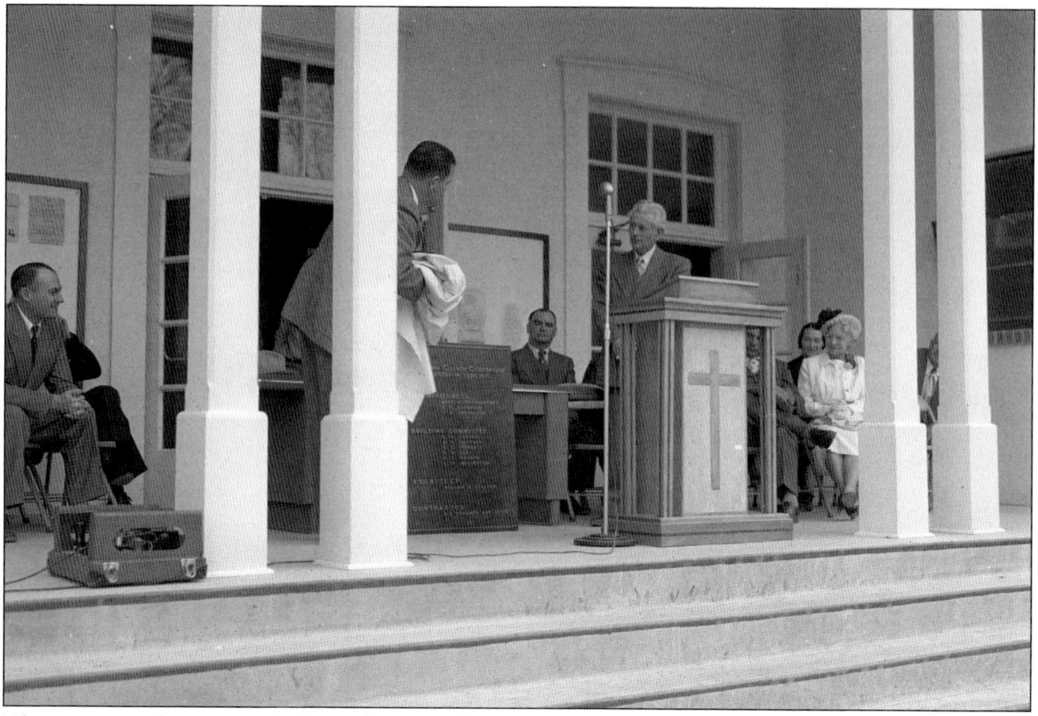

The new courthouse was dedicated on April 17, 1951. Dignitaries in the above photograph include Gov. Merritt C. Mechem, who is handing the plaque to Jack Cline. The image below shows the crowd gathered to hear the speeches and join in the festivities. This building served the county until 2008, when it was torn down and replaced by the administration and court complex on South Oliver Street.

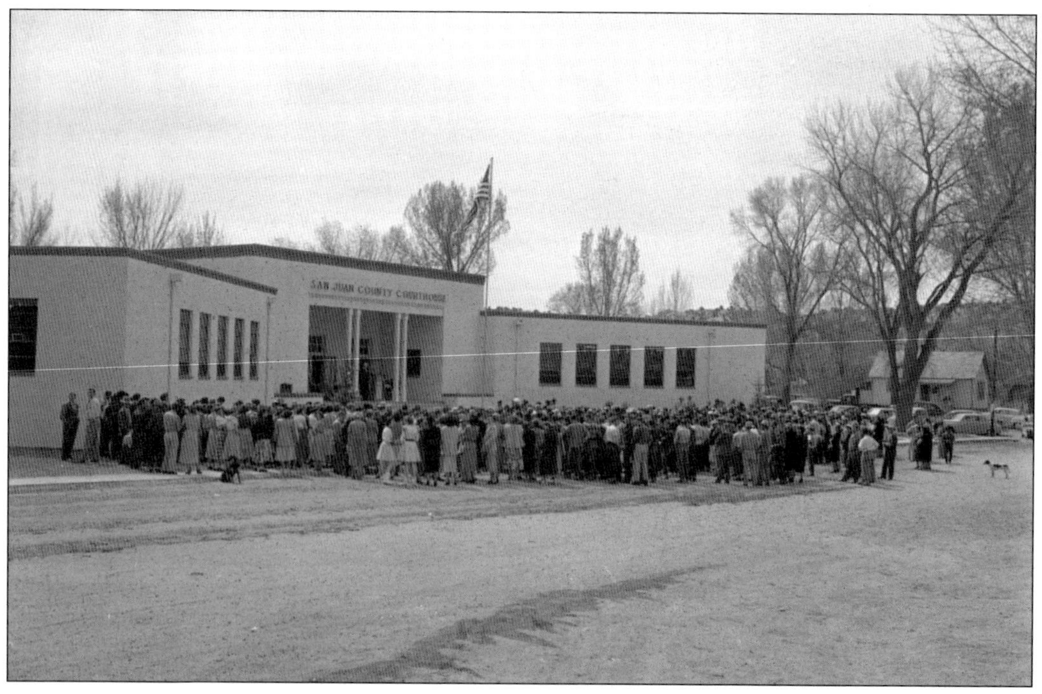

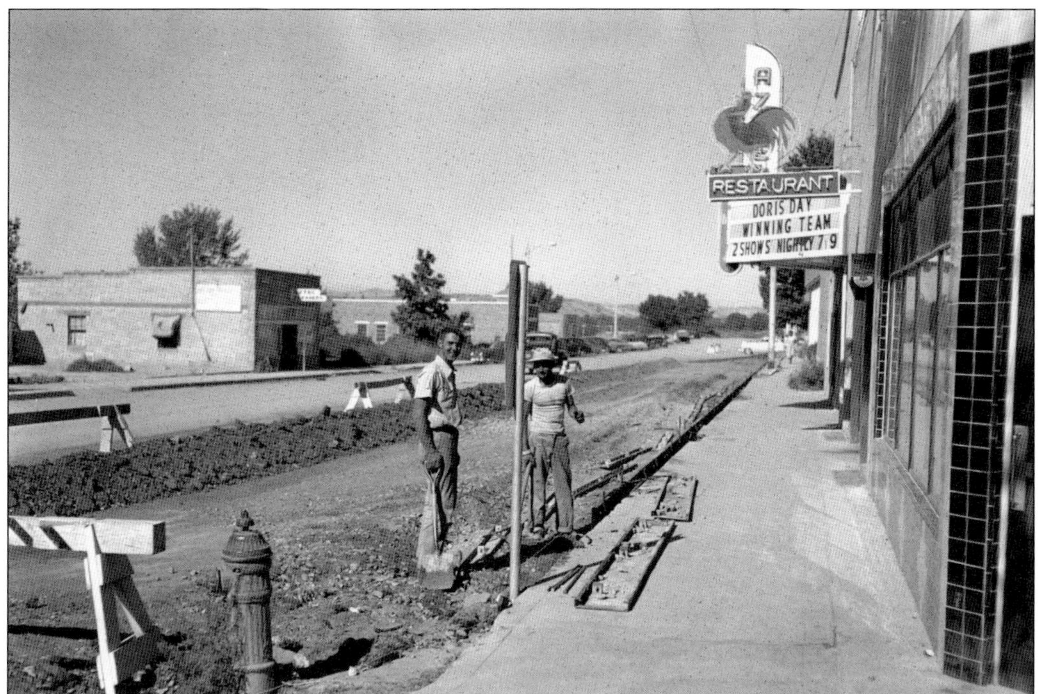

This image shows Main Avenue being prepared for new curbs and paving in 1952. Notice the Cock of the Walk restaurant and the Aztec Theatre. The other side of Main Avenue is still mostly empty, with only the Aztec Cleaners, city hall, and the fire station visible here. The corner building in the foreground at right is a saloon.

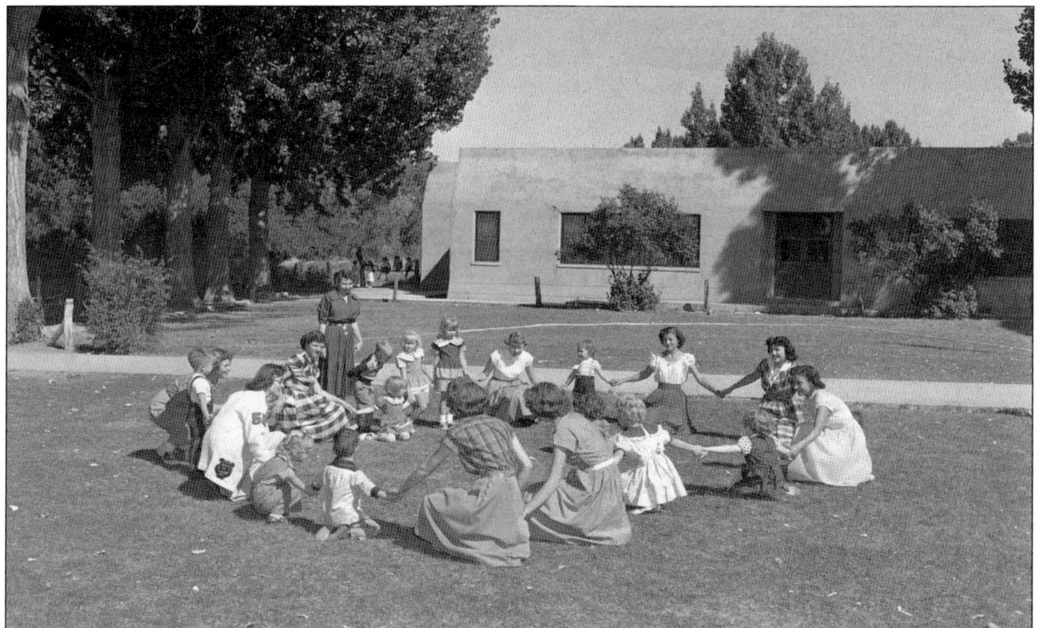

Teacher Wilma White watches while her 10th-grade class plays games with some children in October 1952. Behind the students is the WPA building near the high school. The WPA building was torn down during later expansion.

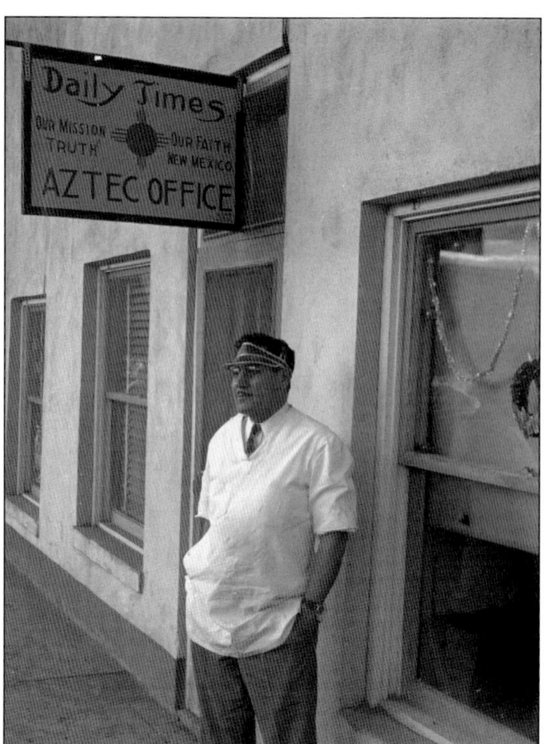

John Padilla stands in front of the Aztec office of the *Farmington Daily Times* on a warm day in December 1952. The building is on the northwest corner of Chaco Street and Main Avenue.

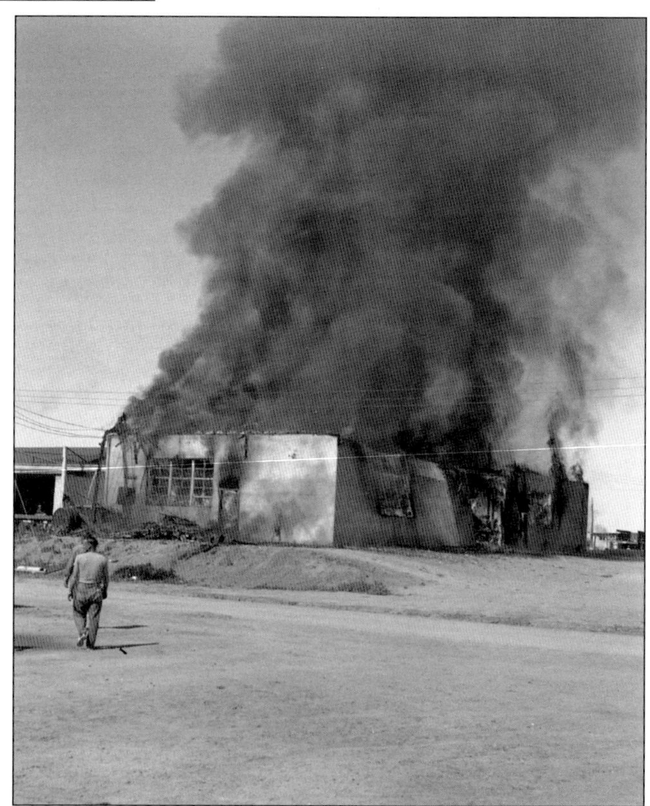

Fire destroyed the Aztec Machine Shop in June 1953. Evidently, the fire got a major head start on the firefighters, as they are not in evidence in this photograph. At that time, most of the town's firefighters were volunteers.

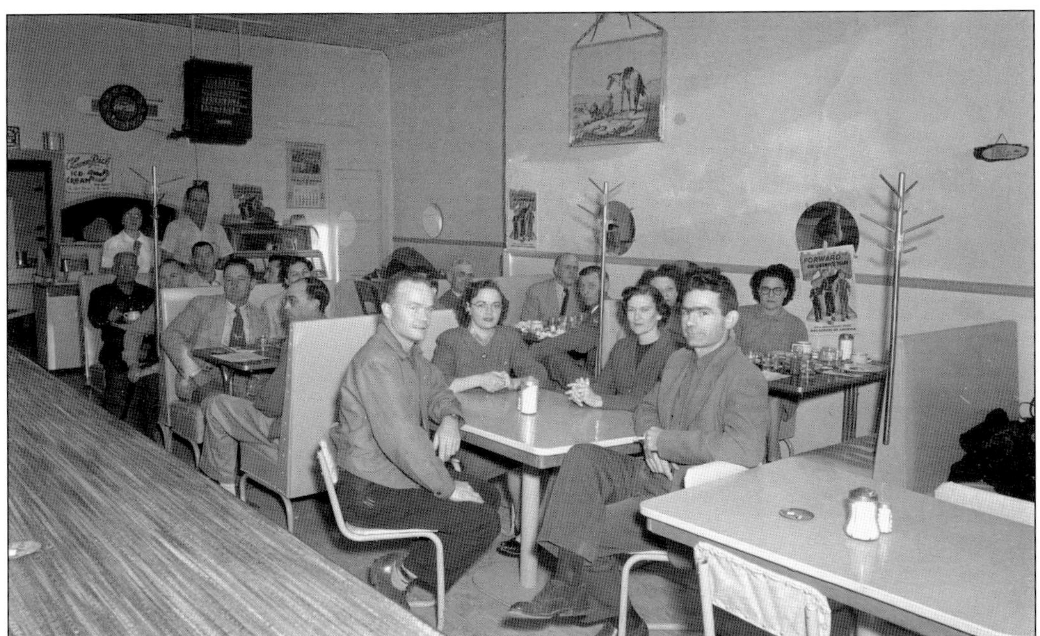

These Boy Scouts of America volunteers gather for breakfast at the Westerner Cafe in the Randall building at 117 South Main Avenue. Old photographs of Aztec show several restaurants in various locations during the years.

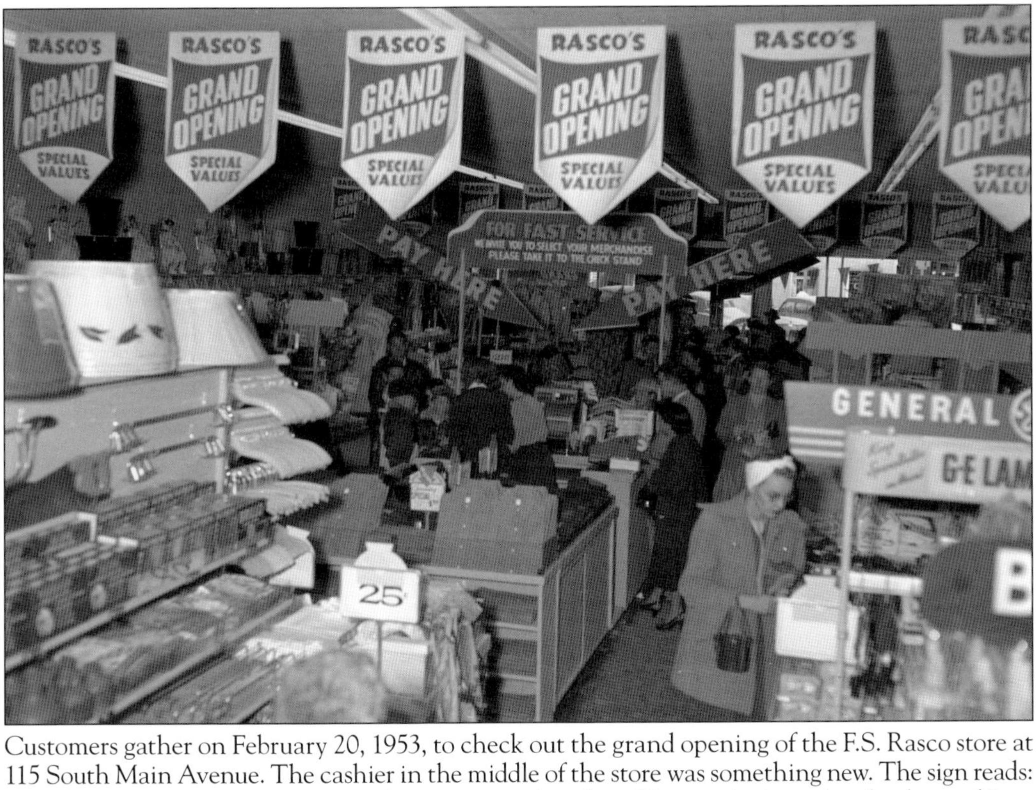

Customers gather on February 20, 1953, to check out the grand opening of the F.S. Rasco store at 115 South Main Avenue. The cashier in the middle of the store was something new. The sign reads: "For fast service we invite you to select your merchandise. Please take it to the check stand."

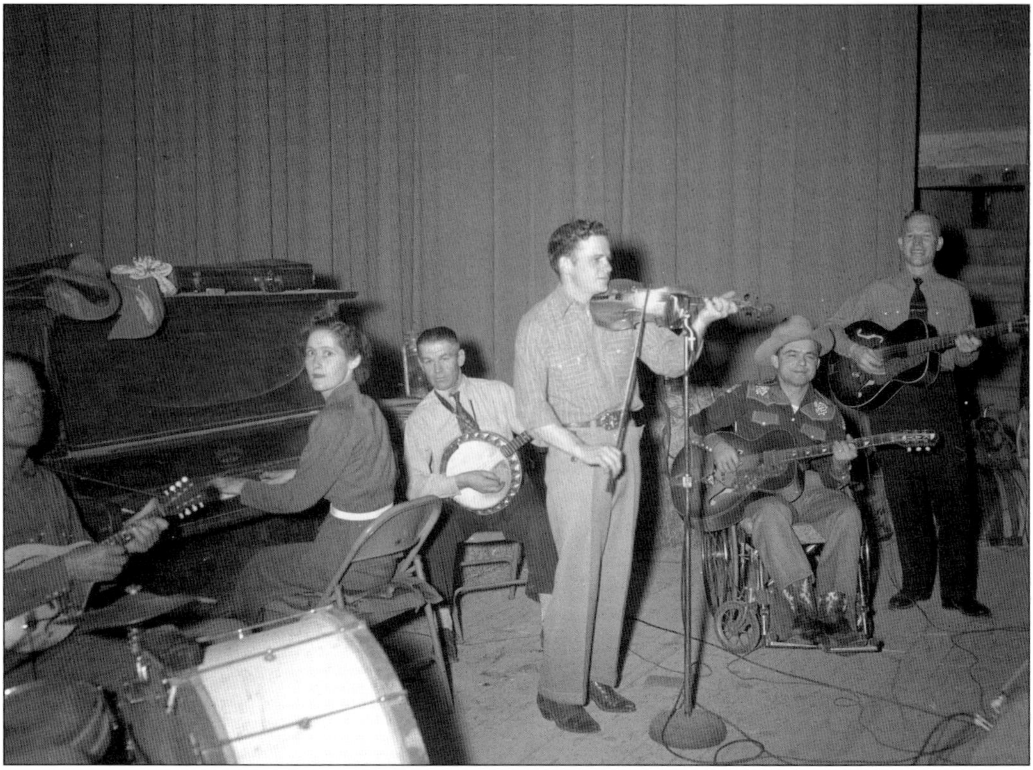

Tom Ruple and the Wagon Wheel Playboys performed at plenty of dances around the area, as well as at their Wagon Wheel dance hall located north of Aztec. Band members include Tom Ruple, playing fiddle at center, Billie Heizer at the piano, and John Ruple (seated right) on guitar. These images are from a fundraising event for polio research held in the Aztec High School gym on February 7, 1953.

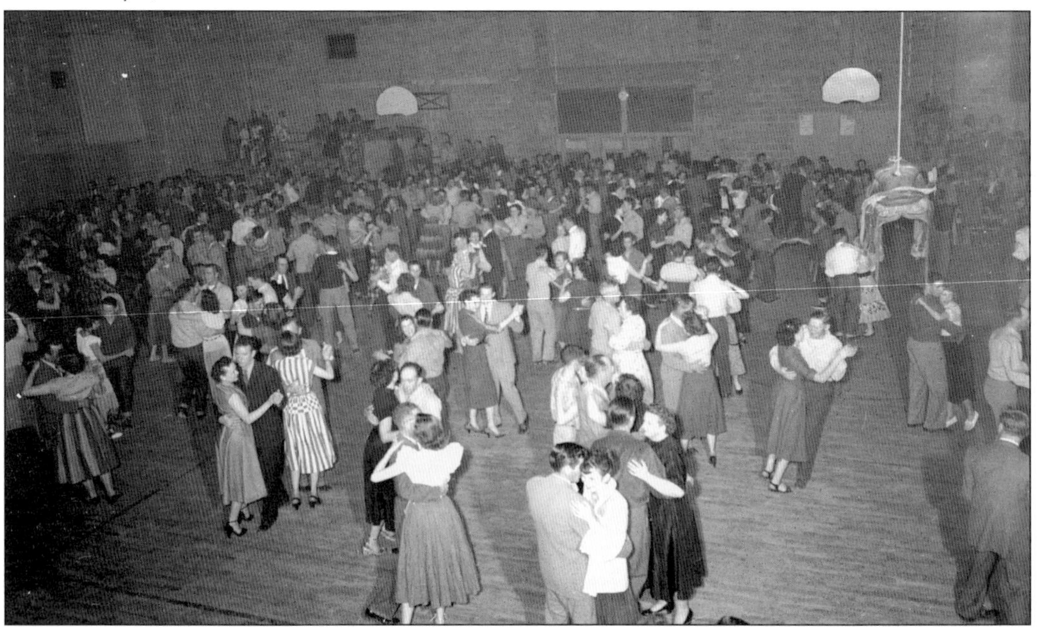

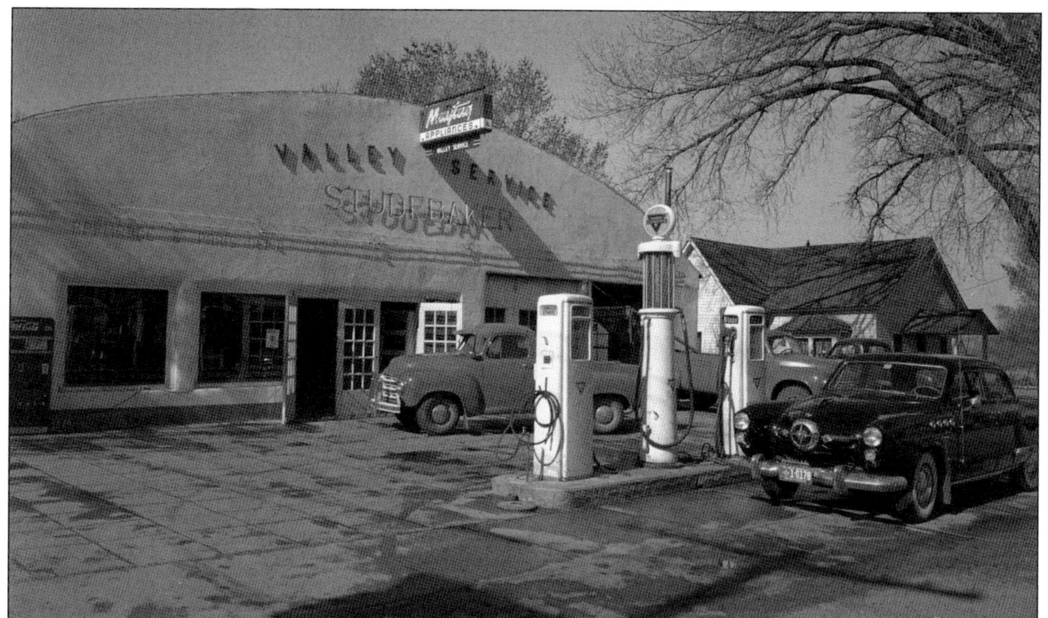

The Aztec area was dotted with Studebaker pickups, thanks to Jim Dusenbery and his Valley Service Company. This 1950 photograph shows one of the area's few remaining visual gasoline pumps with a glass canister (center) that the gas was collected in before being emptied into the car's tank by gravity. A sign advertising Maytag appliances shows the diversity of the company. The present-day business has been remodeled but is still in the same location and still owned by the Dusenbery family. Note the house next door, which was replaced with a car wash.

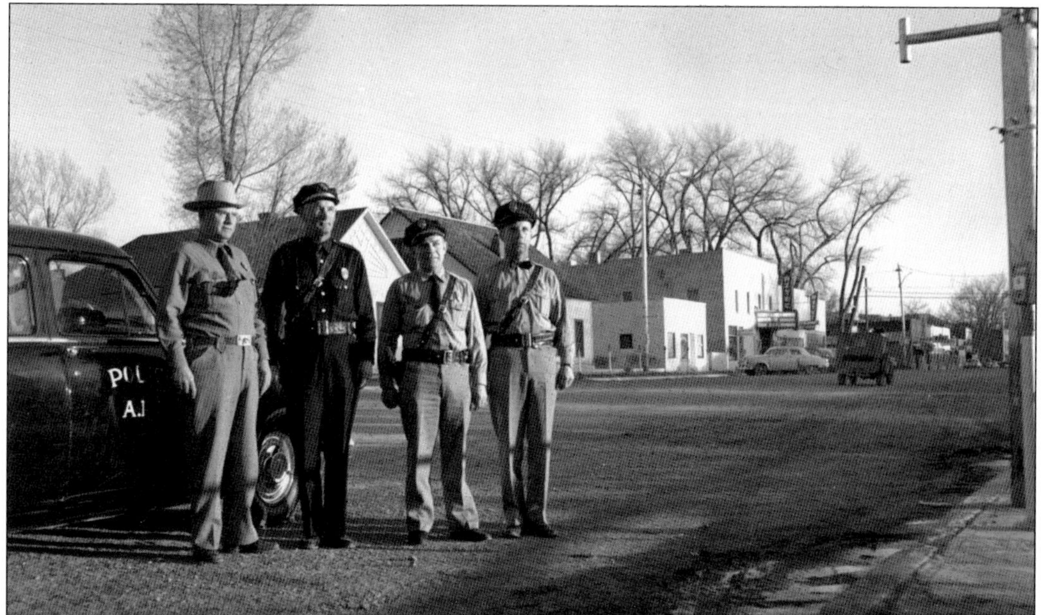

Members of the Aztec Police Department pose on Main Avenue in 1954. They are, from left to right, George Bowra, police chief William E. Perry, Earl Bennett, and Floyd Hazen. Perry was police chief from July 1952 to December 1969. Notice the car with minimal markings and no lights on top.

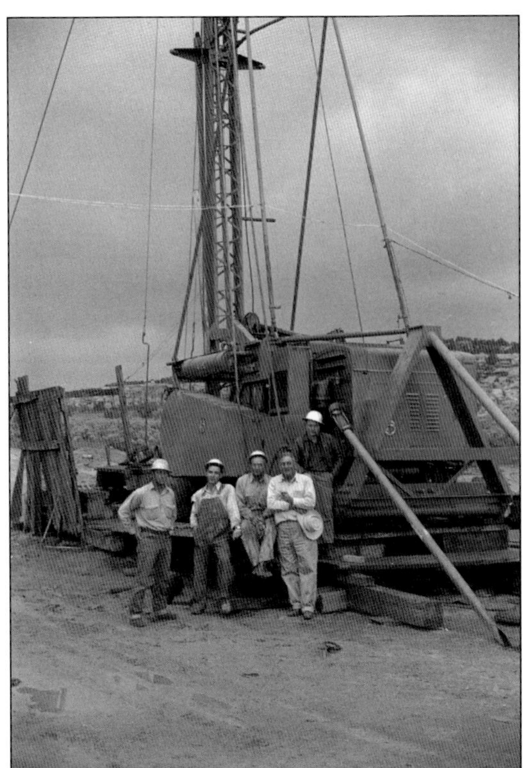

Al "Tuffy" Greer (fourth from left) and his crew assemble at the Riddle No. 1 well in 1949. Greer was a pioneer in the natural gas drilling business in the region. This cable tool rig worked a few miles east of Aztec on what later became Navajo Dam Road. Many roads were created in the area as resource discoveries were made and rigs moved in.

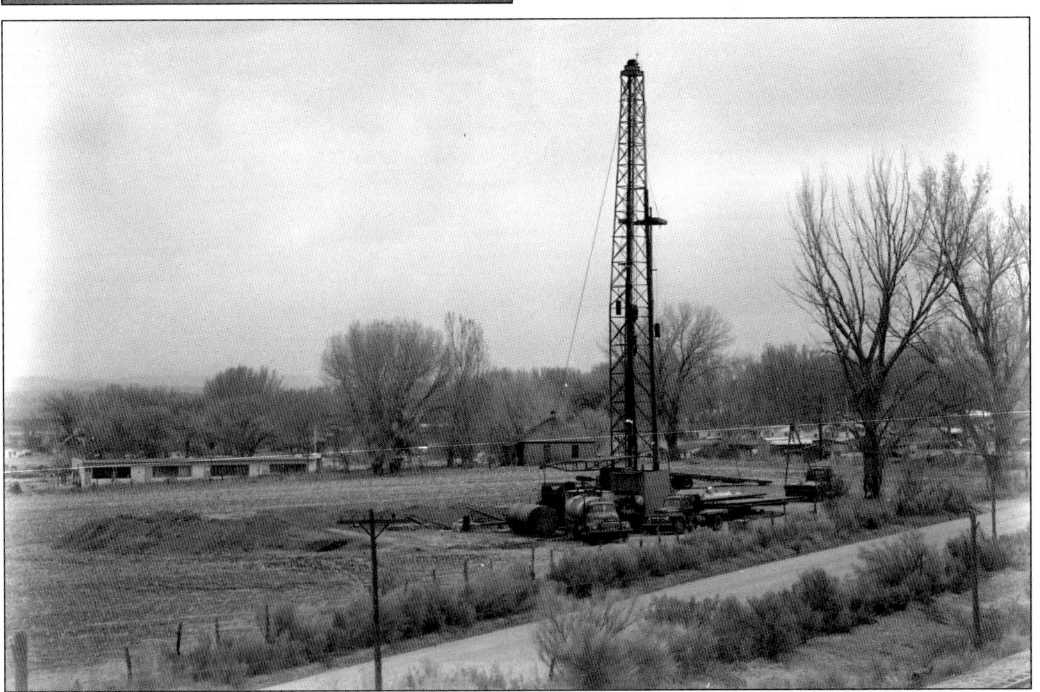

This Greer-Smith Drilling Corporation rig works in south Aztec in 1954. Southside River Road is in the foreground, beside the railroad track. Notice how close the rig is to buildings. This rig was typical of the sights and sounds of the time.

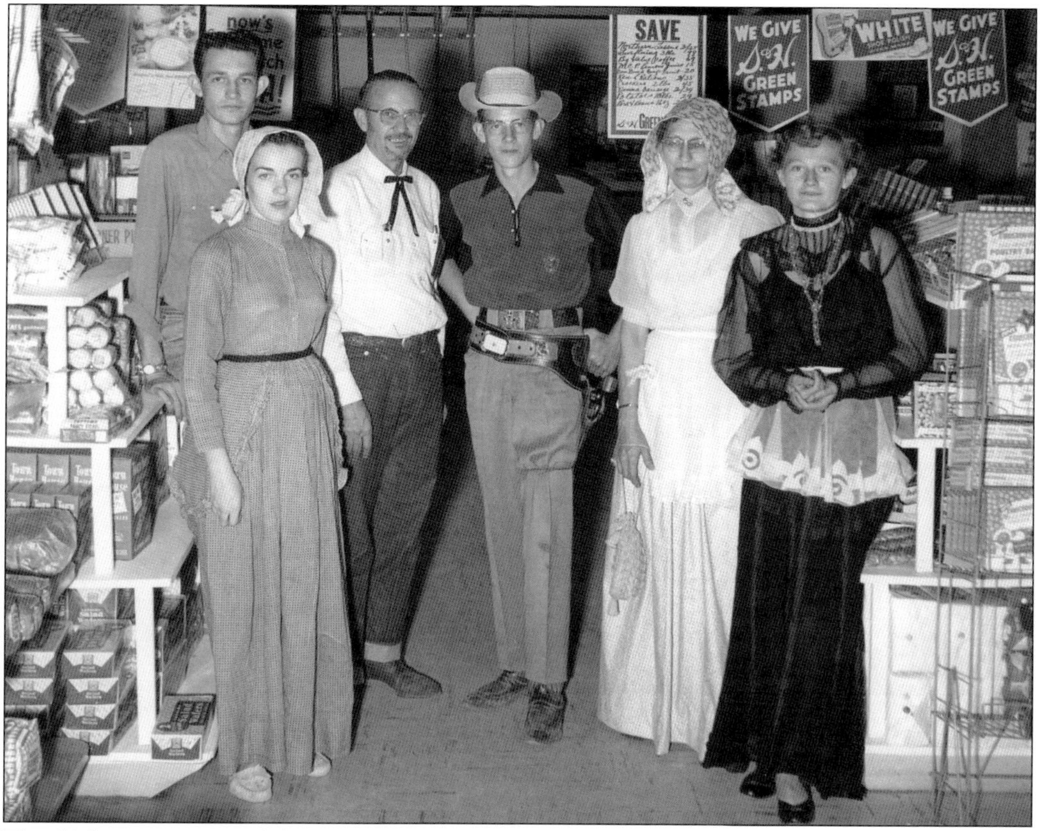

The 50th anniversary of the incorporation of the town of Aztec was celebrated on September 3, 1955. Gathered at Gay's Grocery in the above picture, left to right, are Jerry and Beverly Allen Gay, Don Gay, unidentified, Mildred Gay, and daughter Alize Brescia. The image below shows Jim Sumruld driving his team and wagons in the parade. The sign on the side of the wagon reads, "From Hope, NM, to Aztec in 28 days, 1917." Big Jo Lumber was located at 119 South Church Avenue.

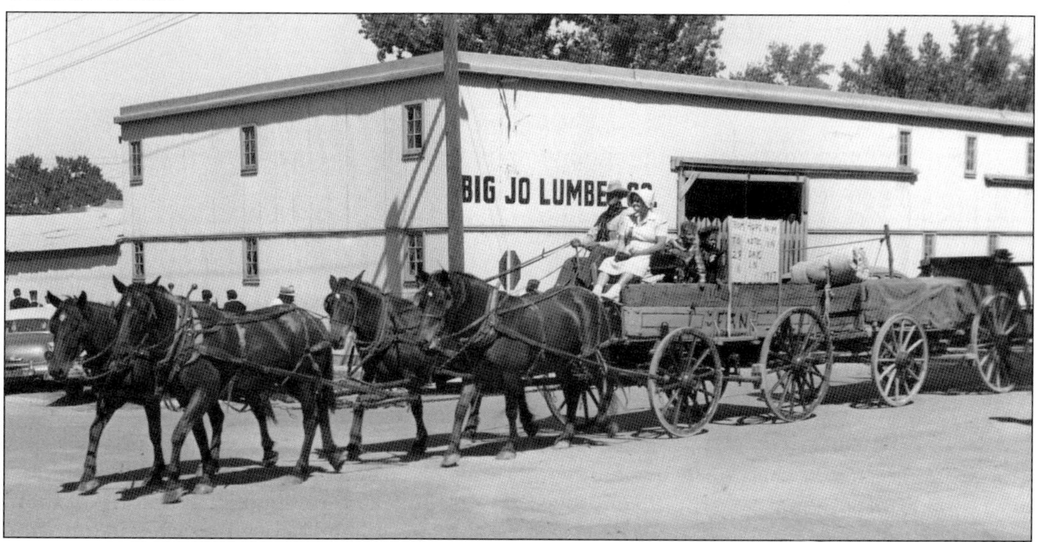

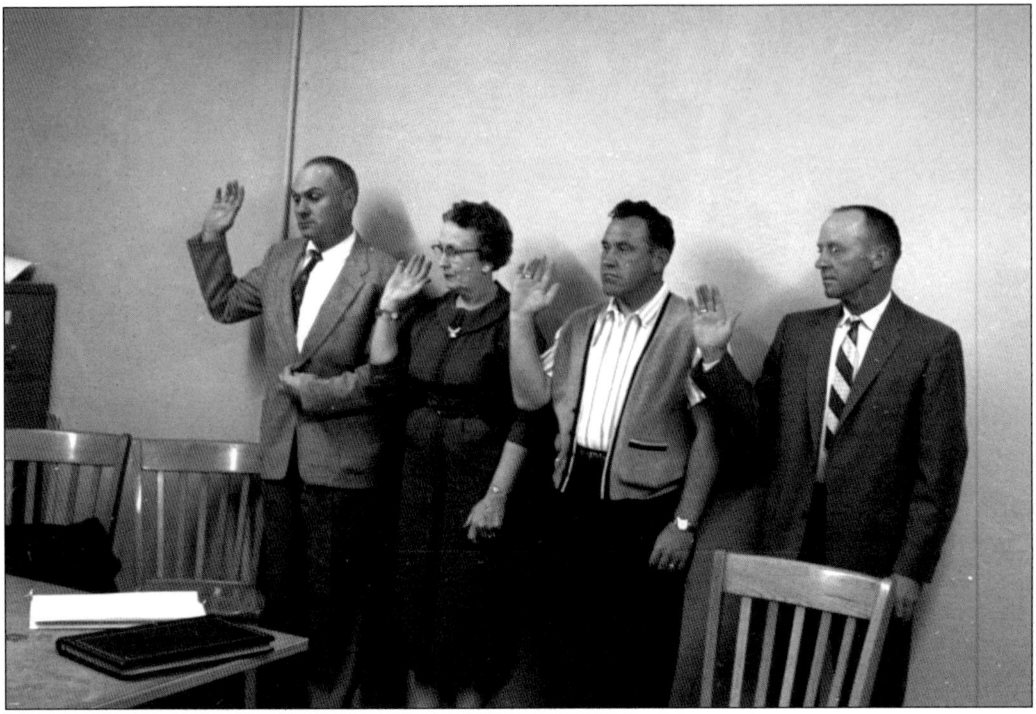

The above photograph shows the Aztec Town Board of 1958 being sworn into office. Pictured here are, from left to right, Johnston Jeffries, Mable Lester, Joe Bosse, and Sandy Scott. In the photograph below, old town board members Charles Maddox (left), Joe Hartman (center), and Emery Arnold watch the ceremony.

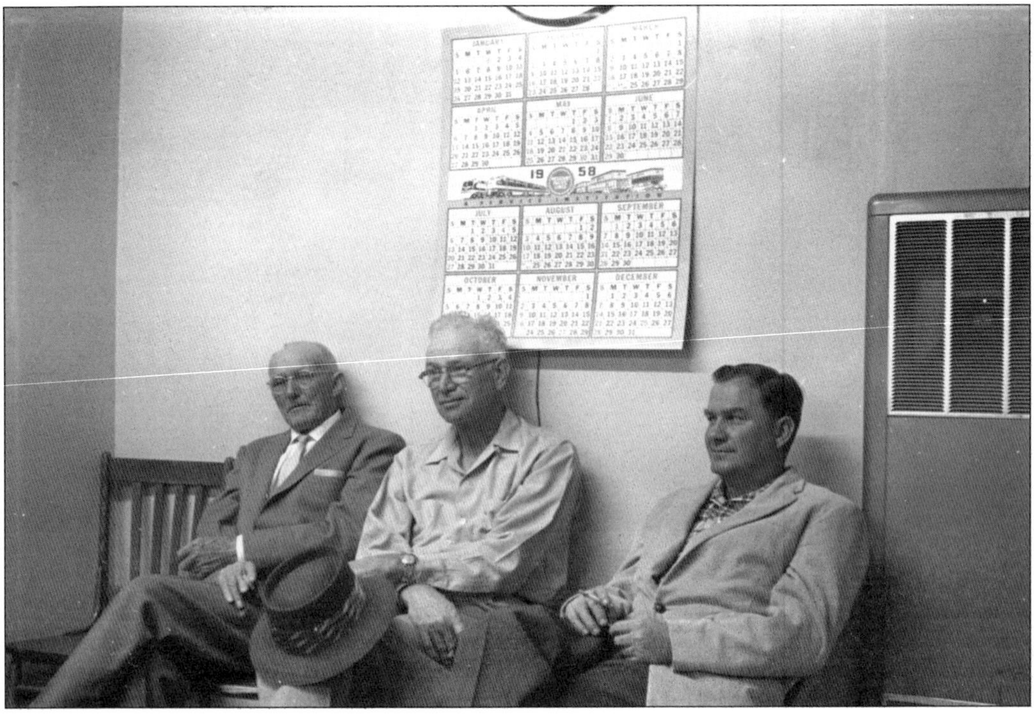

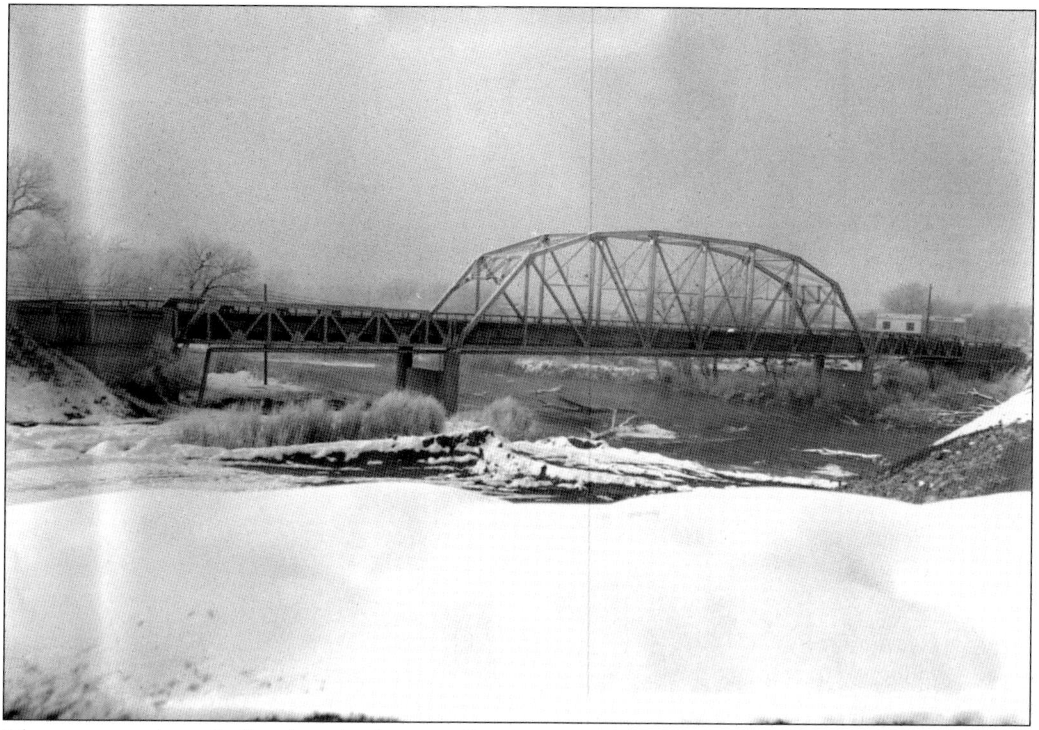

The construction of a four-lane highway to Farmington was an improvement welcomed by Aztec residents. The above image shows the old two-way bridge entering Aztec, which was built by the Pueblo Bridge and Construction Company of Colorado and dedicated on August 1, 1929. The westbound bridge for the four-lane roadway located north of the old bridge is pictured below. Both photographs were taken on December 18, 1960.

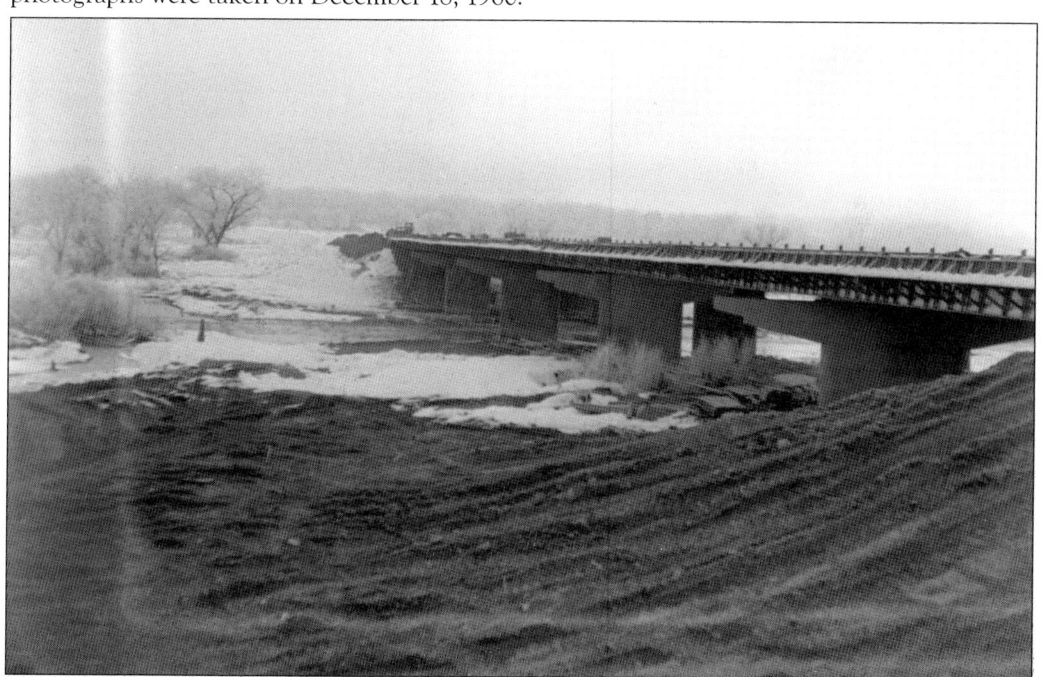

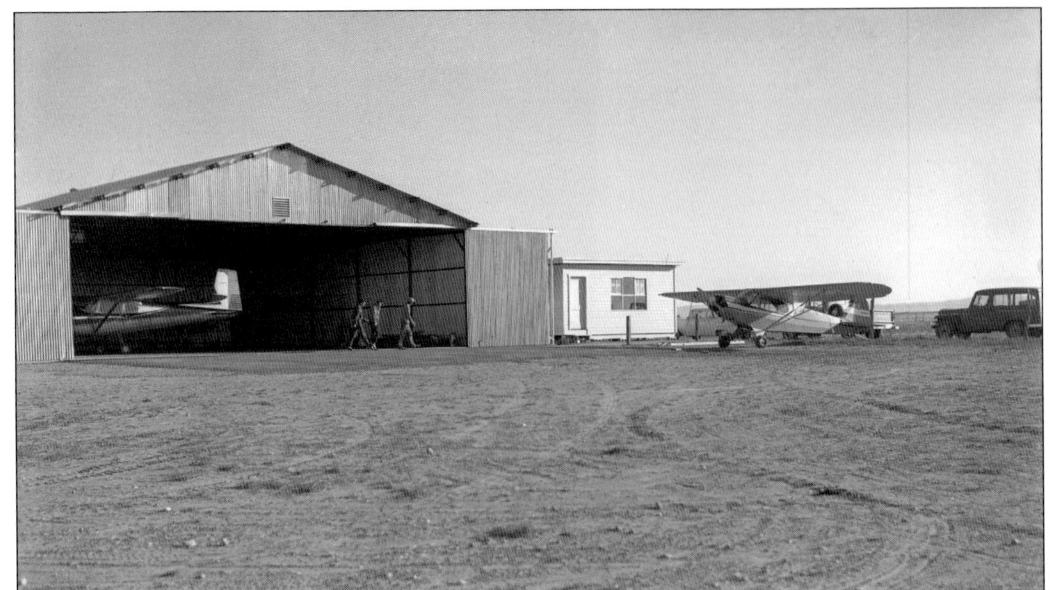

The Aztec Airport became a popular place for pilots of small aircraft. The Aztec Flying Service was in full swing in 1958. The three men inside the hanger are Austin Albert, ? Magee, and ? Johnson. Albert taught many aspiring pilots how to fly.

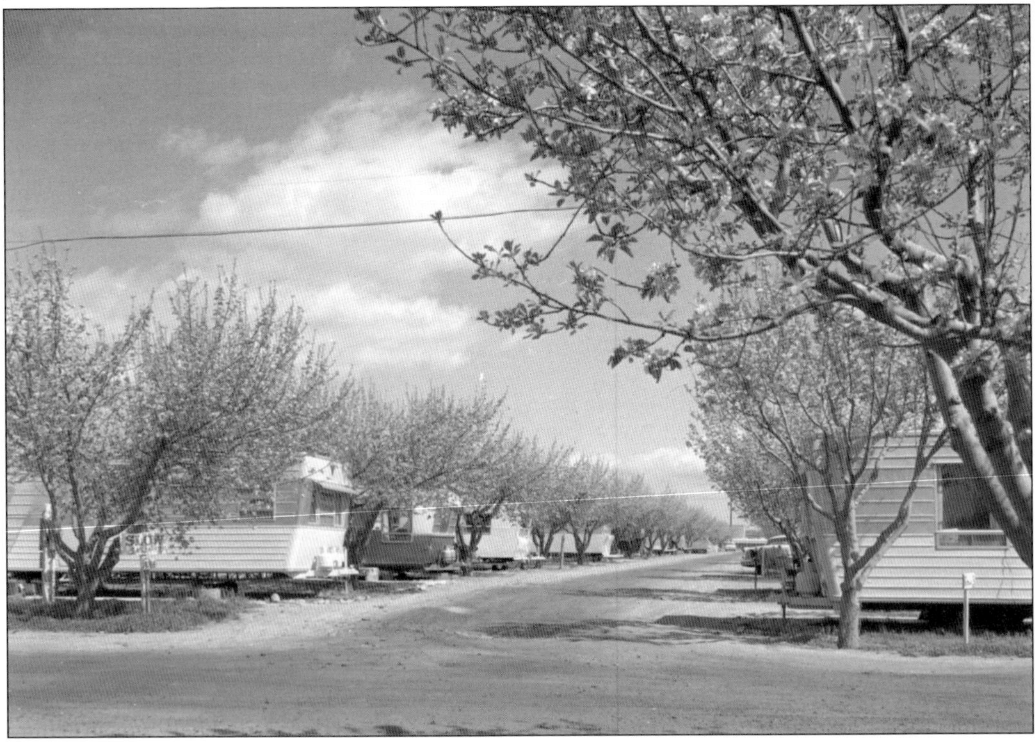

The influx of people in the 1950s resulted in scores of farmers turning their orchards into trailer courts. Some bulldozed the trees away, as housing all over the area was at a premium. When Clayton Hough opened his San Juan Trailer Town, he kept his orchard for shade and fruit. This April 1960 image shows the trees in bloom.

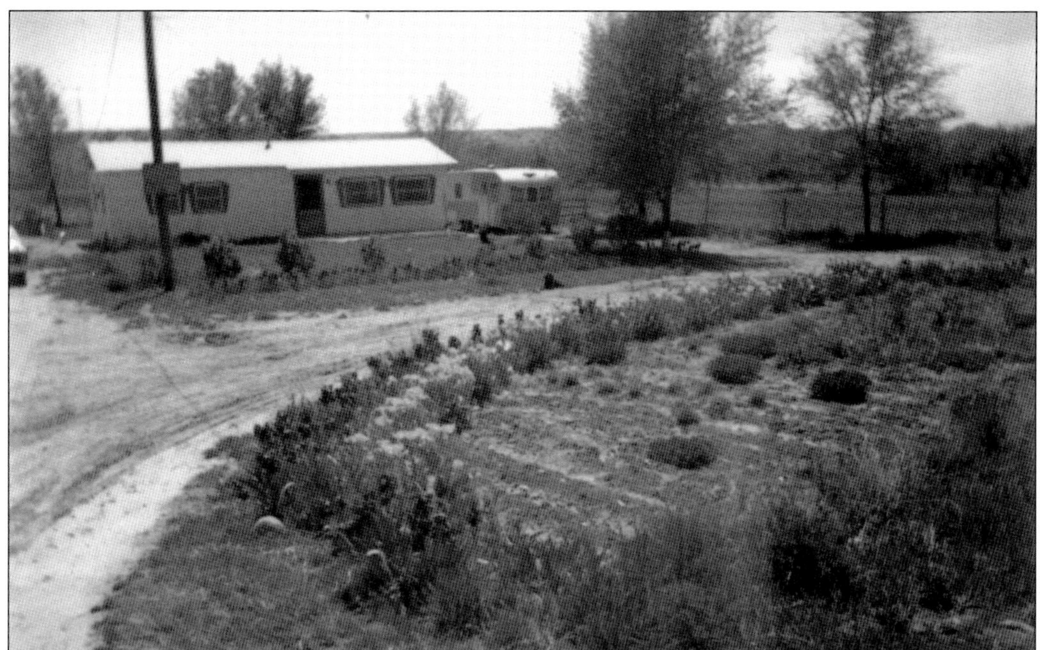

This house, built in 1962, was the first house seen on the right by those traveling east on the main highway (now NM 516) from Farmington to Aztec. Art and LaVada Jones lived here for many years as the neighborhood filled up around them. Finally, they had enough of the fumes and noise from the highway and moved. (Courtesy Art Jones.)

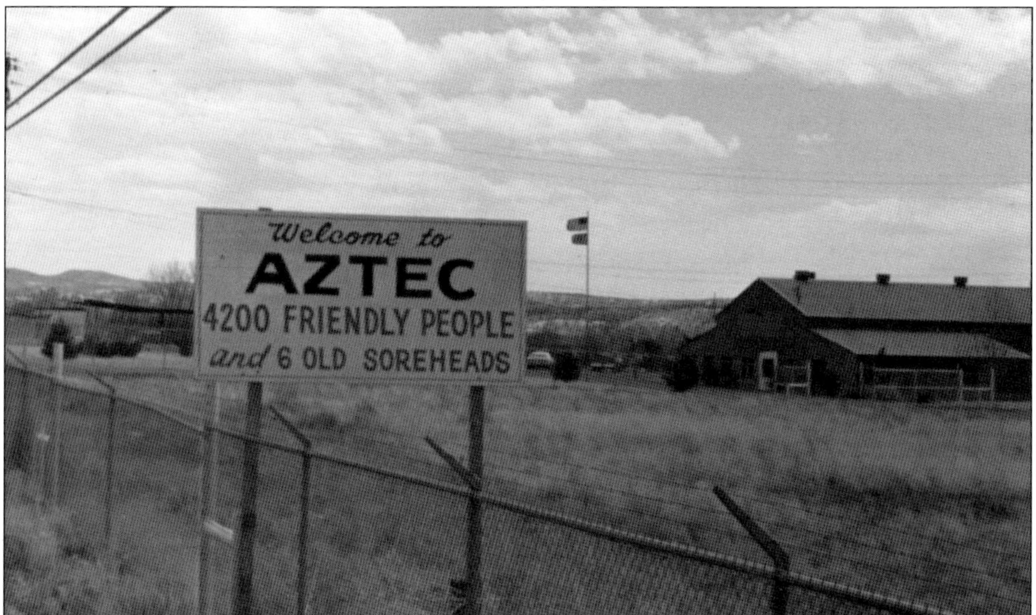

Aztec became well known for the three signs at the entrance into town. One of the signs was placed near the Jones house, pictured above. Emory Minium, former city commissioner, started the practice in 1969 as an entertaining feature of Fiesta Days. Each year, six soreheads would be elected and the names kept secret until an unveiling after the Fiesta Days parade. When the signs faded and the numbers were outdated, they were removed. (Courtesy Aztec Museum.)

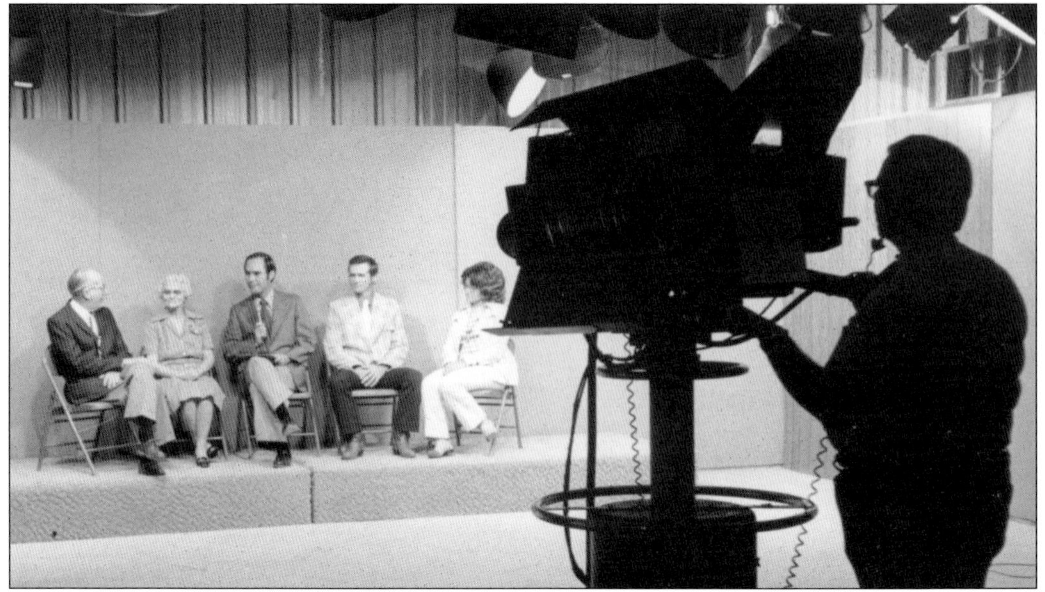

In this image, the Farm Bureau is being interviewed on local television station KIVA. At the anchor's left are John and Lucille Utton, and to his right are Bobby and Rachel Truby. The anchor and cameraman are unidentified. (Courtesy Audrey Glazebrook.)

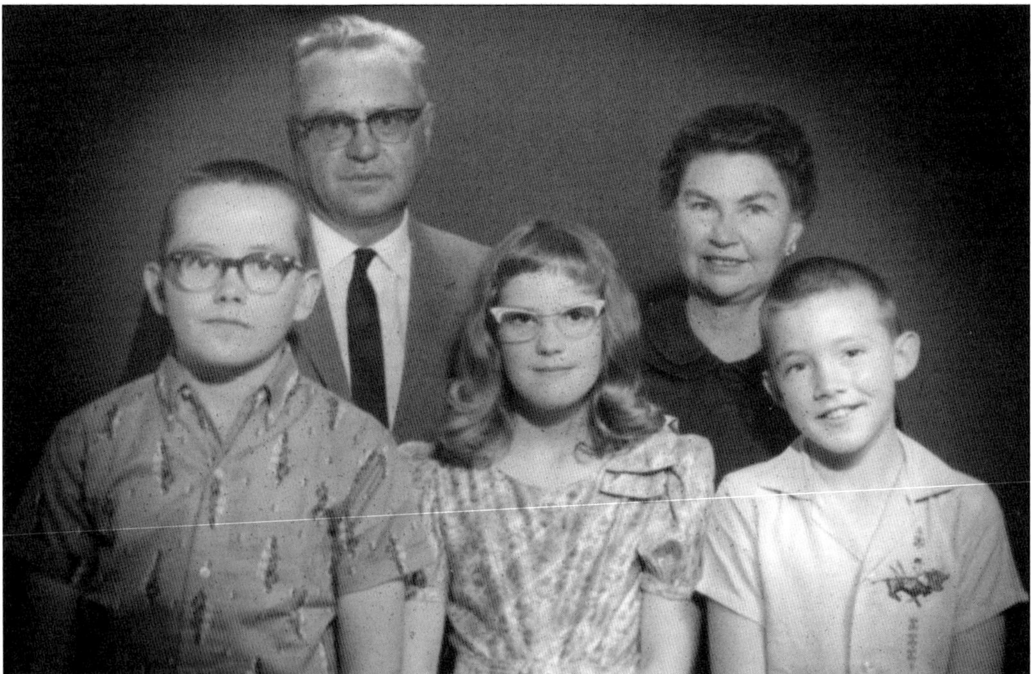

In late 1962, Aztec citizens were gearing up to begin building a direct road to the Navajo Dam. Schoolchildren and teachers were soon involved. Fifth-grade teacher Curn Harvey (second row, left) organized his students, and Bonnie Walls (second row, right) became the food coordinator. The students in the first row, who wrote poems about the project, are Billy Noland (left), Judy Dunning, and Timmy Lane. Dunning's poem was read at the dedication ceremony. (Courtesy Aztec Museum.)

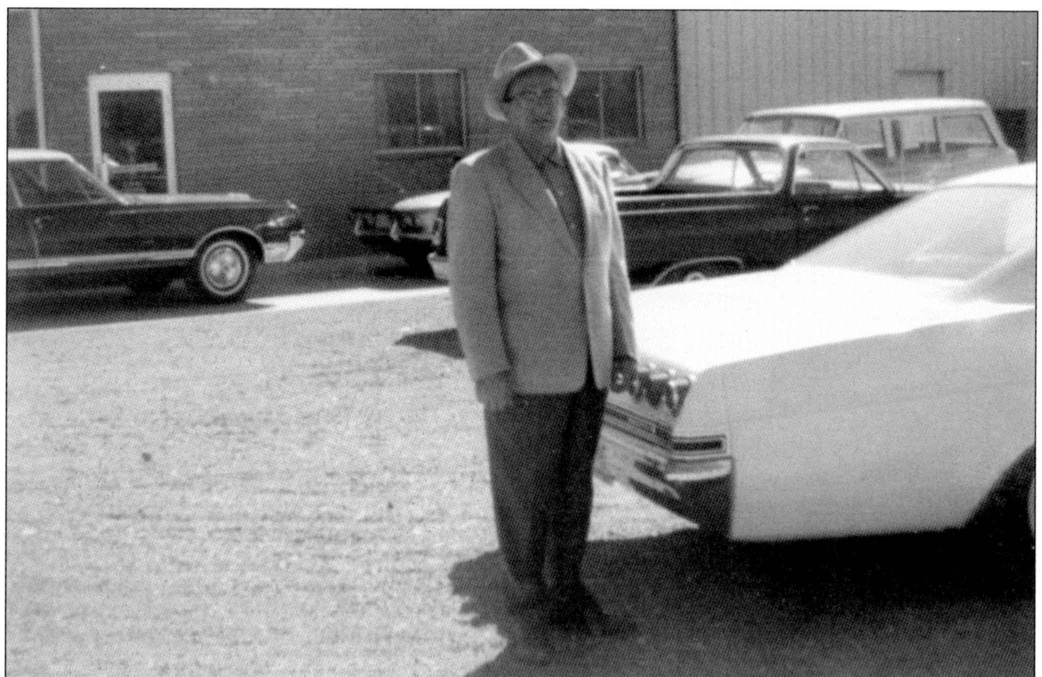

A town meeting on December 5, 1962, resulted in the formation of the Navajo Dam Road Association. The townspeople called it the "Aztec Uprising." Ken Fogle (above) and Al Williams (below) were cochairmen of the association. Fogle was a county commissioner and owned Fogle Chevrolet Company; Williams owned and operated the Stop and Shop Market. The project was conceived as a concerted effort of volunteers, including contractors. One of the eager volunteer groups was the Junior Chamber of Commerce (Jaycees). (Both courtesy Aztec Museum.)

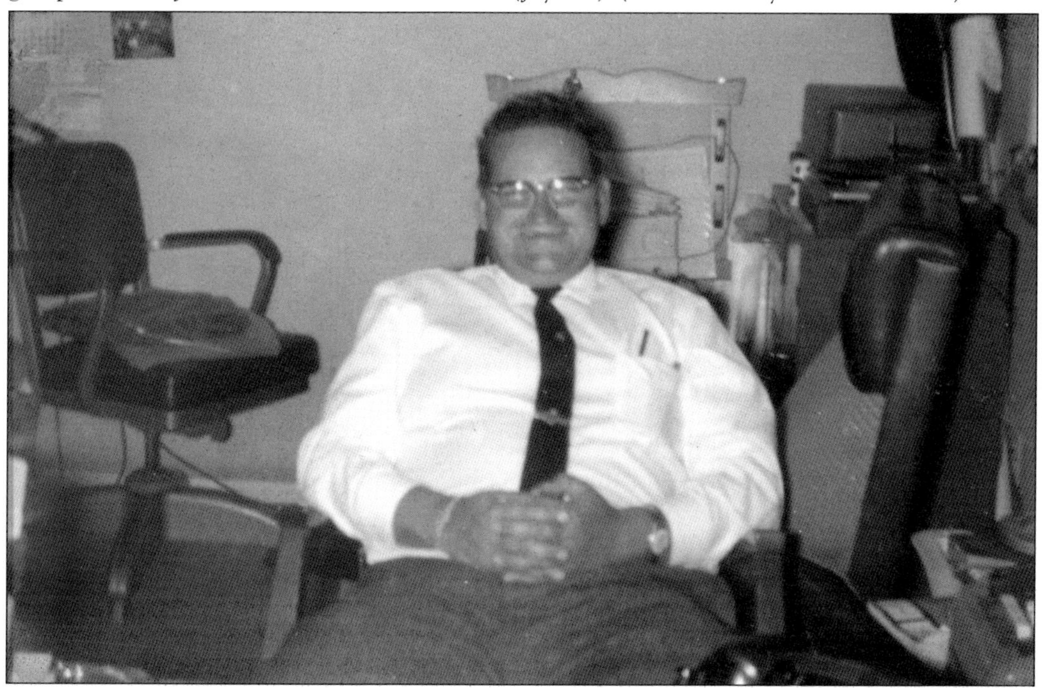

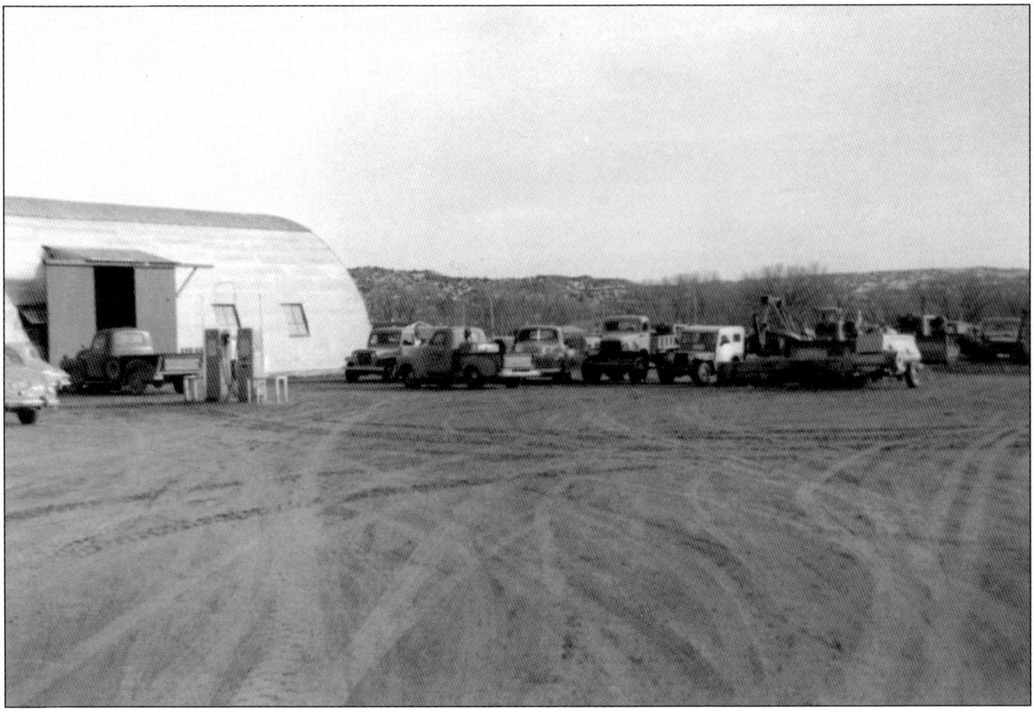

Ray Atchison and his Ray L. Atchison Construction Company were instrumental in the Navajo Dam Road project. Atchison, who started his business in Aztec in 1945, was in charge of equipment procurement and donated his dozers, maintainers, trucks, and other equipment as needed. Joe McKinney, Atchison's foreman, supervised the building of the road. Above is Atchison's yard, and below is one of the trucks he loaned out. (Both courtesy Atchison family.)

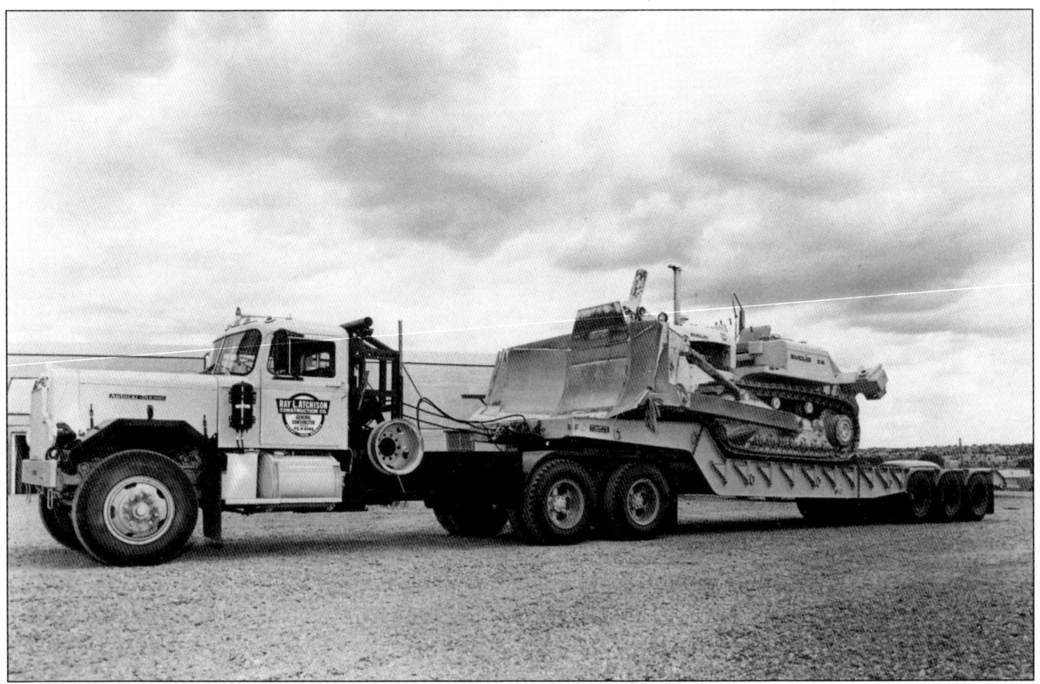

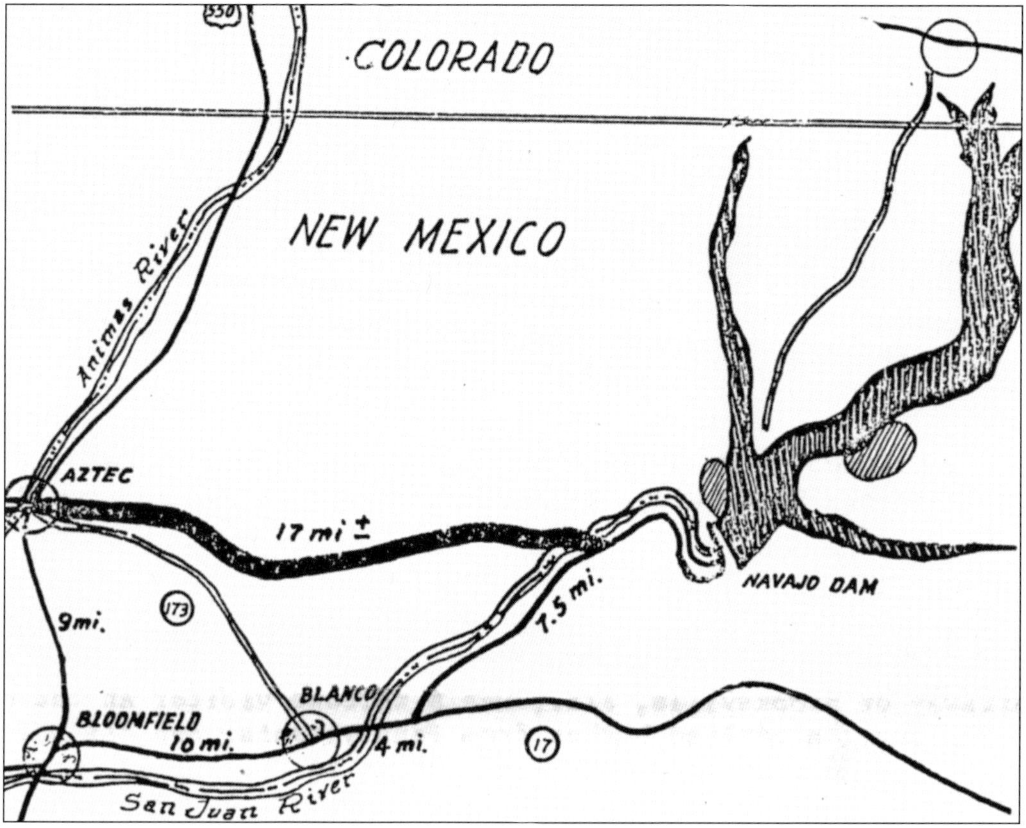

550
COLORADO
NEW MEXICO
Animas River
AZTEC
17 mi ±
173
9mi.
7.5 mi.
NAVAJO DAM
BLANCO
BLOOMFIELD
10 mi.
4 mi.
17
San Juan River

This drawing, which shows the two different routes from Aztec to the Navajo Dam, illustrates the reason for the road. With the new Navajo Dam Road, it would no longer be necessary to go to Bloomfield, then Blanco, and then the dam. (Courtesy Aztec Museum.)

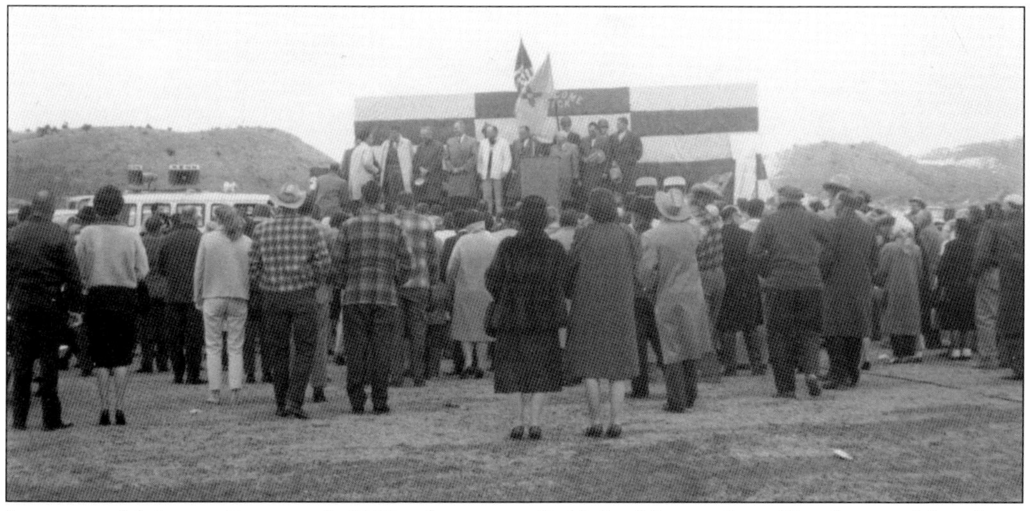

It was a cold day on January 6, 1963, when town held the Navajo Dam Road ground-breaking ceremony. Gov. Jack Campbell was the main speaker; he joined the group with shovels to symbolize that the road was going to be built. The mayors of Aztec, Bloomfield, and Farmington were also present. (Courtesy Aztec Museum.)

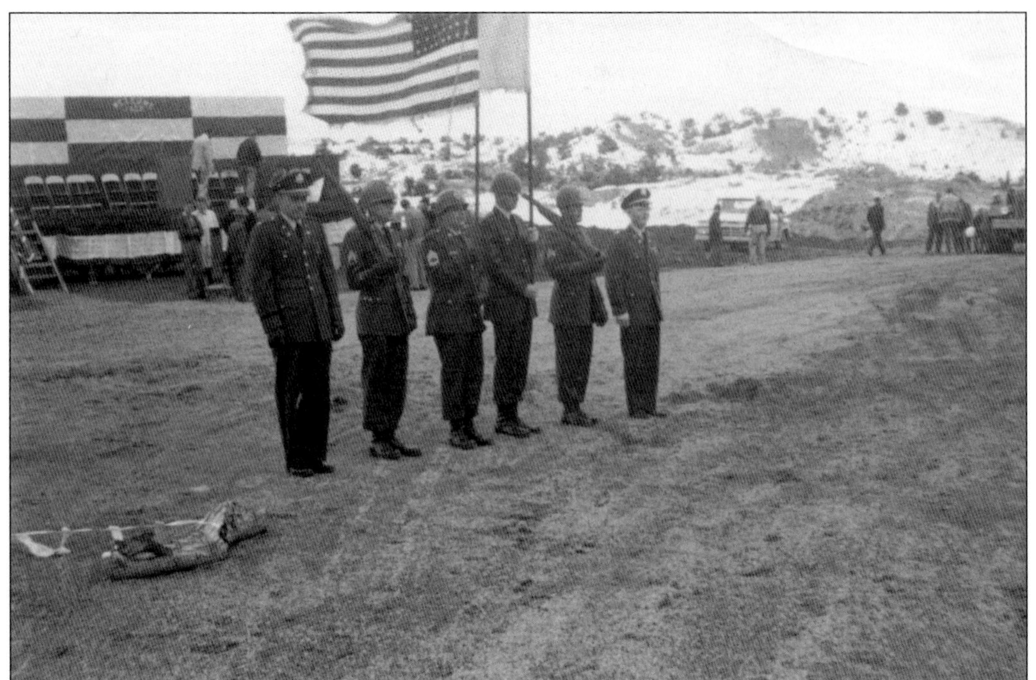

The Honor Guard carried the flags at the ground-breaking ceremony. Cecil Draper, of the First National Bank, and Emery Arnold, of the Oil & Gas Conservation Commission, served as finance directors. Most news articles about the road included the note, "Leave your contribution at the First National Bank." (Courtesy Aztec Museum.)

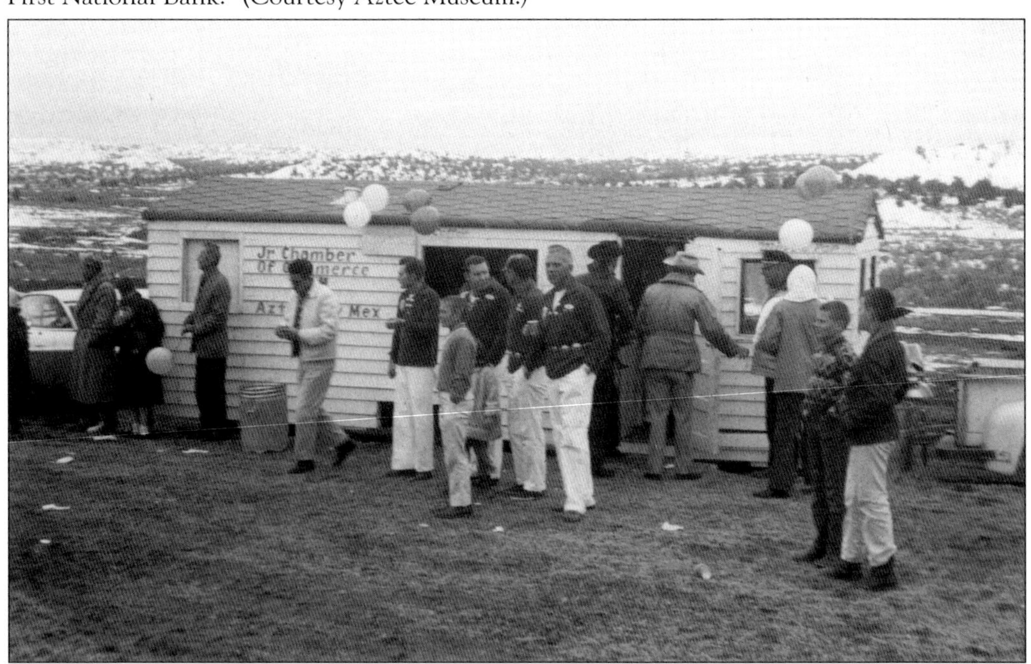

The Junior Chamber of Commerce set up a food building for both the ground-breaking ceremony and for later use during the road construction. The food stand served hamburgers, hot dogs, coffee, and sodas—all donated. (Courtesy Aztec Museum.)

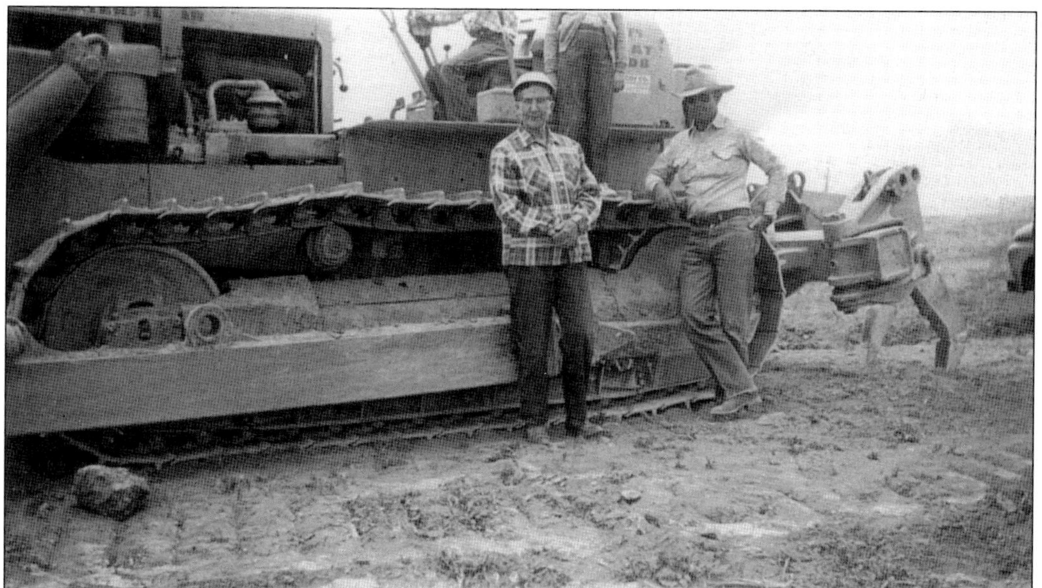

The road construction was fairly informal. Here, Raymond Rhodes (right) is joined for lunch by his mother, Edith Frazier Rhodes. Raymond worked for Jack Fritz Construction. Fritz donated the Caterpillar dozer and operator for work on the Navajo Dam Road. (Courtesy Nellie Howard.)

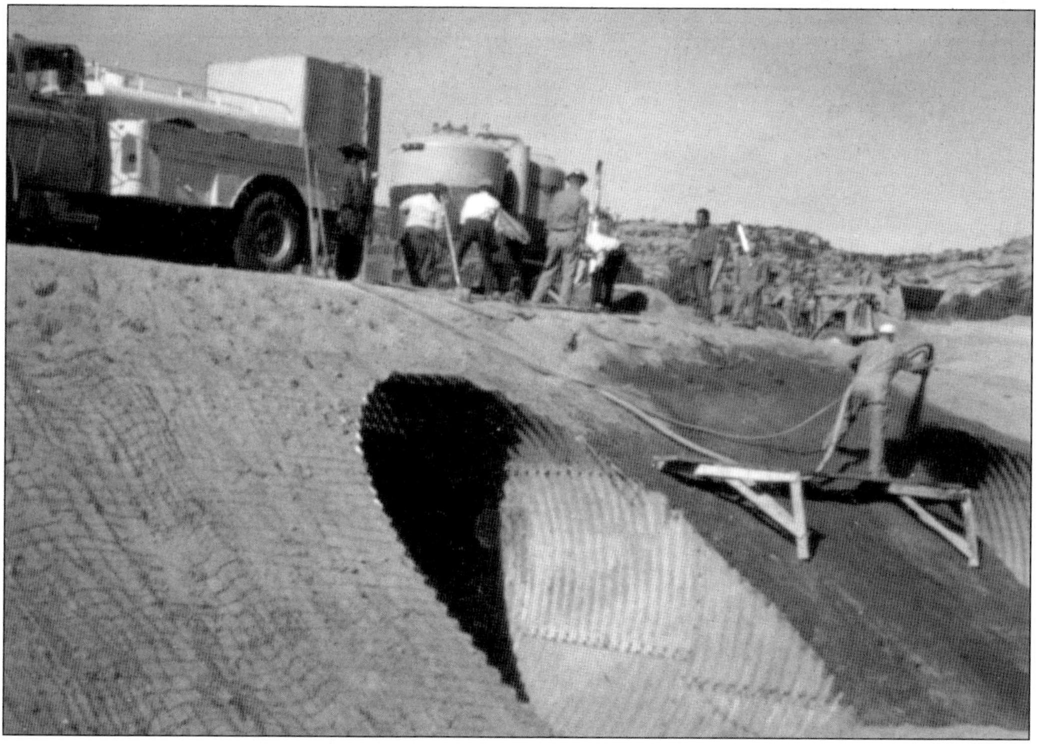

To get to the lake, it was necessary to get to the other side of the San Juan River. Foutz-Bursum Construction Company managed the diversion of the low-flowing river to make way for the new road. El Paso Natural Gas Company loaned the crane and operator to set the three, 25-foot culverts for the river crossing. (Courtesy Aztec Museum.)

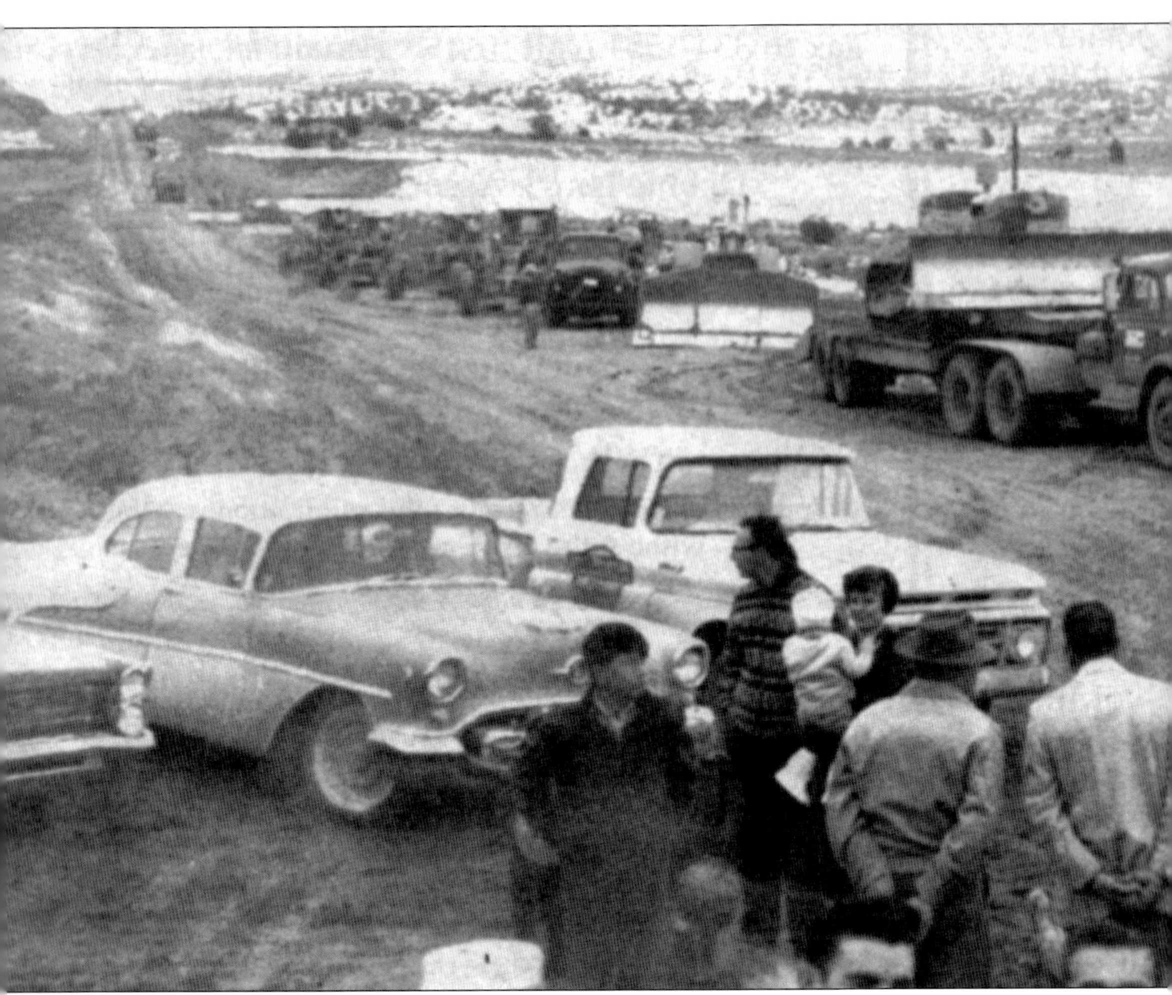

This photograph, taken on ground-breaking day, catches the tone of the Navajo Dam Road project as equipment was lined up and ready to go to work after the ceremony. Equipment came from all over; people brought their children to watch, and workers either took time off their regular jobs

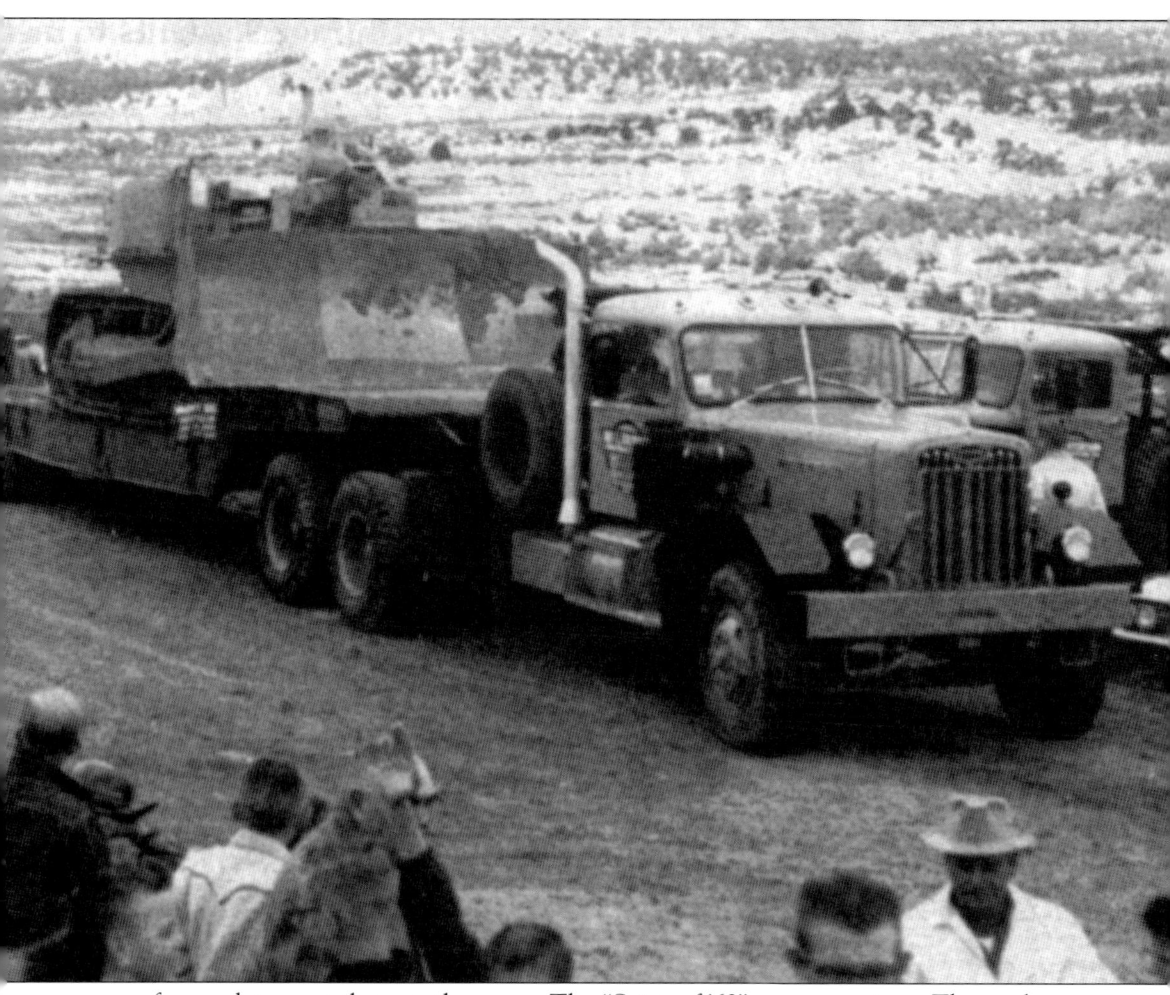

or came after work to contribute to the cause. The "Spirit of '63" was contagious. The road was expected to take a year—it was finished in fewer than four months. (Courtesy Aztec Museum.)

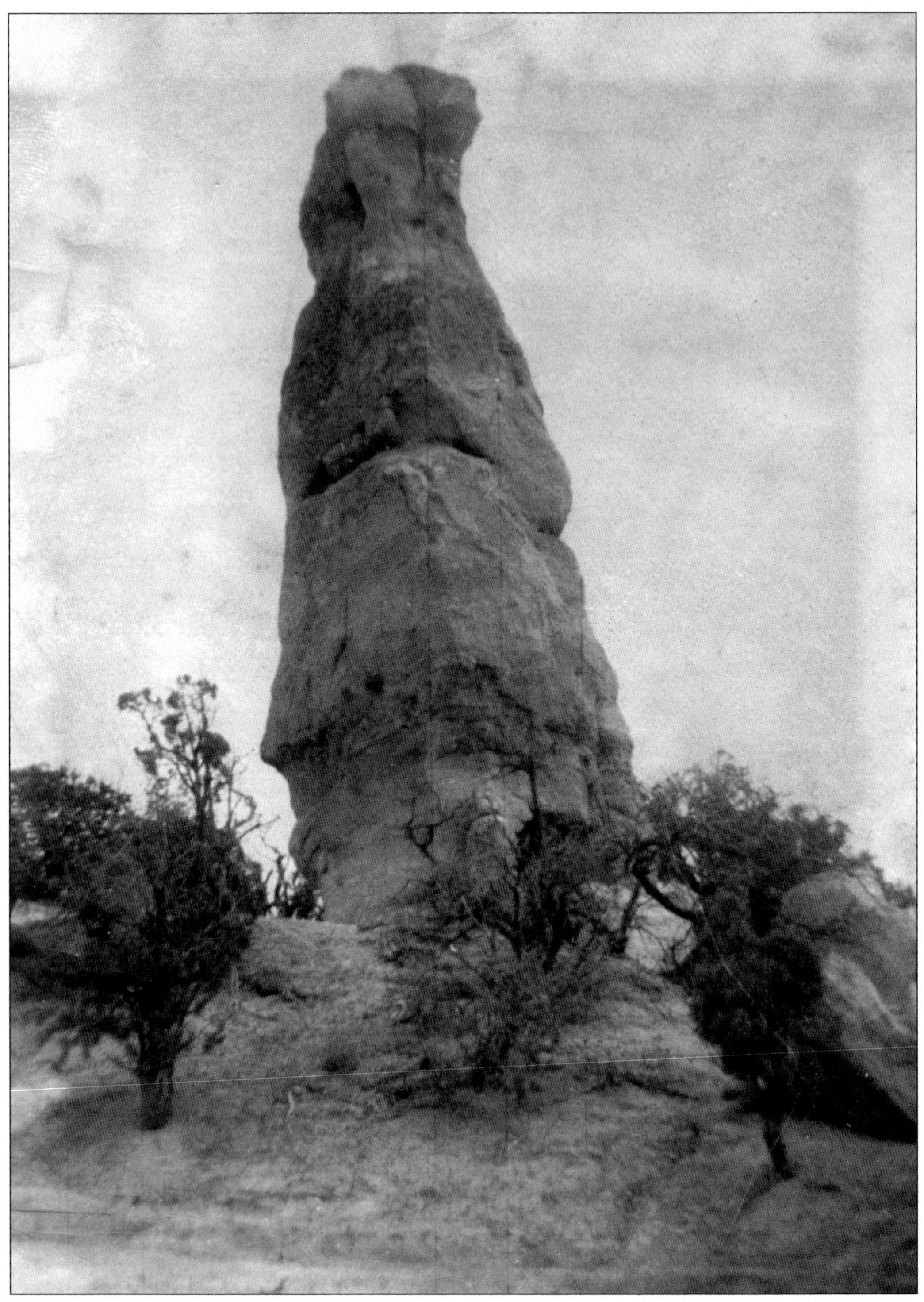

Crews drove by this rock formation each day, and it soon became a landmark. Before long, it was being called "Bonnie Rock" in appreciation of Bonnie Walls, who was in charge of food management and made sure that all the workers on site had plenty to eat. (Courtesy Aztec Museum.)

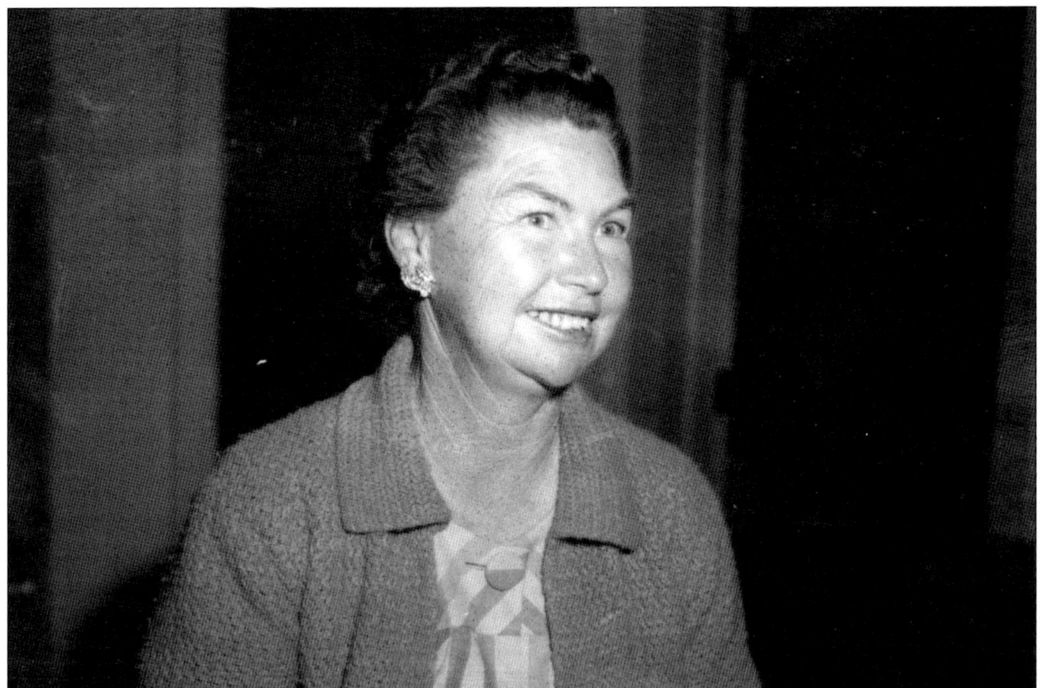

The Navajo Dam Road is not discussed without mention of Bonnie Walls. It is said she had unbounded energy and got the job done. Day after day, Walls served the workers using donated food and volunteer labor. She was the ramrod behind this momentous task. (Courtesy Aztec Museum.)

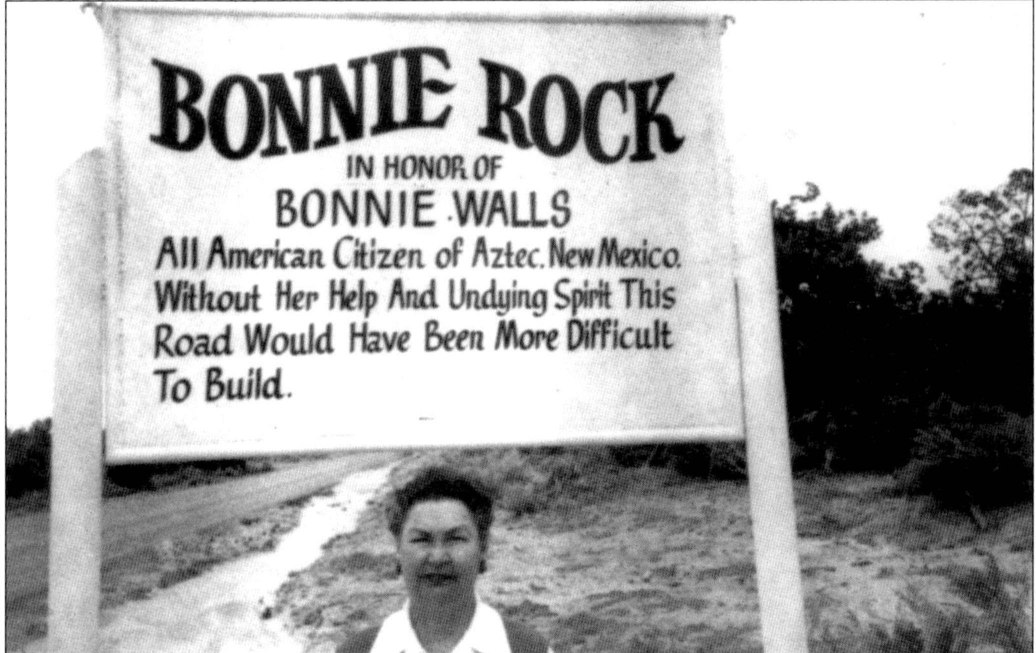

This sign was erected near Bonnie Rock. Walls is shown under the sign in 1963. Today, the trees have grown taller, and there is no marker or evidence that the rock has a name. (Courtesy Aztec Museum.)

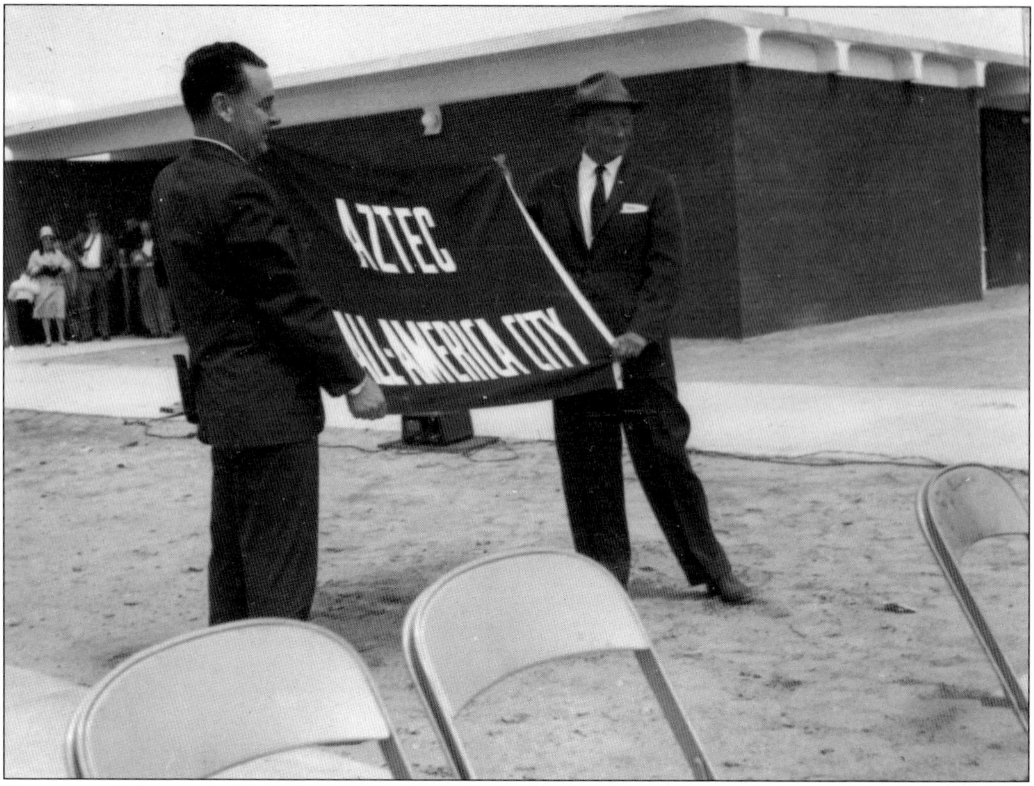

Because of the success of the Navajo Dam Road, Aztec was nominated for and won the *Look* magazine and National Municipal League "All-America City" award. Gov. Jack Campbell, left, and Mayor Cliff Collins carry the banner during the first phase of the ceremonies held in front of the city hall complex in Aztec. In addition to Campbell and Collins, speakers for the event included Lt. Gov. Mack Easley, Sen. Edwin L. Mechem, and Rep. Joseph M. Montoya. Below is one of the signs posted at all three town entrances that declared Aztec a 1963 All-America City. (Both courtesy Aztec Museum.)

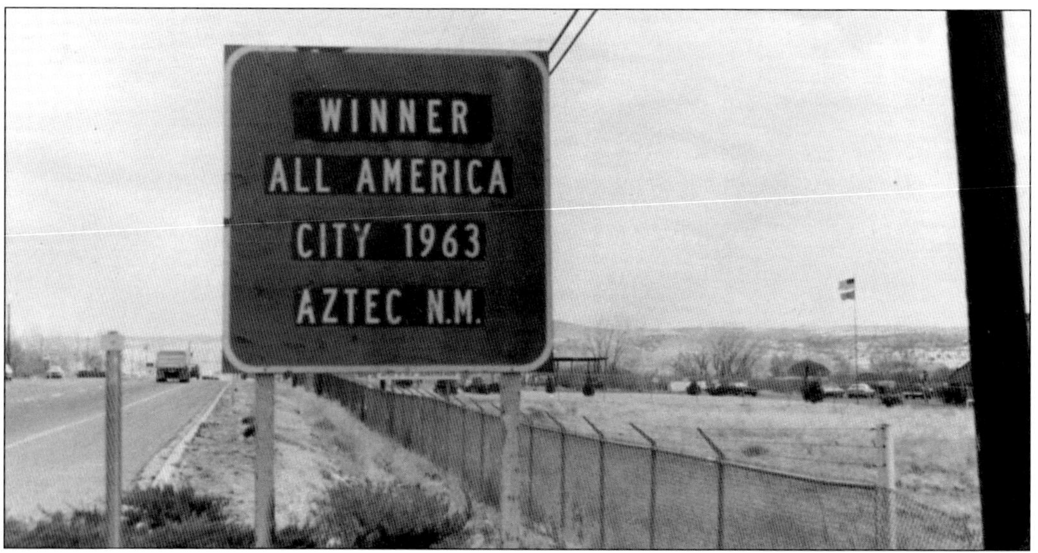

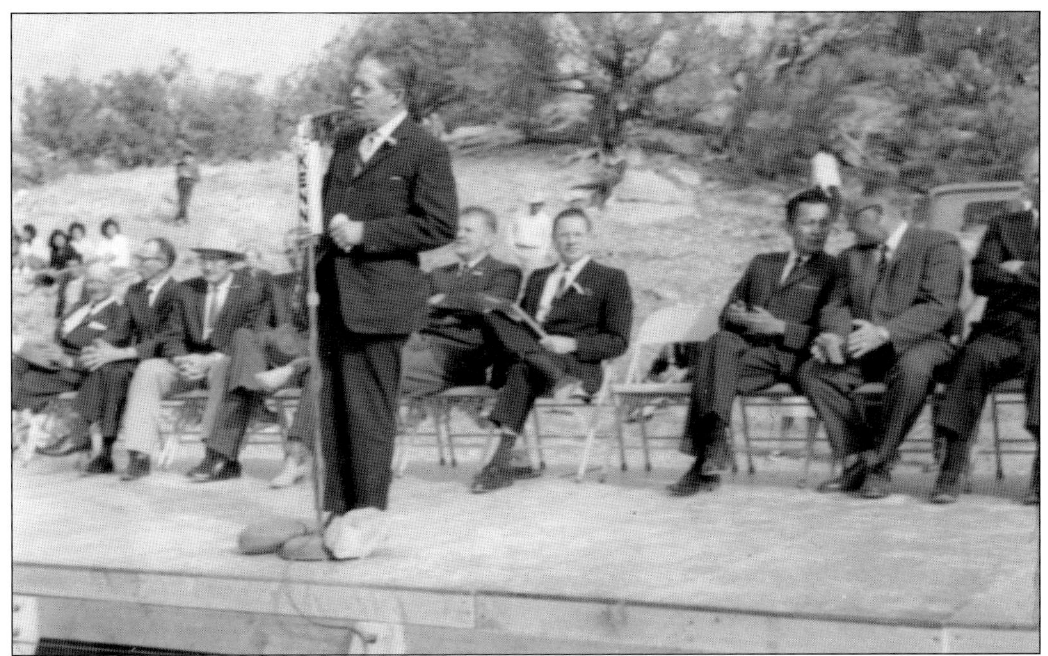

After the meeting at city hall, a caravan proceeded to Navajo Dam for the second phase of the All-America City award festivities on April 19, 1964. Sen. Edwin L. Mechem addressed the gathering while the weather was still enjoyable. Attendance was estimated at over 4,000. (Courtesy Aztec Museum.)

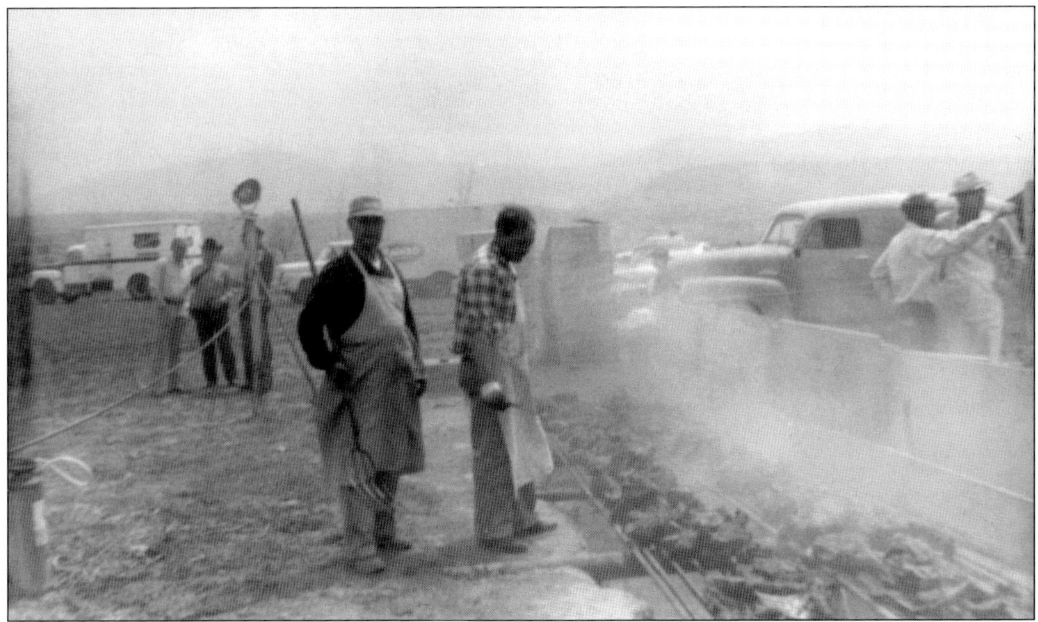

When the speeches were over, the crowd was ready to eat. Dr. K.M. Roberts and Bill Stevens were in charge of cooking and serving 500 pounds of beans and 3,000 pounds of beef from a 40-foot pit. The weather did not cooperate. Winds clocked at 40 mph stirred up sand and blew tablecloths away. According to Emery Arnold, there was a little grit in the barbeque, but it did not dampen the spirits. (Courtesy Aztec Museum.)

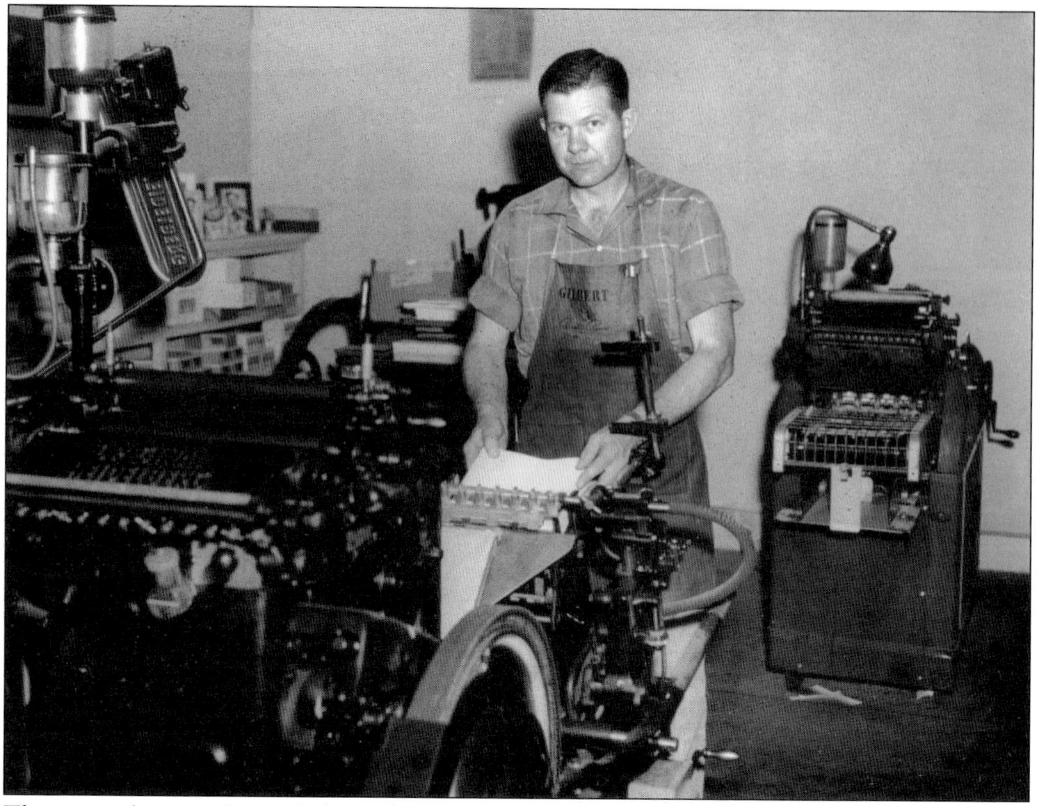

These two photographs mark the end of an era. The image above shows James Bowra at a printing press at the *Aztec Independent Review*. The *Review*, run by Jim's father, George, evolved from other papers beginning in 1888. The *Review* ran weekly from April 29, 1932, until it was sold to the *Farmington Daily Times* in 1984. Below, a Denver & Rio Grande Western train passes the Aztec depot in 1966. After the busy boom years, railroad freight transport slowed considerably. The last train came through Aztec on August 31, 1968. Engine No. 498 is now stored at the rail yard in Durango, Colorado. (Above, courtesy James Bowra; below, courtesy Aztec Museum.)

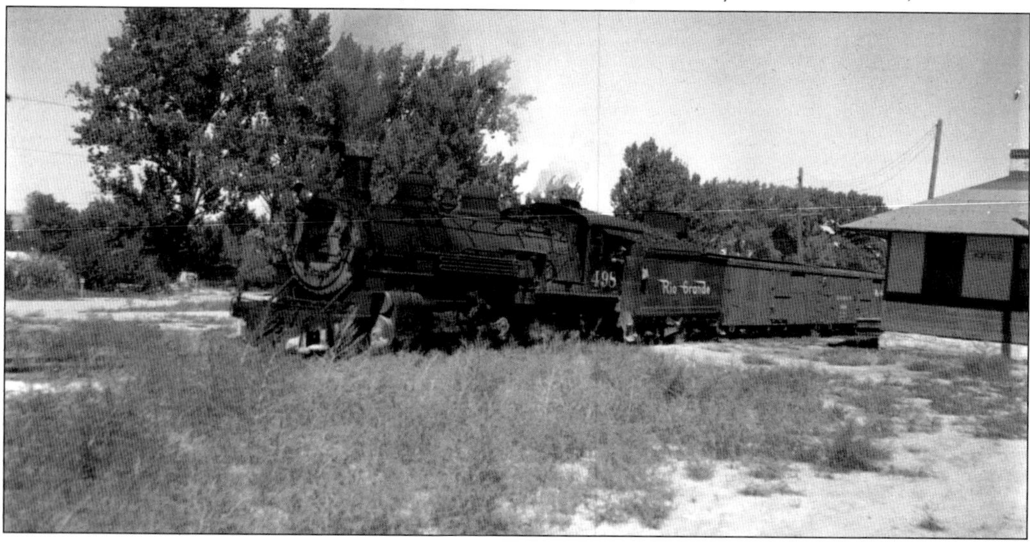

Six

Aztec in 2011

The first five chapters of this book showcased the city of Aztec through the years. This book began with how Aztec got its name, moving on to 1876, when the area was opened up for homesteading. Several pioneer families and early buildings are documented. Aztec survived floods and world wars. The natural gas and oil discoveries and the first commercial natural gas well are cataloged. The Aztec Ruins National Monument fills its own chapter. The Great Depression and the population growth from the 1950s natural gas boom are recorded. The building of the Navajo Dam Road and the "All America City" award are featured. The narrative closes with the death of the railroad in 1968.

Many stories and pictures are missing, as it would take a much larger book than this to cover the full gamut of Aztec's development and growth. Many old-timers were contacted and interviewed, and they were willing to share their photo albums, newspaper clippings, and oral histories. There are many more families that could have been contacted and mentioned in this book. Time and space did not permit that luxury.

The Aztec Museum opened their archives and allowed full access to the photograph collection. Each of the over 6,000 pictures was examined and cataloged. There was so much to choose from that many events with companion photographs could not be included.

To change the pace, this last chapter examines Aztec in 2010 and 2011. Space is a limiting factor again, so sights the reader thinks should be included may not be here. This chapter presents a small glimpse of the current surroundings. This record of what is going on now is included as a benchmark because the area changes every year. The purpose of this final chapter is to establish documentation of Aztec today for future reference. Obviously, Aztec will continue on its progressive path.

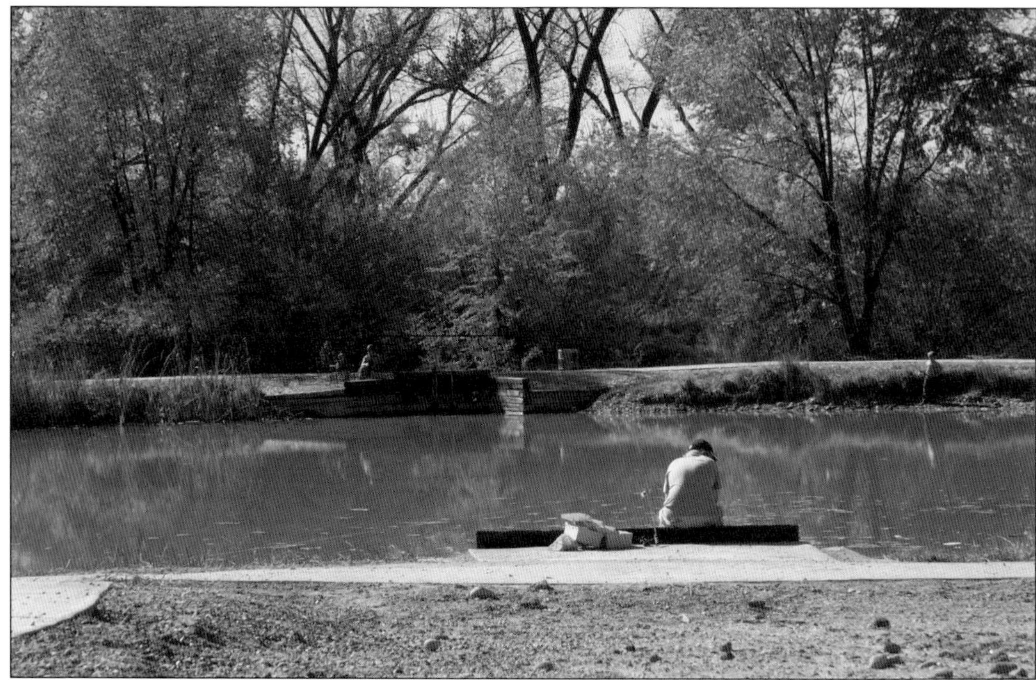

Riverside Park is one of Aztec's greatest assets. It is especially busy during the summer months, with activities going on all over the park. The fishing pond at the entrance is shown above. The pond is stocked, and many youngsters learn to fish here. Below is the rodeo arena, where a couple of riders are enjoying the day. The rodeo arena also hosts a weekly summer gymkhana for the youth. The park also contains a soccer field and a baseball diamond. (Both courtesy Kelly West.)

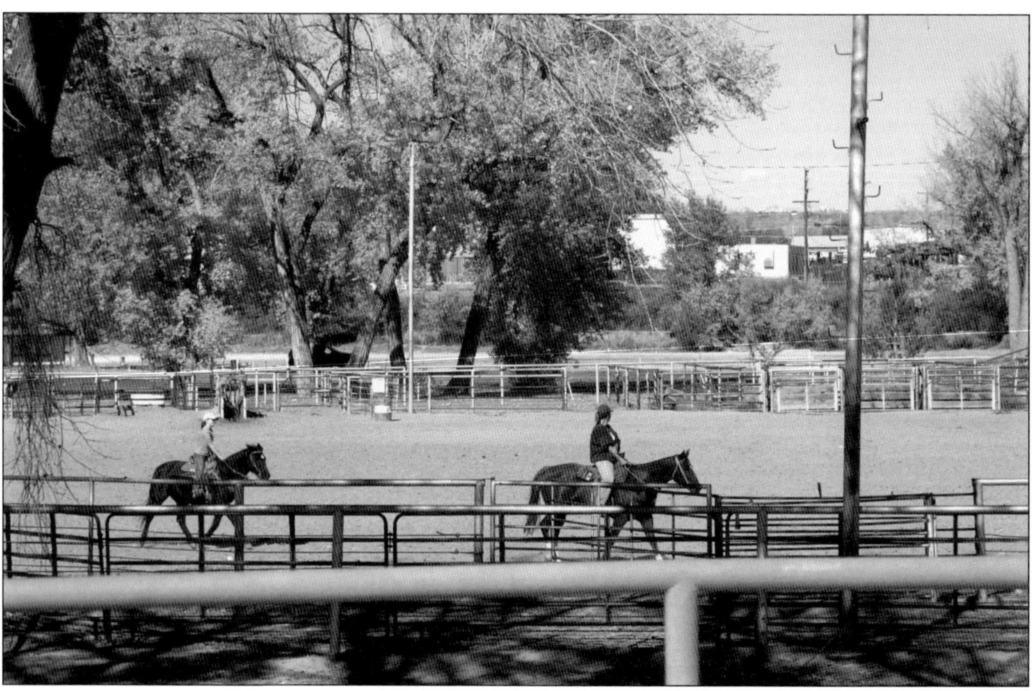

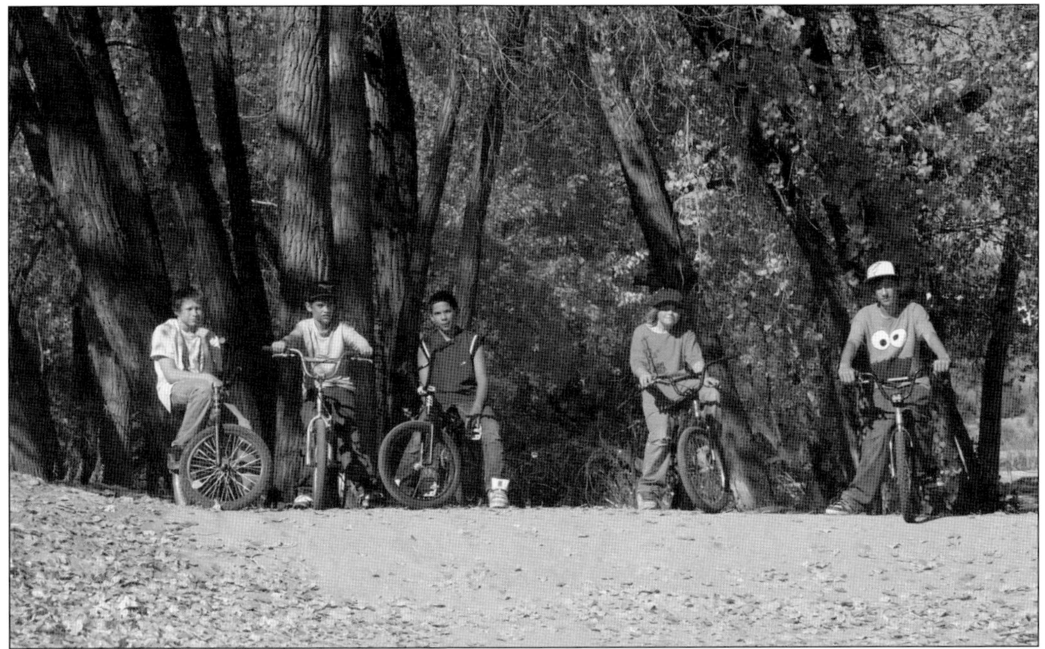

Riverside Park also has a busy BMX track. These cyclists are ready to take a round or two. Numerous events are scheduled during the summer, and sometimes the park resembles a three-ring circus, with some kind of action in each section. Park visitors exercise by walking along the river, using the walker's bridge to cross to the other side. (Courtesy Kelly West.)

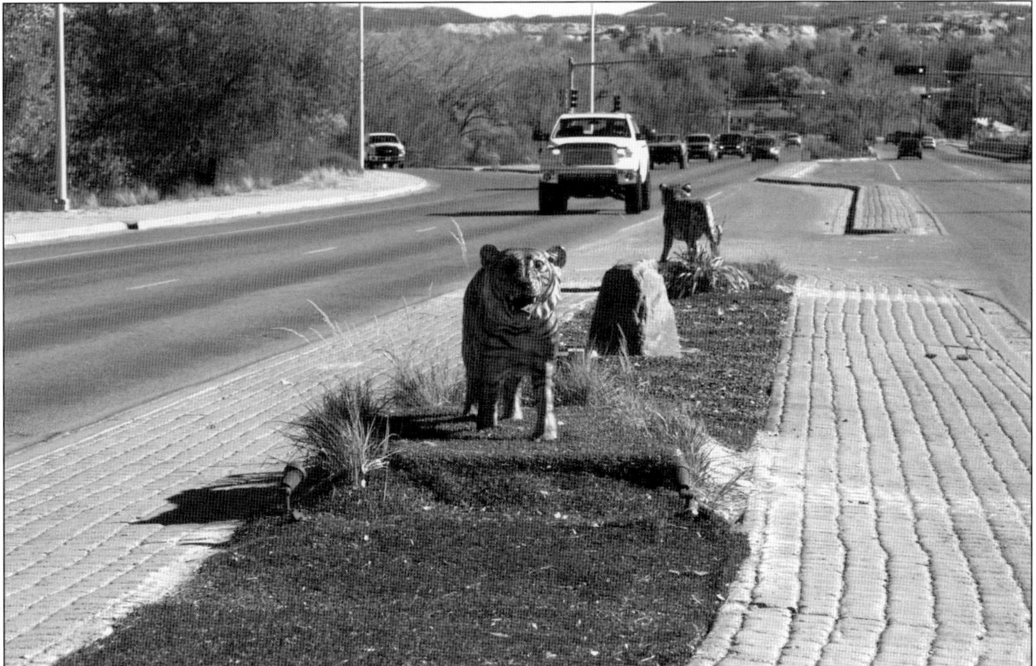

This median near the Animas River bridge features two tigers, the sports mascot of Aztec. All of the high school teams are called the Aztec Tigers; drivers are reminded of this when they arrive in town. (Courtesy Kelly West.)

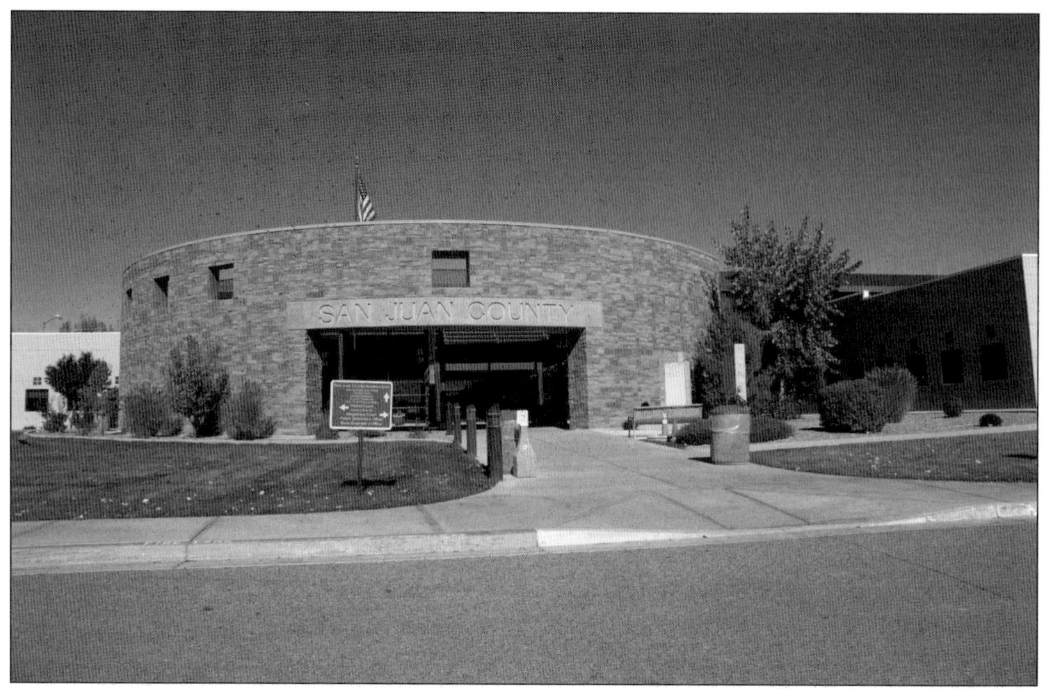

San Juan County no longer has a typical courthouse for all the courts and county offices. In present-day Aztec, these two buildings take that place. Pictured above is the county administration building, and below is the brand-new Eleventh District Judicial Court Building. (Above, courtesy Kelly West; below, courtesy Connie Pruitt.)

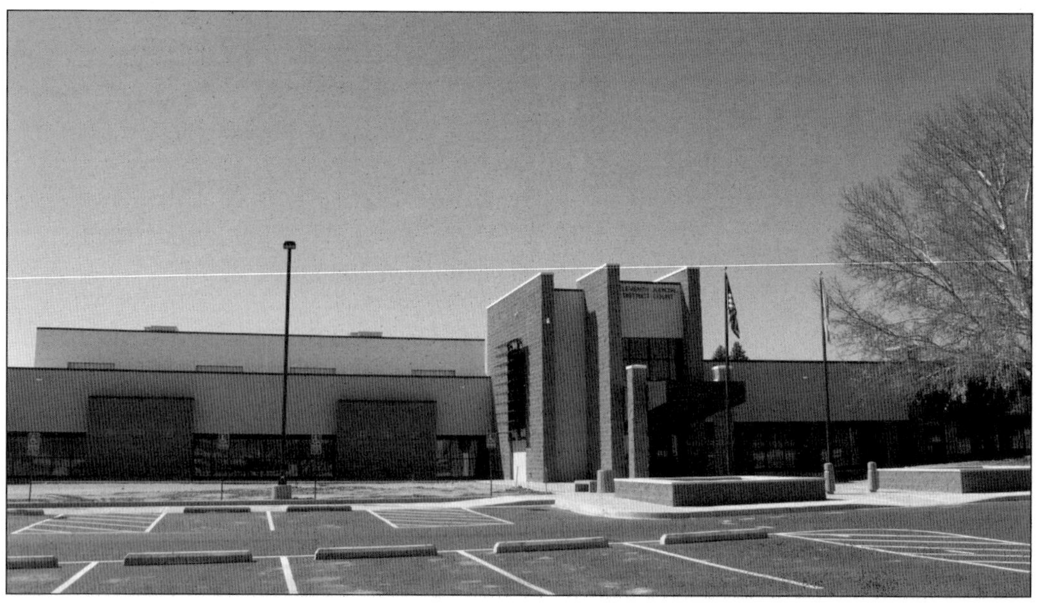

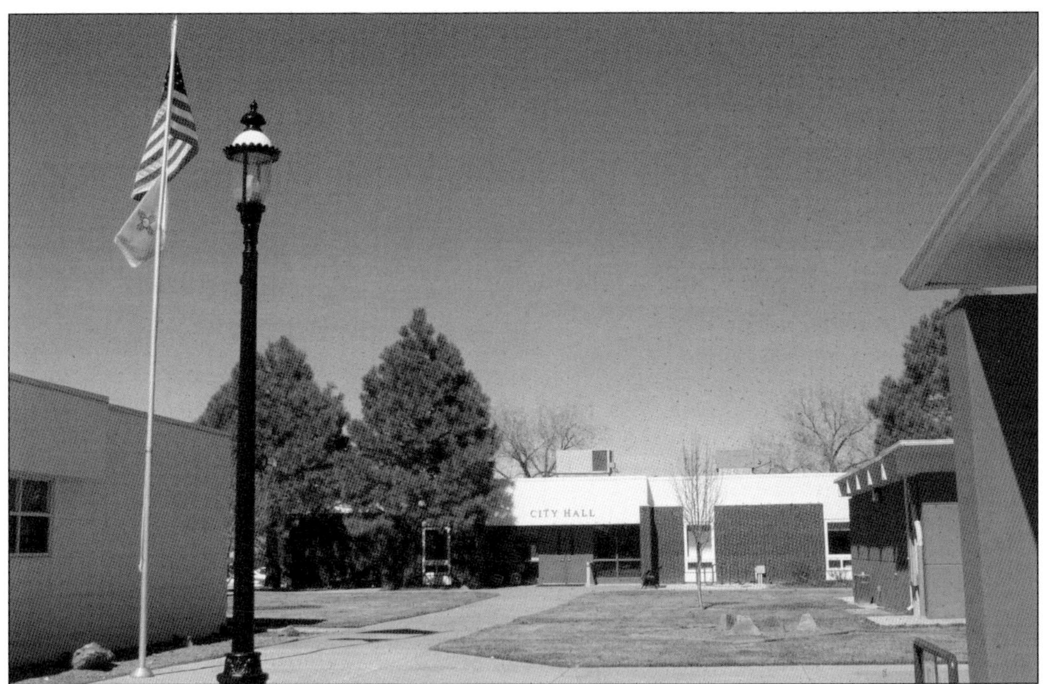

Aztec City Hall is the central building in the city compound. Surrounding structures are home to the police department, motor vehicle department, fire department, and other city concerns. As Aztec grows, so does the compound. (Courtesy Connie Pruitt.)

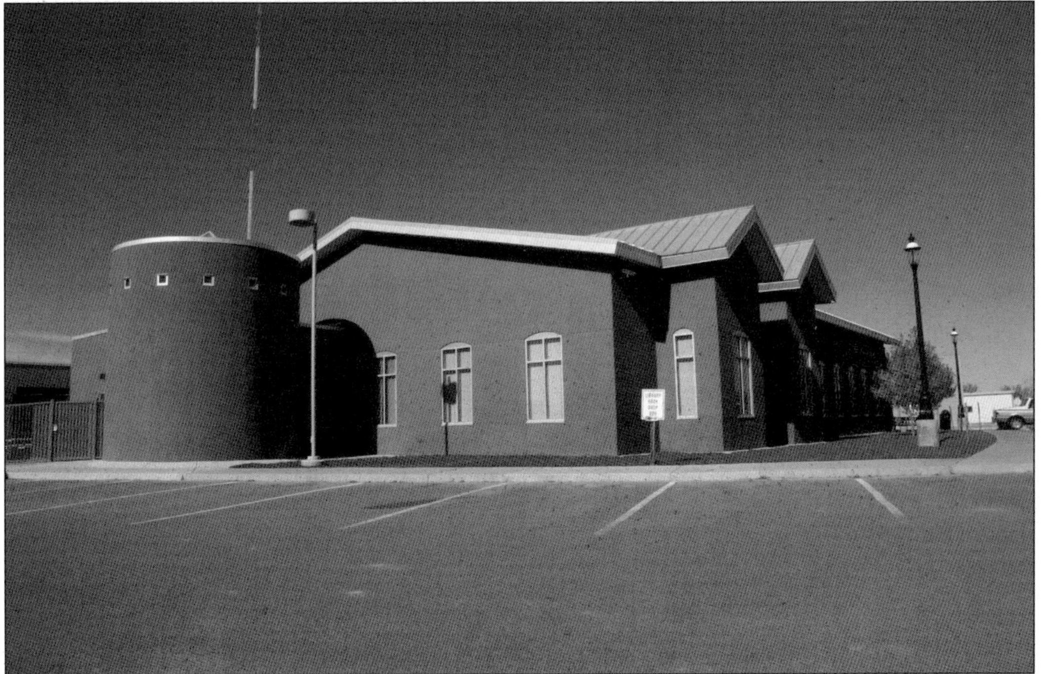

The Aztec Public Library is in another community complex. In addition to the library, the area contains the San Juan College East, Vista Nueva High School, and the Boys and Girls Club. The sign in front reads, "Aztec Family Center." (Courtesy Kelly West.)

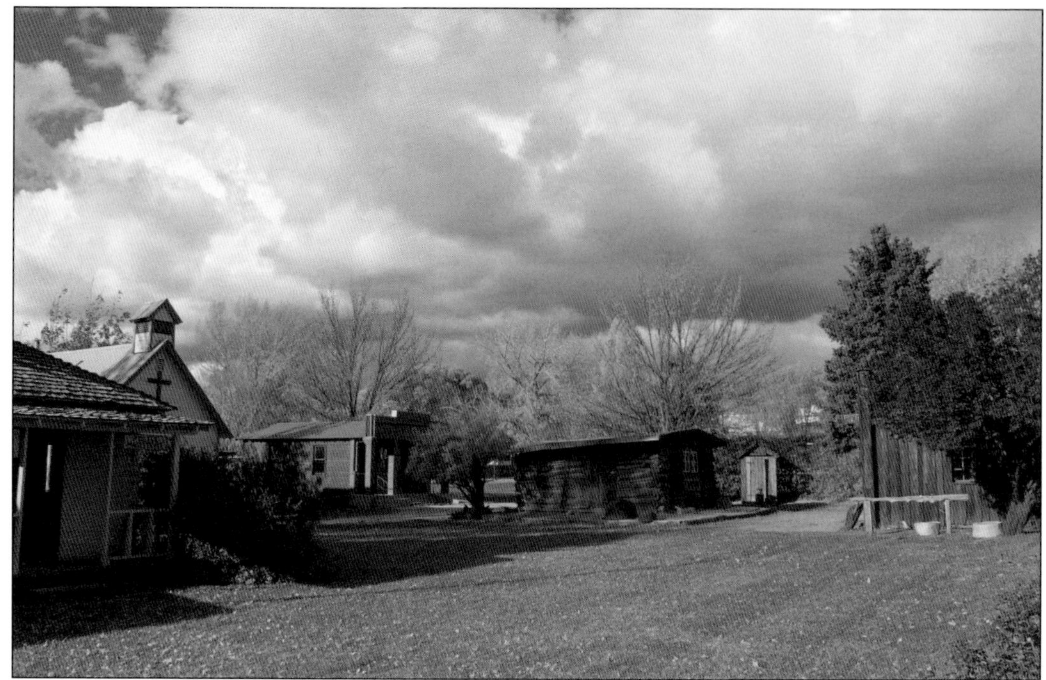

The Aztec Museum and Pioneer Village host thousands of visitors each year. The Pioneer Village, above, houses authentic buildings that were moved in and replicas created to reproduce history. Special events are staged in the village, including printing, horseshoeing demonstrations, and the live pioneer history drama, "The High Noon Shootout." The Aztec Museum, below, is a hub of activity during the annual Fiesta Days in the spring and the Founder's Day held each September. The museum also boasts an extensive exhibit centered on the oil and gas industry in the San Juan Basin. (Both courtesy Connie Pruitt.)

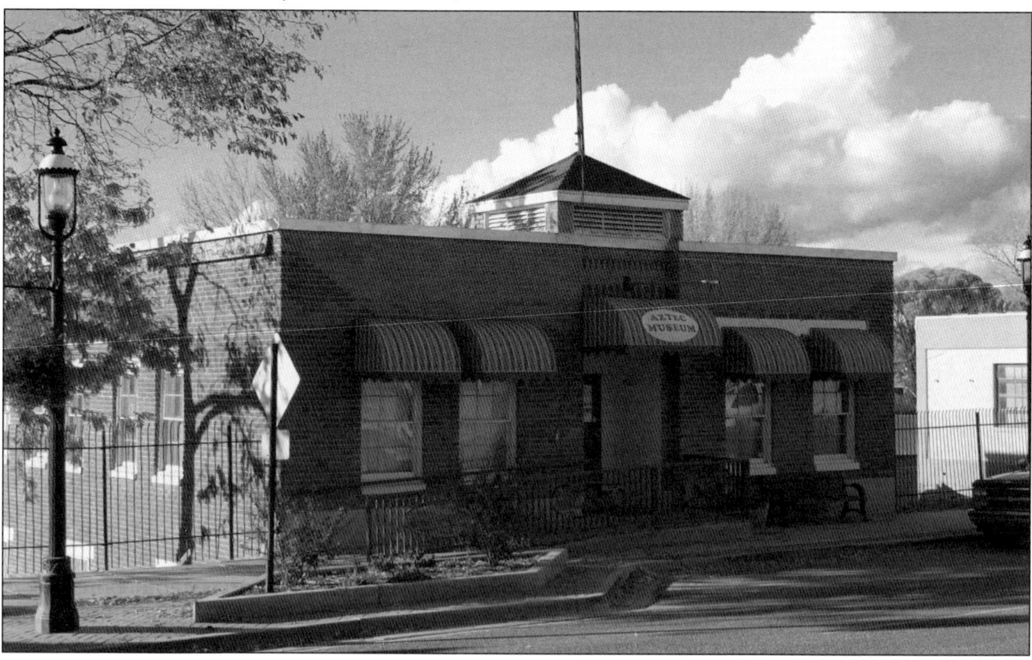

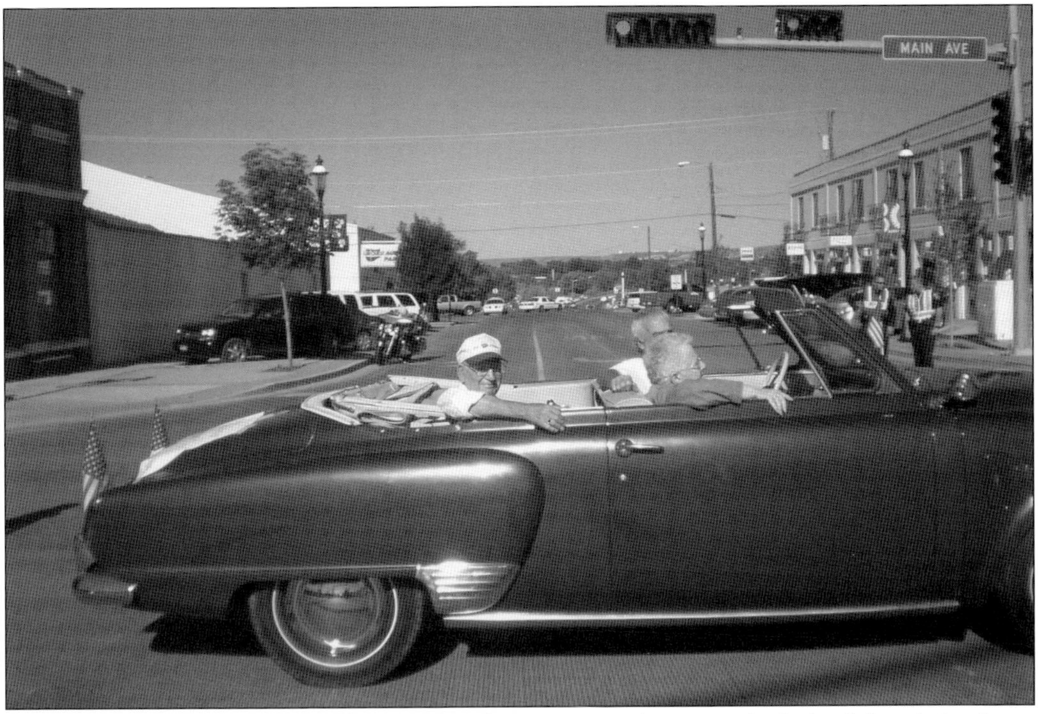

Gerald (left) and Alta Jane Williams, a fourth-generation Aztecan who helped found the Aztec Museum and the San Juan County Iris Society, were named Pioneers of the Year for the 2010 Founder's Day celebration. The driver and owner of the classic Studebaker is Billy Dusenbery, who comes from another pioneer family. (Courtesy Linda Williams.)

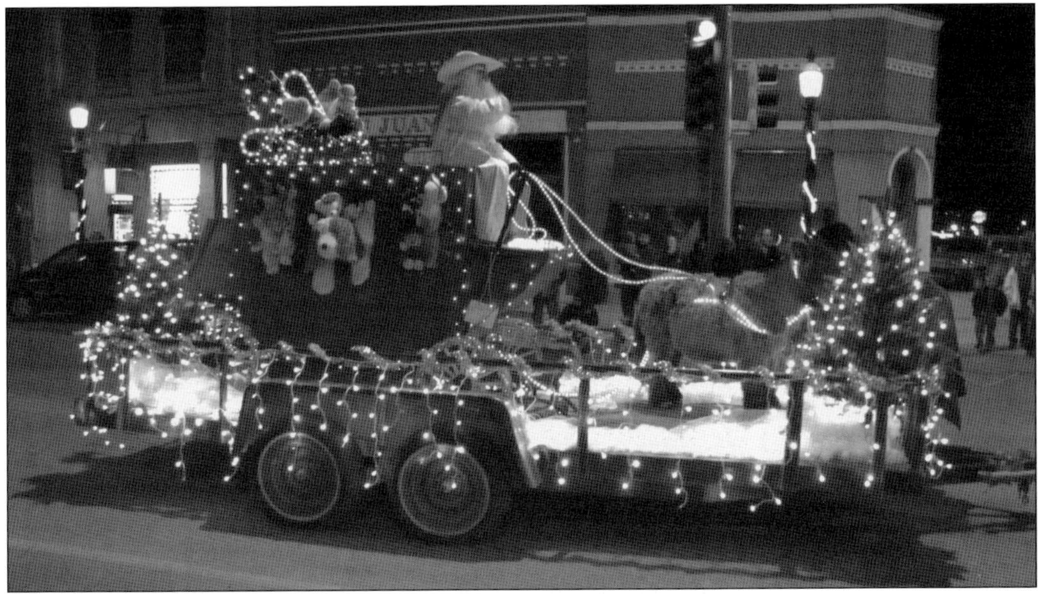

The Aztec Senior Center crew went all out for the 2010 Christmas parade and ended up winning the Senior Division plaque. The float sported a stagecoach stuffed with animals and led by a burro. The cowboy Santa (also known as driver Fred Emery) fits right in with his surroundings. (Courtesy Edward M. Kotyk, City of Aztec.)

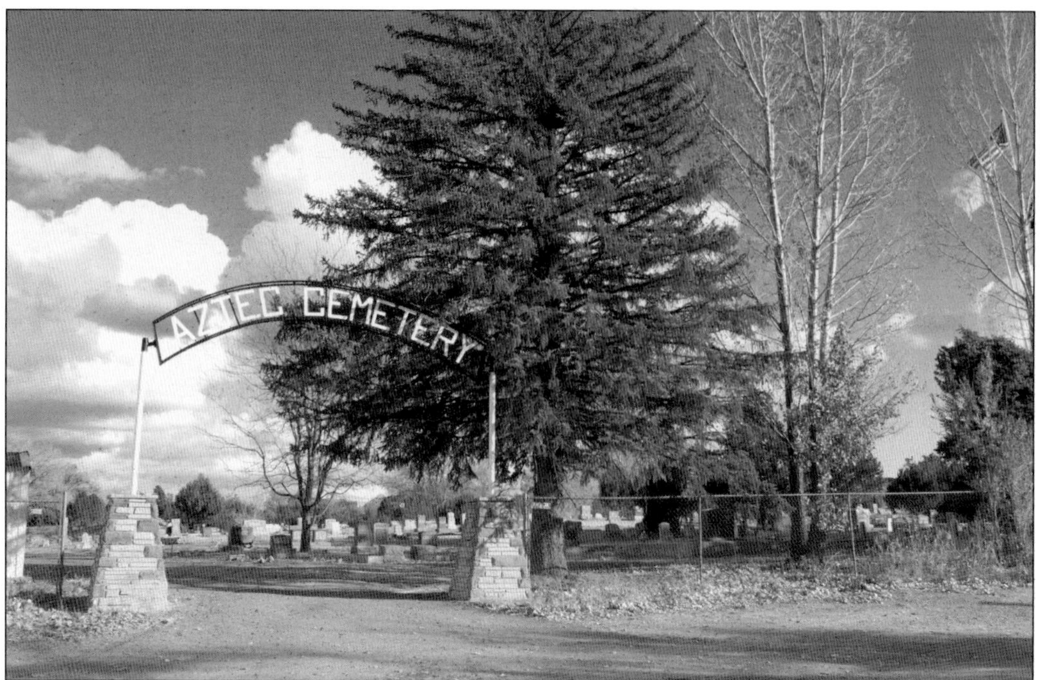

The Aztec Cemetery sits on a mesa above the city. The first recorded burial in the cemetery was Edgar Koontz, who was just two years old when he died on January 30, 1890. The status of this land was in limbo until the Aztec Cemetery Association acquired the 15 acres in 1926. (Courtesy Connie Pruitt.)

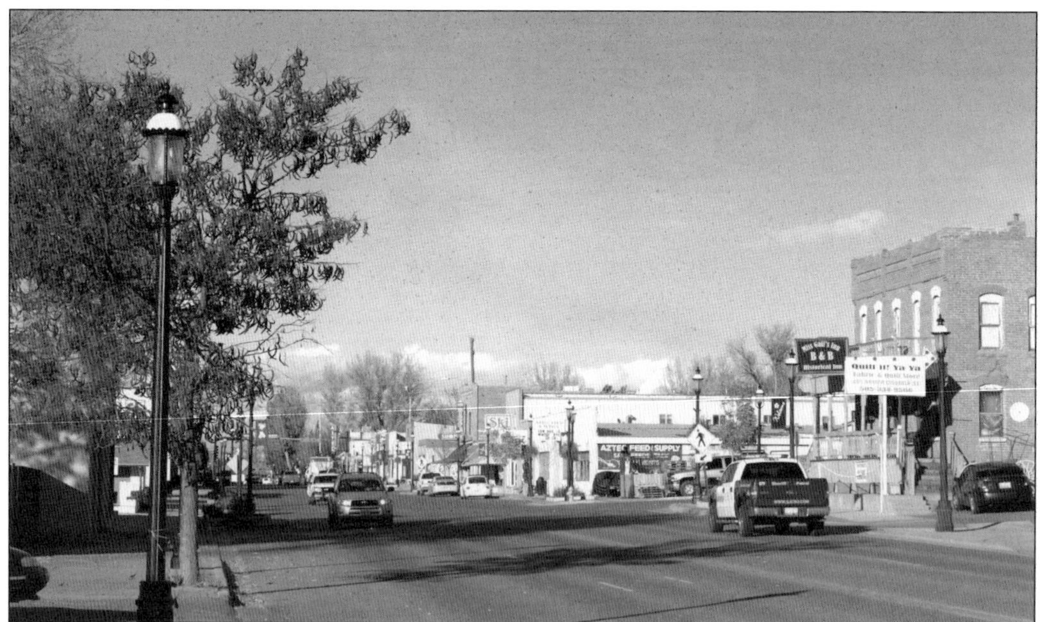

The city of Aztec is shown here, as seen when driving in from the south. Historic buildings, such as the brick structure on the right, intermingle with newer buildings. Main Avenue was recently redone with trees, hanging planters, and wider sidewalks. Aztec is a busy place. (Courtesy Connie Pruitt.)

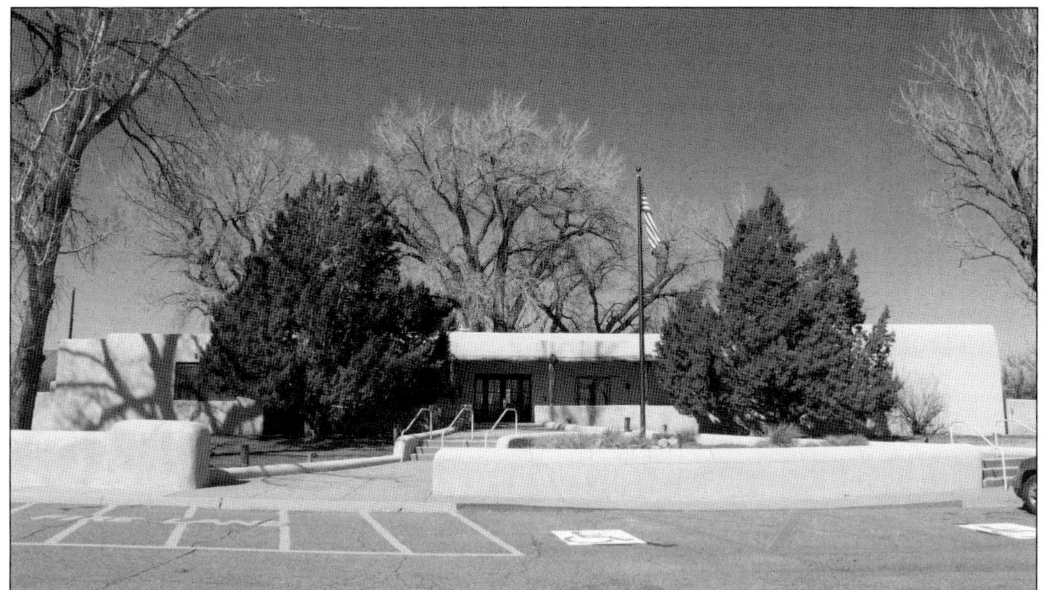

The visitor center at the Aztec Ruins National Monument dominates the entrance to the ruins. The Aztec Ruins represent one of the outlying settlements of the Chaco Culture National Historic Park, a UNESCO World Heritage Site. Visitors can take their time to see the park with a self-guided tour and a museum; over 30,000 people tour the ruins each year. (Courtesy Connie Pruitt.)

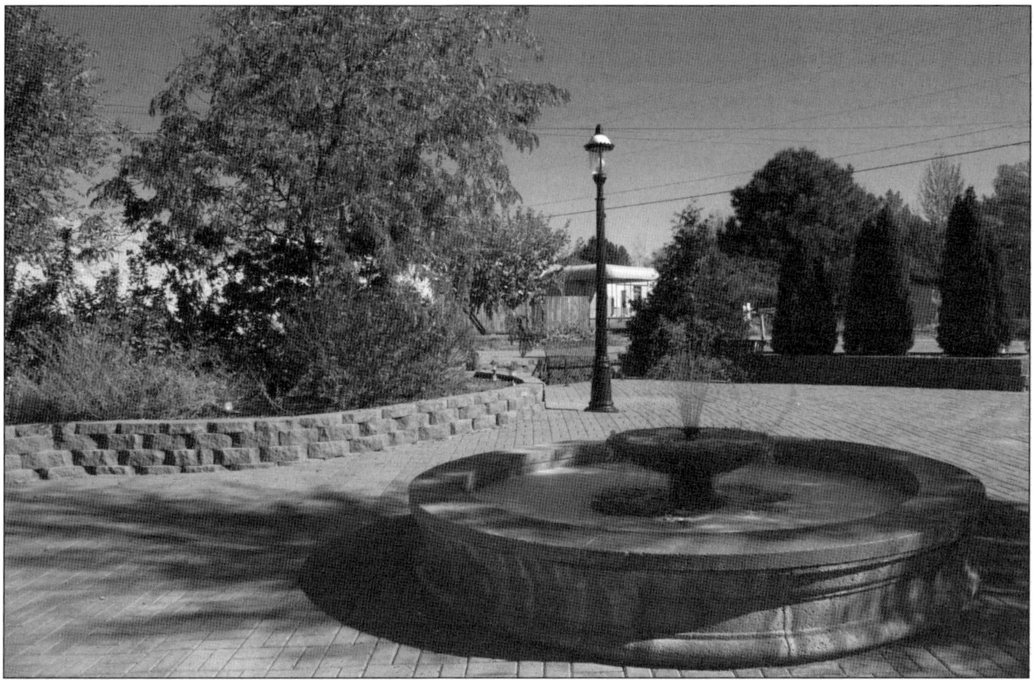

This fountain is the centerpiece of a small, bricked area in downtown Aztec. It has been used for live music, entertainment, and other events. A memorial marker states: "In honor of Ray B. Current and Sadie E. Current whose Aztec Barber Shop served this community at this location from 1903 to 1969." The barbershop interior, complete with Current's equipment, is re-created in the Aztec Museum. (Courtesy Kelly West.)

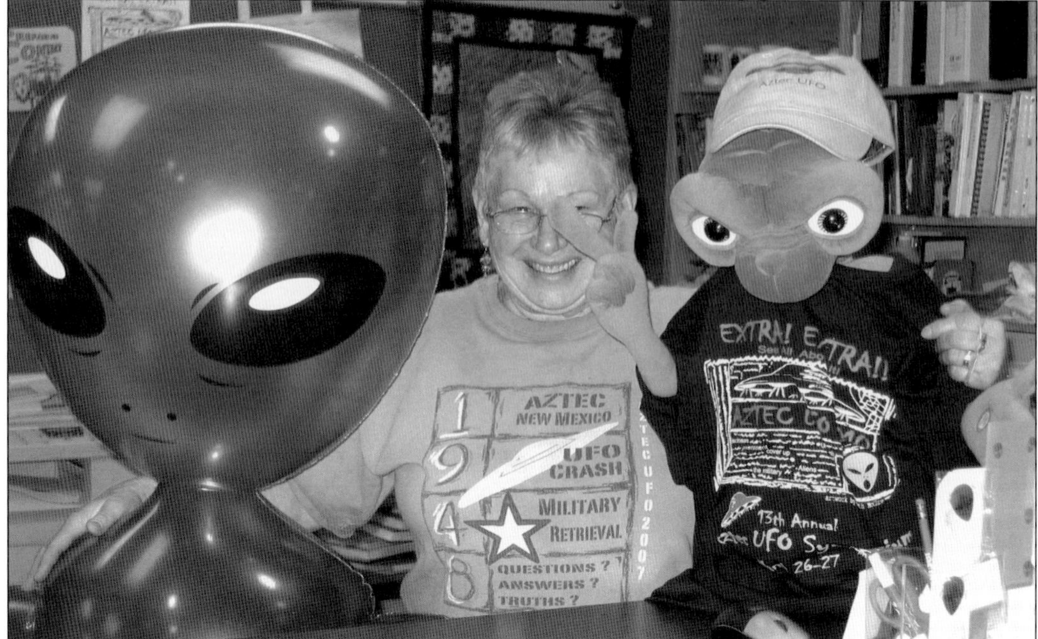

Judy Cowan, also known as "Indiana Judy," greets visitors at the 2010 UFO Symposium at the Aztec Public Library. The UFO Symposium, which commemorates the alleged 1948 UFO crash in Hart Canyon, began in 1998 as a fundraiser for the library and has grown each year—the 2011 event was the 14th annual celebration. Tours of the crash site are on the agenda, and the associated Alien Run Mountain Bike competition continues to gain momentum. (Courtesy Aztec Public Library.)

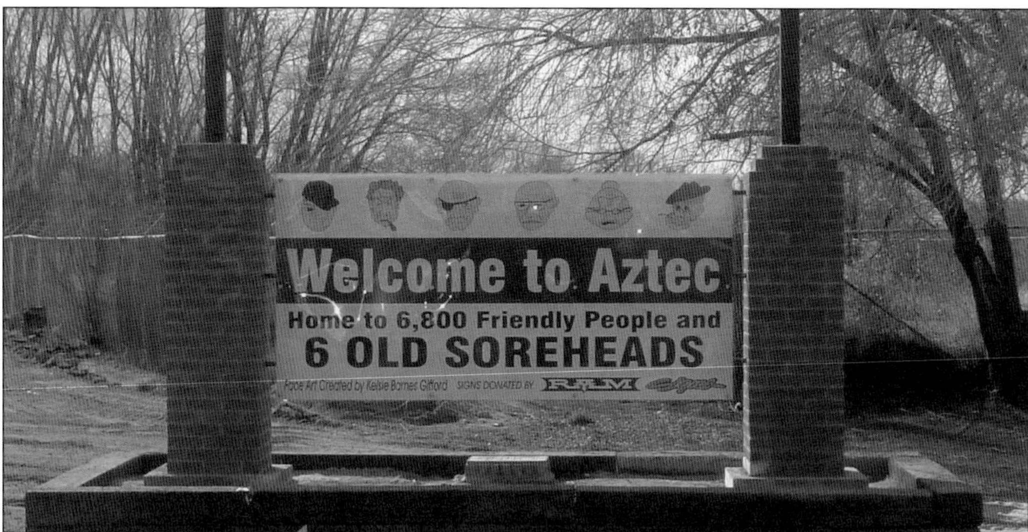

The "six old soreheads" feature of Aztec's Fiesta Days began in 1967. Signs were placed at all three entrances to Aztec, proclaiming that Aztec was the home of "4,200 friendly people and six old soreheads." The signs faded, and the numbers went out of date; they were once repainted with new population numbers, but again fell into disrepair. The signs were removed in 1981, and the uproar began. Time passed on, and in 2010, new signs were made. This sign now greets drivers on the Highway 550 entrance from Durango. (Courtesy Marilu Waybourn.)

Further Reading

Aztec Independent Review newspapers.

Aztec Museum Newsletters.

Bowra, George B., and Willa Bowra Hampton. *The Bowra Legacy: A Journalistic History of Aztec & San Juan County, New Mexico.* Aztec, NM: Inklings USA, 1998.

Davis, Catherine. *A Railroad Here? Meet the Red Apple Flyer.* Flora Vista, NM: San Juan County Historical Society, 2005.

Dugan, Tom, and Emery Arnold. *GAS! Adventures into the History of One of the World's Largest Gas Fields—the San Juan Basin of New Mexico.* Farmington, NM: Dugan Production Corp., 2002.

Duke, Robert W. *San Juan County: The Early Years.* Flora Vista, NM: San Juan County Historical Society, 1999.

Howe, Sherman. *My Story of the Aztec Ruins.* Farmington, NM: The Basin Spokesman, 1955.

Niederauer, George. *Locomotive 315: The Lives, Times and Rebirth of an 1895 Steam Engine.* Durango, CO: Durango Railroad Historical Society, 2010.

San Juan County Pioneer Bulletins.

Waybourn, Marilu. *Aztec: Then and Now.* Flora Vista, NM: San Juan County Historical Society, 2006.

———. *Churches of San Juan County, New Mexico.* Flora Vista, NM: San Juan County Historical Society, 2003.

www.arcadiapublishing.com

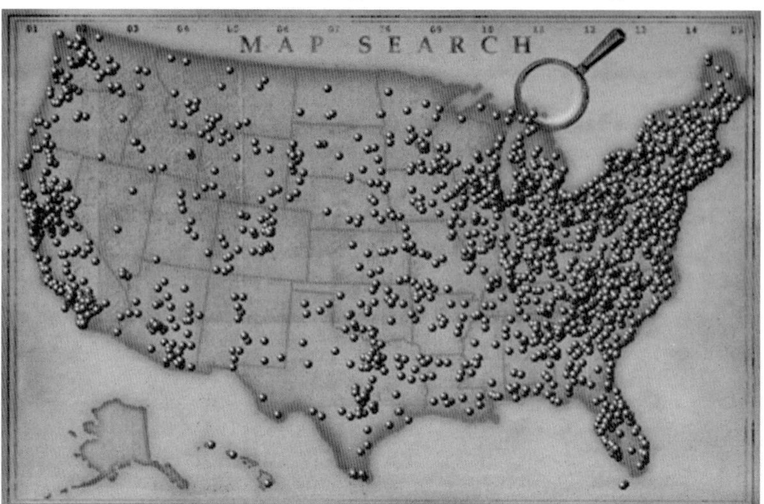

Discover books about the town where you grew up, the cities where your friends and families live, the town where your parents met, or even that retirement spot you've been dreaming about. Our Web site provides history lovers with exclusive deals, advanced notification about new titles, e-mail alerts of author events, and much more.

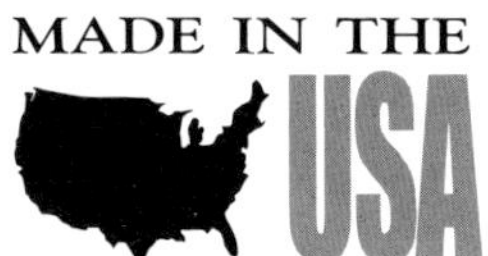

Arcadia Publishing, the leading local history publisher in the United States, is committed to making history accessible and meaningful through publishing books that celebrate and preserve the heritage of America's people and places. Consistent with our mission to preserve history on a local level, this book was printed in South Carolina on American-made paper and manufactured entirely in the United States.

This book carries the accredited Forest Stewardship Council (FSC) label and is printed on 100 percent FSC-certified paper. Products carrying the FSC label are independently certified to assure consumers that they come from forests that are managed to meet the social, economic, and ecological needs of present and future generations.

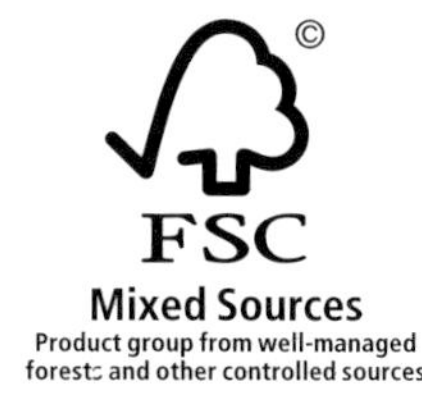

Cert no. SW-COC-001530
www.fsc.org

Find Your Place in History.